DATE DUE

JUN 0 1990

JUN 1 3 '90   RED

MANAGERIAL JOB DESCRIPTIONS
IN MANUFACTURING

AMA RESEARCH STUDY **65**

MANAGERIAL JOB DESCRIPTIONS IN MANUFACTURING

Gordon H. Evans

AMERICAN MANAGEMENT ASSOCIATION, INC.

This Research Study has been distributed without
charge to AMA members enrolled in the Manufacturing Division. Those who are enrolled in other
Divisions, or who wish extra copies, may order the
Study in a hard-cover edition at $8.00. Price to non-
members, $12.00.

Library of Congress catalog card number: 64-20404

The photographs on the front cover are reproduced
by courtesy of Ford Motor Company.

About This Research Study

IN 1958 THE AMERICAN MANAGEMENT ASSOCIATION published *Defining the Manager's Job,* a 446-page book giving the results of a research study on industry practice in the preparation and use of managerial position descriptions. The report included numerous examples of position descriptions for company officers and other top-level managers in almost every area of managerial specialization.

Since its publication, AMA has received numerous requests for job descriptions in further depth—for middle-management levels of production, sales, finance, and even narrower functional areas such as production control and quality control. This present Research Study is intended to fill the need for information on a wide range of managerial and supervisory positions in manufacturing or production. It is based on a questionnaire survey of the practices of 217 companies and on a careful examination of more than a thousand descriptions generously supplied by companies assisting in the research.

Why should a company compile managerial position descriptions? Most frequently the goals are equitable salary administration and refinement of organization structure, participating companies report. In both the previous study and this one, however, it soon became apparent that one of the chief benefits of such a program is that the *process* of writing the descriptions is as beneficial as the use of the finished documents. Again and again research participants say they intended at the outset to use their descriptions exclusively for salary administration purposes, and for this reason they wrote the descriptions as accurate "snapshots" of the way in which the job under analysis was being done. But, in discussing the first drafts of these true-to-life descriptions, numerous organizational flaws, awkward relationships, and disagreements as to job emphasis were uncovered. In the give-and-take between superior and subordinate manager during the preparation of a description, such defects are often corrected. Without the description program they might go undiscovered until they caused serious damage to company efficiency. In reading and using this volume, then, it is hoped that managers who undertake managerial position descriptions in manufacturing will be aware of the "extra" benefits even though they may have started their efforts with good salary administration as the primary goal.

To a large extent, the present research found that practices do not change merely because the jobs being described are positions in manufacturing or production management. For a detailed road map and a statistical study of such matters as organizing to get job descriptions written, the reader may therefore consult the previous report, *Defining the Manager's Job* (AMA Research Study 33). To avoid repetition of what has been previously published, this Study reviews only briefly the important issues covered in detail in the earlier work.

Gordon H. Evans is a Survey Associate in AMA's Research and Information Service. He has a Wall Street background, has been a consultant to the General Electric Company, and has also been on the staff of the National Bureau for Economic Research. He has written on many business and economic topics, including money and banking, the social effects of automation, and public policy toward big business. Mr. Evans is a graduate of Columbia University, from which he also holds a master's degree.

JOHN W. ENELL
Director of Research

MARY M. STANTON
Editor of Research Studies
DOROTHY MACDONALD and SALLY BROBSTON
Editorial Assistants

Contents

Tables

Exhibits

Indexes

PART ONE

Job Descriptions in Manufacturing
And Their Preparation

1. An Introduction to Job Descriptions in Manufacturing

How do men describe the work they do in manufacturing management and supervisory positions? The vehicle they use is one that has evolved over many years of trial and error in management practice: the job description. In its present state of evolution, the job description has become a catalyst of clarity for complex organization structures in industrial corporations. It is the tool by which corporate objectives are broken down into smaller segments, and by which responsibility for achieving those goals is delegated throughout the organization.

The job description has become indispensable to the process of breaking down work into manageable components, for it is one of the important means by which the energy of the organization is unified in constructive channels. As such, the job description is a tool worthy of use by every manager. In the old days when "seat of the pants management" was in vogue, the boss had to have a clear perspective—even if unwritten—of the duties his men would perform. In this respect, the difference between him and the modern professional manager is easy to see: the professional has learned the value of writing job descriptions down on paper. He does this because he knows that the very act of formulating the duties and responsibilities of individuals, and writing them down in clear language, *in itself* provides everyone concerned with a finer understanding of how the company's work gets done.

In this study the focus of attention is on managers and supervisors

TABLE 1. *Usage of Managerial Job Descriptions in the Manufacturing Function in 217 Companies*

NO. OF EMPLOYEES IN COMPANY	NO. OF COMPANIES OF THIS SIZE IN SAMPLE	PERCENTAGE USING JOB DESCRIPTIONS
1,000 or less	68	75
1,001–5,000	90	87
5,001–20,000	40	88
Over 20,000	19	89
All sizes	*217*	*83*

—line and staff—in the manufacturing or production component of the company. The material comes from a survey, supplemented by interviews, of 217 firms. Almost 83 per cent of them describe positions in manufacturing management and supervision in writing. As shown in Table 1, the larger the company, the more likely it is to have such descriptions. The proportion extends to approximately three-fourths of all companies with 1,000 or fewer employees and nine-tenths of those with 20,000 or more. These written descriptions are statements of duties, responsibilities, and job relationships, which is the definition of "job description" used in this study.

Job descriptions are often used with job specifications. The difference between them is that the job specification (or "man specification") is usually a statement of minimum hiring requirements, outlining the skills, knowledge, and other qualities that a candidate must have if he is to be considered acceptable. Written specifications of this kind almost always exist at the level of the first-line supervisor. They are rare, however, at higher levels of manufacturing management. Almost 50 per cent of the companies surveyed use both job descriptions and job specifications. In companies with fewer than 500 employees it is fairly common for both descriptions and specifications to be lacking; hardly 25 per cent of the surveyed firms in this size category reported using them. But, the survey revealed, almost no company develops job specifications without first developing adequate job descriptions.

ESSENCE OF BLUE-COLLAR PROGRAMS

During the research for this study, based as it was on many hundreds of job descriptions in manufacturing organizations—from the blue-collar ranks up to the level of the vice president of manufac-turing—it became clear that managerial position descriptions are written for reasons that often are sharply different from those under-lying description programs for blue-collar jobs. While the two types of programs share certain purposes, such as the accumulation of data for wage or salary administration, they differ in one principal respect. The difference is that one of the main reasons for establishing writ-ten job descriptions at supervisory and managerial levels is to im-prove the organization of manufacturing management.

Many managers in the production end of a business are familiar with the job descriptions prepared for blue-collar employees. These descriptions are almost always part of job-analysis programs aimed at setting wage rates. In them, the content of the work is described in detail and great care is taken to be exact about such factors as dangerous working conditions, the amount of physical effort in-volved, excessive heat or cold at the workplace, and the degree of manual skill required.

Almost invariably, these descriptions portray the employee's job *exactly as it is being performed,* so that they form a basis for job comparison, through which equitably graded compensation rates can be set. Some companies compare jobs by ranking them in order of value to the firm. Others use "factor comparison," in which the various elements of a job are reduced to numerical values. Take working conditions, for instance. The dirtiest job in a foundry may be assigned a numerical value of 10, while an inspector's job in the same shop—work that is relatively clean and comfortable—may rate a value of only 2 or 3. Again, the degree of manual skill achieved by a master machinist may have a value of 10, while that of a shop laborer may get a rating of 1 or 2. The factors which are given numerical values vary from company to company, but the principle is the same: the greater the point total for all factors, the higher the salary grade. If a company has a large number of very different jobs, a large number of salary grades will probably be required to allow sufficient gradation to accommodate everyone from, say, a janitor to a diamond cutter. If, in contrast, the company's jobs are quite homogeneous, very few salary grades may be needed—indeed, the firm may simply rank them by other methods and employ no formal minimum-maximum grades at all. In the former case, job descriptions are likely to be very detailed so as to point up small differences between jobs. In the latter case, they often consist of only six or seven sentences.

It is also noteworthy that job descriptions for blue-collar manufacturing employees almost invariably include fairly accurate "man specifications," "job specifications," or—to use the familiar shop abbreviation—"specs." Commonly these state, for example, the years of education and experience deemed necessary or desirable, and in most companies the job analyst will have numerical equivalents for these requirements. The job description for a maintenance plumber, to cite one example, may state that most incumbents "do the full work of a union construction trades journeyman" and, also, that they "read complex blueprints and layouts." The analyst, depending on his particular system, may give this job fairly high ratings for both education and job experience, and these ratings then serve as the base from which job specifications are derived. Thus the plumber's job is said to require a man with "two years of vocational school training in plumbing with either a full apprenticeship certificate or, in the absence of a formal apprenticeship program, three years of on-the-job construction trades experience."

MANAGERIAL DESCRIPTIONS DIFFER

For the purposes of this study, "managerial" may be said to include everyone from shop foreman to the highest executive exclusively concerned with manufacturing or production—usually a vice president. It also includes managers in closely allied staff functions —quality control, production control, materials handling, inspection, and so on.

Examination of the position descriptions for these managers and supervisors, together with a review of survey responses, indicates that while differences in approach may not *always* be present in a given company, they exist to such extent that a clear line of demarcation can be drawn between the typical job-description program for blue-collar workers and that which is customarily found at managerial levels. Many survey respondents stated that they use their managerial position descriptions *entirely* for purposes unconnected with compensation rates. Rather, as we have seen, the principal goal of their programs is to improve organization, using the job description as a diagnostic tool to uncover defects. Following the usual practice, these companies first describe each job exactly as it is being done by the present holder. But, after comparing adjacent jobs, line management may make extensive changes in the descriptions to set up new procedures and reporting relationships. The original "as is" descriptions can be used for compensation purposes; however, the new "as should be" descriptions are, in fact, formalized directives from management involving *change* in organization and methods. The second set can serve as a basis for setting salary scales only when the incumbents are actually performing their work in the way described.

An anecdote contributed by a job analyst illustrates this distinction quite well. He wrote a set of descriptions for the foremen, middle managers, and top managers of his company's manufacturing department. These, being of the "first round" type, outlined the work as it was being done. When they were submitted to departmental management, it was evident that the organization was in real need of change; in attempts to draw up organization charts based on the descriptions—primarily the "relationships" sections—lines of authority were often duplicated or were hopelessly vague. Management's reaction was that it would take some time to rewrite the descriptions so as to alter reporting relationships in a satisfactory manner; so, while a full-fledged organization study was being conducted, the "as is" descriptions were filed with the personnel department. When lower-level management vacancies occurred in manufacturing, personnel used the descriptions to get a general idea of the type of person needed. More than that—once an acceptable candidate was found, the job descriptions were used in orienting him.

Eventually the department head discovered what was happening. "Why," he asked irritably, "are we perpetuating a form of organization we already know to be bad?" Upon which the descriptions were immediately altered so that they would embody, not actual practice, but, rather, the sort of performance that would be acceptable in the future.

Practice in the Standard Oil Company of California also is pertinent here. This company writes two very different descriptions for each managerial job; a so-called management guide and a job description proper. The latter, written for salary-administration purposes, describes the job "as is." The management guide, on the other hand, is used for orientation and on-the-job training; and, when appropriate, it is the primary vehicle by which the content and reporting relationships of the job are changed. Quite often, a Standard of California management guide describes a position, not as it is being currently performed, but *as management wants it to be performed in the future*. A company manual states the difference between job description and management guide as follows:

> Job descriptions within the company are terse, factual, and designed primarily for job evaluation. . . . Management guides, on the other hand, not only expound the intangible aspects of positions and their interlacing relationships, but they also serve to inspire the occupants of the positions with which they deal to set a goal of achievement and stir the individual to pattern the fulfillment of this position to the ideal as expressed in the guide.

2. How Companies Use Managerial Job Descriptions

THE RESPONDING COMPANIES were asked to indicate in detail, by means of a checklist, the specific uses to which they put position descriptions written for jobs in production management. The question was open-ended in that they could fill in uses which had not been thought of when framing the checklist. One hundred and eighty-three respondents gave answers that could be tabulated, and the results are shown in Table 2. One respondent could obviously check more than one use; in fact, the majority did so. The 183 companies gave a total of 708 answers.

Of these 183 respondents, a total of 135 (73.8 per cent) indicated that they write job descriptions to obtain data for wage and salary administration. Slightly more use them "to clarify relationships and responsibilities," an item checked by 139 companies (75.8 per cent).

The next largest group of responses relates to training and orientation. Job descriptions, these replies indicate, are used to give the manager or supervisor better job understanding (112 responses); to acquaint new employees with their jobs (99); and to discover training needs (55).

A total of 105 responses (57.3 per cent) affirm that descriptions are useful in assessing performance on the job. In some of the companies represented, they serve in periodic merit reviews as a form of checklist against which to measure how well managers have been

TABLE 2. *Purpose of Using Supervisory and Managerial Job Descriptions in Production Management in 183 Companies*

	NUMBER OF COMPANIES USING	PER CENT OF COMPANIES USING
To clarify relationships and responsibilities	139	76.0
To obtain data for wage and salary administration	135	73.8
To help managers and supervisors get a better understanding of their jobs	112	61.2
To assess performance on the job	105	57.4
To acquaint new people with their jobs	99	54.1
To discover training needs	55	30.1
To review or improve the work flow	48	26.2
Other answers	15	8.2

doing. Most often, a description is used for this purpose by the manager's immediate superior or by a merit-review committee. The very process of description development, some respondents pointed out, may help to determine the level at which the manager is performing.

It is apparent, then, that the staff personnel man or the line manager embarking on a job-description program in manufacturing will want to keep in mind that the descriptions probably will not be used exclusively for compensation purposes. In fact, a number of the survey respondents noted a change in the purpose of their programs. At first, the effort was mainly devoted—in the usual way—to describing jobs as they were actually performed. But, in the process of writing, organizational shortcomings inevitably showed up, hence the final versions of the descriptions often pointed the way to more effective working arrangements.

In these companies job-description programs are presently aimed at objectives other than salary administration, but the first "as is" description of a given position is still used for setting compensation rates. If the job is found to be poorly organized, if the reporting relationships prove to be defective, or if any other major problem comes to light, a second version is written which, in time, becomes the "as is" description. In other words, a periodic review of jobs is maintained through the job-description program, whereas in many firms new descriptions commonly are written only when substantial changes in jobs take place—that is, at irregular intervals.

Brief labels of the sort used in a checklist are, of course, not always immediately clear. For this reason the survey respondents were also asked this specific question: "What use does your company make of its manufacturing job descriptions?" This called for a fairly detailed statement, and some of the answers which were received may perhaps point the way to better understanding of management thinking and practice.

CLARIFYING RELATIONSHIPS AND RESPONSIBILITIES

In some cases, the writers evidently had in mind the utilization of finished job descriptions. These are used "for pointing up duties, responsibilities, and authorities . . ."; ". . . to clearly define areas of responsibility and authority, and stress the aspects of jobs thought to be of major importance"; ". . . to provide understanding and coordination of duties and responsibilities between the individual and his supervisor and associates." In certain other cases, respondents stated that the descriptions ". . . acquaint [the incumbents] with the responsibilities of other persons at all levels." Naturally this requires that the incumbents see the descriptions of many other people in the company besides their own—usually by means of a complete job manual which is made available to members of management. This manual generally contains an over-all company organization chart, several departmental charts, and all departmental or companywide descriptions.

Even this limited use of job descriptions reflects some awareness of the value, to managers, of the process of formulation and comparison. For "understanding and coordination," a manager must see the descriptions of other managers' positions. If these overlap and conflict with his own job, there will be a certain amount of protest; and if the defects are serious enough, they will be remedied by rewriting. Thus one respondent said:

> In our program the line head of each manufacturing unit reviews all new job descriptions with the manager in the job and with those to whom he reports and those who report to him. If discrepancies or conflicts are discovered by comparing all the job descriptions, the line manager makes it his business to see that changes are made and the descriptions re-issued.

Another puts it this way:

> Our analyst, who works closely with us despite the fact he comes to
> our plant from Central Personnel, makes it a point to describe the
> job as he finds it being performed. He takes several interlocking
> jobs at a time and works on them. Quite often he finds that there
> are conflicts—particularly when there is a newly instituted job. In
> the review of the description carried out by line management,
> changes are often requested, and—if approved by top management—
> these go through in the form of a revised official version.

Such comments make it clear beyond any doubt that companies are
definitely finding job descriptions a tool in, first, uncovering instances of faulty organization, reporting relationships, and work
flow and, second, correcting them.

There are obvious reasons why defects in organization are fairly
common. One executive explains it as follows: "Our company is
undergoing rapid growth; both the organization and our jobs within
it change constantly. Of course we want our employees to expand
their responsibilities as far as they are able, but they must do so
without overlapping. . . ." And firms which have undergone merger
or acquisition experience similar problems. For example: "Because
of several mergers, we have reorganized along decentralized lines.
Job descriptions are required to clarify confused areas of new responsibilities for hiring new people and in transferring old employees."

Managerial position descriptions might well include quantitative
restrictions to prevent conflict. A respondent who uses his descriptions primarily to clarify relationships and responsibilities wrote:
"The description should detail the limits, the maxima and minima
of authority as to purchases, expenses, and people." Yet few descriptions examined in the course of the research for this study give such
limits in quantitative terms. Most common, of course, is the simple
statement that a given manager may not authorize expenditures
above a certain money value. Apparently other limitations on managerial authority are less easy to reduce to writing.

BETTER UNDERSTANDING OF THE JOB

There were two types of statements about the value of managerial
position descriptions in producing a better understanding of the

job. One simply pointed out that the finished description gives the incumbent a fuller picture of this work. It was noticeable that these statements came mostly from companies in which the first draft of the job description is written either by a staff specialist—usually a personnel man—or by the incumbent. Subsequently, the line superior revises the draft to include his own ideas of how the job should be performed and organized. Plainly, these respondents think the written description is of great assistance in *telling* the jobholder what he is to do.

Once again, however, a large number of respondents emphasized the value of the formulation process. For one thing, the act of defining the jobs of subordinate managers and supervisors forces the higher-level manager to take a clear-eyed look at the work of his unit. This is particularly beneficial, some respondents reported, when large groups of managers are going through the job-description process together.

Assessing Performance

Most of the responses that mentioned the use of job descriptions in assessing performance spoke of periodic merit reviews or appraisals. Sometimes, though, the respondents indicated that the exact terminology of the description is kept in mind during the ordinary course of supervision, so that the superior manager forms an accurate idea of the subordinate's performance. Usually, the jobholder is appraised according to the "demands of the descriptions," or these are used as a "basis of performance" or to "estimate and appraise. . . ."

Occasionally, however, the respondents revealed something of actual techniques used: "In our shop . . . [job descriptions] are primarily helpful to the committee which undertakes group appraisals. . . ." Here appraisal by committee has become standard practice, it being regarded as fairer than appraisal by a single line superior. A special committee is selected and charged with rating managers in a given department. This committee always includes the line superior of the person undergoing appraisal, but it also includes several of his peers and, also, his boss's immediate superior. According to this company's spokesman, the incumbent's job description is especially useful in this situation, since all committee members may not be intimately acquainted with his exact duties.

A few respondents said that the job description becomes a written "standard of performance." In other words, it is reviewed with the incumbent at the time of appraisal to determine whether he has performed effectively all of the duties spelled out in the description. (Indeed, some analysts think of the job description as a "charter of authority and responsibility," which states, in no uncertain terms, what is expected of the incumbent.) In contrast, a very few respondents reported using a separate set of written standards of performance in conjunction with the job description. The description states what work is to be done. The standards of performance state how *well* the work is to be done.

Needless to say, adequate standards of performance cannot be developed unless an accurate statement of job content exists. For instance, a quality control director may be charged with maintaining satisfactory quality in the firm's product. This is the broad "grant of authority and responsibility" written into the general part of his job description which precedes the detailed listing of duties and the specific ways in which he is to carry them out. Standards of performance for the job usually concentrate on a few key points or criteria which can be used as a constant check on performance. For instance, one quality control director's standards say "his work shall be so effective that no more than 5 per cent of the finished product shall be returned to the company with statements from customers about defects which originate because of manufacturing failures."

Obviously, standards of performance rest first of all on accurate job descriptions. Second, they usually require good record keeping so that conformance to standard can be checked. The example given is a numerical or "quantified" standard. Sometimes these are very difficult to develop, and the company is forced to fall back on nonquantifiable standards. In one set of standards for a divisional superintendent in a manufacturing firm, the point is made that the incumbent is to "establish standard costs for major grades and operations and supervise so as to meet such standard costs." And immediately the job description continues: "Performance is up to standard when actual manufacturing costs meet standard costs." The superintendent is also called on to ". . . build and maintain a loyal and efficient group of assistants and supervisors to progress toward goals of production, quality, waste [control], and budgets." Performance is up to standard ". . . when able and efficient assistants and supervisors direct their efforts toward meeting of production goals and budgets." For every major point in the description, in short, there is a standard of performance which is included in the same document. The danger in these non-numerical standards is that they may become mere repetitions—in different words—of exactly the same idea previously stated in the outline of duties. Still, they may be of real help in framing points of inquiry for an appraisal.

As yet, the practice of including standards of performance in job descriptions seems relatively uncommon. Of the hundreds of descriptions submitted to AMA in the course of the research for this study, only six or seven included anything like a formal statement on standards. Apparently many companies do not feel the need to add them; they find a clearly written description of the job an adequate tool for appraising performance.[1]

Job Orientation for New People

Ninety-nine out of the 183 companies responding to this question use descriptions to acquaint new managers and supervisors with their jobs. One wonders why the number is not larger.

A job analyst who has had much experience with managerial programs believes it may be simply the old story that numerous job descriptions, originally written for wage-and-salary purposes, therefore assume primarily the "as performed" point of view. "In many companies," he goes on to say, "the desire is to alter jobs in accordance with new ideas. Wage-and-salary descriptions are useless for this purpose."

A clear and definitive statement of job duties would seem to be the best possible orientation tool. However, constant updating in terms of top management's perspective on the job would be essential if it were to serve any practical use.

---

[1] For an extensive discussion of performance standards see *Setting Standards for Executive Performance*, AMA Research Study 42, 1960; also, Virgil K. Rowland, *Managerial Performance Standards*, American Management Association, 1960.

IDENTIFICATION OF TRAINING NEEDS

Unfortunately none of the 55 companies which cited the identification of training needs through job descriptions provided any detailed statement of how this is done. Several did, however, mention
"convenience for the company training director." Descriptions, of
course, give clear statements which can easily be translated into job
specifications. And, if a clear record exists of the incumbents' previous experience and training for managerial work, it should not be
difficult to find areas of weakness and set up a training program to
remedy them. In cases where key personnel are found to lack some
quality essential to managerial effectiveness, individual plans may
even be developed.

REVIEWING AND IMPROVING THE WORK FLOW

Only 48 of the 183 companies mentioned the possibility of improving the flow of work. Apparently it is the least common of the
major uses of managerial position descriptions, possibly because
work-flow studies at supervisory and managerial levels have been
very few indeed. Numerous analyses have been made of clerical and
blue-collar operations. Work systematization and simplification have
in fact been preoccupied with repetitive, non-discretionary jobs;
in the plant, studies have been directed mainly toward production
operations themselves or, sometimes, maintenance. Very rarely has
any comparable formal effort been made to examine the more complex organization and timing of executive or even supervisory work.

Some of the respondents, however, say that accurate managerial
job descriptions are useful in checking lines of authority from the
point at which a decision is made, to the manager whose approval
is needed, and back again to the point of origin where the decision
is put into effect. One job-description specialist remarked that, even
without the benefit of a great deal of theory, sometimes "authority
chains" are so long and complex that the need for improvement is
apparent once they are drawn.

It is worthwhile questioning whether this lack of time- and work-
flow analysis for managerial and supervisory levels is important.
E. D. Chapple and L. R. Sayles, in their book *The Measure of Man-*

agement,[2] propose work flow as the basis for organization design. They contend that efficiency is undermined by a confusion of formal and informal organization structures—referring, of course, to the often-cited conflict between the formalized authority structure of the business, usually as laid down in organization charts and job descriptions, and the informal structure which builds up by dint of custom, the superiority of one man over another, and other non-authoritarian forces. To these authors, the informal organization is more nearly based on the real flow of work through the company. When artificial chains of command intersect this real but informal work flow, they feel, there is a "point of stress." For them, the goal of administration ". . . is to minimize the incidence of organizational deviations from the established interaction patterns of the work process." The theory has much to recommend it when applied to the middle and lower tiers of management. Even at these levels, however, many managers sharply question deviations from the authorized, formal flow of authority and legitimate decision channels.

If job descriptions are to be useful at all in this area, it is fairly obvious that they must be accurately written and that subsequently they ought to be used as a diagnostic tool by someone with enough line authority to correct any defects brought to light in the process of analysis.

SPECIAL SALARY-ADMINISTRATION USES

Of the 135 companies citing wage and salary administration, the majority confined themselves merely to stating that accurate managerial job descriptions are useful in evaluating jobs and placing them in equitable salary grades. Several respondents, however, pointed to other salary-administration uses.

One firm feels it is desirable to have accurate descriptions so that they can ". . . prove to the employee that he is in a correct job level by analyzing his job in terms of the several factors which bear on classification of level." Others stress "equity" factors, one respondent saying, "Unless we have descriptions, there might be several employees in a similar job, doing the same duties, but with entirely

[2] E. D. Chapple and L. R. Sayles, *The Measure of Management,* The Macmillan Company, New York, 1961.

different salaries. To an extent this might be justified by different appraisals and ratings of the persons involved—but there are limits beyond which we cannot go." Again, another company says: "We must maintain a sound wage structure and prevent inequities. Our descriptions eliminate many grievances." This last comment almost seems to take a bargaining point of view; it is as though the respondent were dealing with a trade union. His questionnaire shows that his program includes many first-line supervisors, and at their level this "bargaining" attitude toward job descriptions probably is fairly appropriate. One wonders, though, whether it would really be helpful in setting the compensation of a company officer.

Some firms state that they use managerial position descriptions as a basis for outside salary comparisons. The general tenor of their responses indicates that they must describe their managers' work accurately so that they can evaluate their compensation rates against those of other companies. They also, of course, must have access to the managerial position descriptions and compensation rates of competing companies. Fortunately, there are a few independent organizations which regularly make confidential surveys of compensation rates for various kinds of professional people on many different levels. The results of the most helpful of these surveys are published with fairly detailed listings of executive duties; for instance, AMA's own Executive Compensation Service offers subscribers salary data for managerial and supervisory positions, accompanied by short composite job descriptions and classified by industry, sales volume, and the like. Such guides are best utilized when the company has an accurate idea of the content of its own supervisory and managerial jobs—as is the case when an effective job-description program exists.

Some firms make comparisons on a more limited basis, particularly at levels up to foreman or junior supervisor, by matching figures directly with neighboring firms or by using a regional association as a clearinghouse when cooperation has grown sufficiently to make this possible. As a respondent explains: "We match duties and responsibilities with similar companies; we could not do so on the basis of job titles alone, which often do not indicate very much about what a given job actually consists of." Similarly: "Job descriptions are used to check against like positions in other organizations."

3. The Description-Writing
Process Explored

THE RESPONSES of the survey participants indicate that there are two basic situations in which a production or manufacturing department undertakes managerial position description:

- A companywide effort in which all managerial positions are being described.
- A departmental program in which the production department and, perhaps, allied groups are making the effort.

The key in either situation is cooperation between line and staff. Staff personnel people (most often wage and salary specialists) quite commonly participate; they may interview the job incumbents, survey them or observe them at work, and write the first drafts of the descriptions. Otherwise the descriptions are written by the incumbents or by their immediate superiors and then re-worked by a staff specialist so that the format will conform to that of other groups.

In any case, the job analyst or wage and salary administration specialist can be of great help in compiling managerial position descriptions. He can also be a source of conflict.

In companywide programs, the staff specialist usually appears on the scene with the blessing of top management. Quite commonly, the top people in the firm have decided that position descriptions are needed, and the entire effort has been delegated to the specialized personnel staff. If the program is aimed at determining compensation, and the jobholders are allowed to write the originals of the descriptions, there will be a distinct effort to put the best foot forward. One staff specialist wrote:

> Our firm makes porcelain items of all types, and the manufacturing department is organized along product lines. Each unit manager has one or more products under his direction in the production stages. You would be surprised how many people who really had nothing to do with them claimed to make or manage not only the kitchen sink but bathtubs and a lot of other things.

A staff-managed program devoted to "organizational clarification" and other non-compensatory purposes can run into the same sort of trouble. "Sometimes there's an effort of those who feel insecure to exaggerate their role in company affairs in order to preserve their positions," was the way one staff specialist put it. The problem of empire building is also encountered. An aggressive man may write the draft of his description to include the management of units which often respond to his informal direction though officially they are under the control of another man. In one instance, a plant manager stated that the plant personnel director reported exclusively to him when, actually, he reported to the vice president of personnel at company headquarters. There are, in short, many varieties of exaggeration and many motives for it. But if a manager can insert a new responsibility into his description, and if that description is subsequently issued as official, he may be able to transform the puff into reality.

A line-oriented program may run into just as great difficulties. In such a situation, manufacturing management has usually undertaken the program for the sake of benefits which will accrue to the manufacturing group (this also applies to any other functional group which is managing its own program). The tendency is to write descriptions which organize manufacturing to the satisfaction of manufacturing managers. Authorities and relationships are stated so that they will make life easier for manufacturing—perhaps ignoring the needs of finance, marketing, and other functional divisions of the firm.

Staff assistance can be very useful here. The specialist from personnel may be able to look at position descriptions for managerial jobs in manufacturing with a less one-sided attitude. And, if the manufacturing department's program is intended to dovetail with those of other departments, the staff man may be able to use his position of neutrality to point out conflicts and overlaps to the company's line managers.

Cooperation between line and staff, however achieved, can prevent many fumbles and resulting inaccuracies in position descriptions.

INTRODUCING THE PROGRAM

Difficulty is most likely to be encountered when the job-description project is first introduced. Unless the objectives are clearly explained, the effort to obtain written descriptions of managerial jobs may cause insecurity and even hostility.

To cite the report on an earlier AMA survey in the managerial-job-description area:

> It is easy to see that if the program is introduced carelessly, at least a few executives may believe that an effort is being made to prune deadwood, to adjust compensation (sometimes downward), to cut some jobs down to a smaller size, or to inflate other jobs. Prestige and status are definitely involved.

> What should be done about it? Most of the survey respondents believe that the program will get off the ground best if it has the full force of the company's top management behind it. Often, the introductory announcement outlining the program to the managerial group is sponsored or conducted by the president of the firm. The favored method appears to be a group meeting of top company executives at which the need for descriptions is outlined and the method to be used in describing their positions is explained. Each of these executives then may hold a meeting of his department's officials and explain the program to them as fully and as frankly as possible. Some companies, in contrast, prefer to announce the project by means of a letter signed by the president, and a few firms feel that the matter is vital enough to require both a meeting

and a letter. If a consultant is employed, it is generally felt that he should be introduced at the meeting. It is also advisable to state what each executive may expect and what he must do in order to prepare himself for the job analysis.

. . . Often, reassurances are given that compensation will not be reduced as a result of the description program and that no one will lose his job. Sometimes it is carefully explained that the study is being conducted for equity in compensation only and that job content will not be altered as a result—or, on the contrary, that the balance of duties is being reviewed and compensation will not be affected.

In reassuring the managers affected, it is well to remember how many companies find that their descriptions are later used for markedly different purposes than those in view at the outset. In other words, when promises are made, one must be sure that they can and will be fulfilled. Suppose, for example, a large group is told that no one will be discharged as a result of the program and, after a long study of the descriptions, it is found that several jobs could be dropped. Then the company has only two real choices: to make transfers or to wait for retirement or normal attrition to take effect.

The need for top management support and reassurance applies equally to manufacturing management where a departmental job-description program is undertaken. There are usually "more pressing matters" to occupy people's time if the project has not received full approval at the highest departmental level.

SPELLING OUT THE OBJECTIVES

The guidance given in writing the descriptions will depend on the objectives of the program. If exact descriptions of the job are needed for salary purposes, the analyst will be most concerned with eliminating views of how they *ought* to be done. If the incumbents are to write the first drafts themselves, it may be necessary to guard against overly optimistic thinking—writing the descriptions to portray what, hopefully, they will be "a year or two from now." If, on the other hand, the top managers already have a fairly good picture of how jobs are currently being done and are now interested in possible improvement of organizational structure and reporting relationships, they will look for precisely those creative or forward-looking thoughts which are rejected in salary-oriented descriptions.

Standard Oil Company of California makes the distinction aptly in its manual, "People and Paychecks":

Taking Jobs Apart. Finding out what the package contains is called job analysis, an art requiring an open mind, a wide knowledge of jobs, and a willingness to ask many questions. The objective of a *job analysis*, as opposed to *job engineering*, is simply to determine the job's duties and responsibilities—"How and why and what is done?"—and the job qualifications—"What kind of man does it take to do it?" Since this analysis is the basis for most of what is to follow, it is worthwhile to discuss a few of its basics:

1. The job is studied, not the man. This applies to all phases of the job. Determining job qualifications is a good example. A job which normally would require a degree in business administration is that kind of job, even if the man filling it happens to be an unusually capable high school graduate. On the other hand, the fact that the person on a job is a college graduate does not necessarily mean the job requires one. Whether it does or not is determined by the duties and responsibilities of the job, not the qualifications of its holder. This is not to say, however, that if a job is being well done by a person under- or over-qualified for it, a change should *necessarily* be made.

2. What the job is, not what it ought to be, or is thought to be, is the first, but not the last, question. It is too easy to make a mistake by taking appearance as fact. We are surprised to find out just how much the quiet little fellow over in the corner is doing. The only way to know the job is to dig for facts, study them, taking little for granted.

3. Each job is part of an organization. The more that is known about the jobs over, under, and around the one under study, the easier it is to determine how that one fits into the organization and what its contribution can be.

4. It is essential, though not always easy, to see *the whole job*. Some can be quickly and easily observed. Others may have long work cycles. Many accounting jobs have monthly, quarterly, and annual cycles. Other cycles depend on the specific assignment: for example, a Project Engineer. Still others have important responsibilities which are seldom exercised, such as those of refinery operators in case of emergencies.

5. Ideally job analysis should only be fact-finding—but in practice it necessarily involves judgment. What is significant in the job, the difficulty and importance of its duties, the qualifications needed to perform it—none of these may be absolutely determined. A good and usable answer to these questions depends upon the perspective and objectivity of the job analysis.

Putting Them Back Together. So much for the job "as is." Normally the next step would be to record this information on a job description. However, we prefer instead to take a highly important side trip. This is to ask the question, "Is the job organized properly?" and, if not, to make changes so that it is, a process sometimes referred to as *job engineering*. The subject of organization is broad, but here are some of the most important questions asked about any job:

1. Is everything done on this job really necessary? Habit and inertia keep people doing the things they are used to doing, even though the need for some of these operations may have disappeared.

2. Is this the best way to get the necessary work done? New equipment, ideas, and organizations often make possible more efficient ways of reaching the same end.

3. Does this job fit well with other jobs around it, and related to it? Is there duplication of effort or working at cross purposes? In short, does the job as constituted help out teamwork?

4. Does it provide training for more responsibility? And thus fit into a good promotional sequence? If not, and if the job cannot be redesigned so that it does, it should be earmarked and watched carefully to avoid "deadending" some unlucky and undeserving employee.

5. Does it have a reasonable mix of duties? For example, including many simple routine duties in the same job with involved responsibilities is undesirable. A man capable of difficult and responsible work will be wasting a substantial part of his time, and the company will be paying a high price for accomplishment of the simple duties.

6. Is it engineered for the normal work day? It is clearly unfair and unwise to overload one man and leave another idle for much of his time.

The advantages of good job organization are obvious. An employee has to work no harder to do something worthwhile and to do something we know is productive than something we suspect doesn't really matter. In short, this step is a big contributor to productivity, the goose that lays the golden eggs. Jobs properly engineered and organized are seldom problem jobs.

To re-emphasize: "Job engineering" is beyond the scope of the staff personnel man who is conducting a salary-oriented description program. His objective is to describe the job as it is, not as it ought to be. This applies, moreover, to those who are writing first drafts of descriptions to give management a look at the current organization with the idea that these factual descriptions will be used as the basis for an organization study which *may* result in changes. A good analyst, or a man working on his own description or those of his subordinates, may find it appropriate to make written records of the changes he feels are needed to improve the job. If he does not have them ready when the time comes, he may find that someone else is making sweeping changes with which he does not agree.

WHO DOES IT?

The actual drafting of job descriptions is about evenly divided between staff specialists and the regular manufacturing chain of command, the AMA survey found. Table 3 gives the answers of 183 companies to the question, "Who usually writes your descriptions of managerial and supervisory jobs relating to manufacturing?" Some companies reported that several people normally take part in the work, which accounts, of course, for the total of 254 responses from 183 companies.

The jobholder or his immediate supervisor is the job-description writer mentioned in 41.7 per cent of the responses. Staff specialists were named in 39.0 per cent, and consultants—who might also be viewed as staff specialists even though they are not on the regular company payroll—were designated in another 4.3 per cent of the answers. Over all, then, it appears that at least as much writing of descriptions is done by experts in description writing as is done by experts in the details of the work being written about. What seem to be the pros and cons of the two arrangements?

The staff man mentions three principal advantages of having the descriptions prepared by a specialist: (1) He can schedule the writ-

TABLE 3. *Persons Who Prepare Job Descriptions for Manufacturing Management in 183 Companies (By Size of Company)*

PERSON WHO WRITES JOB DESCRIPTION	TOTALS		NUMBER OF EMPLOYEES									
			1,000 OR LESS		1,001 TO 5,000		5,001 TO 20,000		OVER 20,000		NO. NOT REPORTED	
	No.	Per Cent	No.	Per Cent	No.	Per Cent	No.	Per Cent	No.	Per Cent	No.	Per Cent
*Totals**	254	100.1	74	100.1	106	100.1	48	100.1	23	99.8	3	100.0
Line personnel:	106	41.7	33	44.6	39	36.8	22	45.8	11	47.8	1	33.3
Jobholder himself	41	16.1	13	17.6	10	9.4	12	25.0	6	26.1	0	0.0
His immediate supervisor	65	25.6	20	27.0	29	27.4	10	20.8	5	21.7	1	33.3
Staff personnel:	99	39.0	22	29.8	48	45.4	19	39.7	8	34.6	2	66.7
Wage and salary administrator	30	11.8	0	0.0	21	20.0	6	12.5	2	8.7	1	33.3
Industrial relations specialist	7	2.8	5	6.8	1	0.9	0	0.0	1	4.3	0	0.0
Personnel administrator	23	9.1	10	13.5	11	10.4	1	2.1	1	4.3	0	0.0
Job analyst	10	3.9	0	0.0	3	2.8	3	6.3	3	13.0	1	33.3
Industrial engineer	5	2.0	2	2.7	1	0.9	2	4.2	0	0.0	0	0.0
Other specialists	24	9.4	5	6.8	11	10.4	7	14.6	1	4.3	0	0.0
Other:	49	19.3	19	25.7	19	17.9	7	14.6	4	17.4	0	0.0
Consultant	11	4.3	6	8.1	5	4.7	0	0.0	0	0.0	0	0.0
Other answers	37	14.6	13	17.6	13	12.3	7	14.6	4	17.4	0	0.0
Title not reported	1	0.4	0	0.0	1	0.9	0	0.0	0	0.0	0	0.0

* Because of rounding, the percentages do not add up to exactly 100.0 in each column.

ing and get it done without so much conflict with the demands of other duties. (2) Being a specialist in the analysis of jobs, he knows what factors to look for, he can cover points more consistently, and he can make the language of the descriptions more accurate. (3) As mentioned, he generally brings a disinterested point of view to the task and is not so likely to be involved in departmental politics; therefore, he is not so prone to exaggerated statements of responsibility and authority.

Yet there are disadvantages to letting a staff specialist write the first draft of a manager's job description. The incumbent certainly loses most of his sense of participation, and even his superior may feel that the description program is a "personnel gimmick" of little benefit to his organizational group. Virgil K. Rowland, assistant to the president of The Detroit Edison Company, argues as follows: "Staff should do nothing that line can do better itself." Mr. Rowland firmly believes that most of the benefit of a job-description program is lost if line superior and subordinate do not come together in open and frank discussion sometime during the description process.

Actually, there may be more interchange of ideas than has been suggested so far. Often a description is not completely written in final form by a single individual. Instead, several people may participate in varying degrees. Many respondents report that the first draft may be written by the incumbent and revised by his superior, or written by either the superior or the incumbent and brought into line as to style and format by a staff specialist. There seem to be two main patterns:

1. If the first draft is written by a staff specialist, the review and final version are undertaken by superior line management even if they only give a few directions to the specialist on the content of the final version.

2. If the first draft is written by those with line authority (often the incumbent and his superior), the draft is reviewed mainly for style and format by the staff specialist.

Still a third situation was mentioned by a few companies. By way of explanation, let us say that the original drafts have been examined and that final versions have been prepared. Most often these are inserted in a manual and circulated to the managers authorized to have them. It is possible now to run through all the jobs in a given department or company and compare them. At this point, the top management of the firm may call for still another revision. This happens when major relationships, often between primary functional divisions, are judged to be out of line. Some description programs conducted on a companywide basis have resulted in major reorganizations which were not envisioned at the program's start.

In Table 3, it is interesting to note that as the size of the company increases, there is a greater tendency to allow the managerial job incumbent to write the first draft of his own description. Of the 71 firms with more than 5,000 employees, 18 (25.3 per cent) follow this practice. The percentage is considerably smaller for companies with fewer employees. Do larger firms with a larger number of professional managers respond to new trends in management more quickly than their smaller counterparts?

Certainly there is a great emphasis on "shared objectives" and "participative" management in the literature today. If a manager prepares the first draft of his job description, it is apparent to him that he has much weight in determining what he is doing. If his superior changes that first draft to bring it more into line with *his* objectives, the subordinate still has had his say. When, however, the superior writes the first draft and shows it to the subordinate with the injunction that he is to "look it over and report back," the subordinate will often jump to the conclusion that he is actually being given a rigid guide to his work. And often he may be right in this conclusion. Occasionally, of course, this is precisely the way to handle the situation; some subordinates stand in great need of strong direction. But in many companies the "participative" approach is highly valued. It is felt that when duties and targets are worked out in give-and-take discussions between a subordinate and his chief, the subordinate will be more strongly committed to meeting the goals agreed upon.

This point of view is especially appropriate for managerial job-description programs in which the emphasis is not on salary administration. In preparing descriptions for salary programs, the neutrality of the staff specialist or even an outside consultant may be very beneficial.

4. Methods of Gathering
Job-Description Data

THE MOST POPULAR SINGLE METHOD of gathering information for managerial position descriptions in manufacturing is to interview the incumbent manager himself. The interview is most often conducted by a staff specialist; however, the companies participating in the survey often use two or more methods to collect needed data. Table 4 gives the responses of 183 companies; as usual, the fact that these companies gave 381 different responses makes the multiplicity of approaches clear.

The respondents mentioned only three methods by which a person other than the jobholder can gather information for a description:

- Observation.
- Interviewing.
- Questionnaires.

There is, however, a fourth method which is sometimes recommended. This is the use of a "job diary" or "job log" in which the incumbent notes different phases of his work during the course of a typical working cycle. Clerical and blue-collar employees often fill out "time cards" noting which jobs or activities they have been pursuing. This information is then used by cost accounting in deter-

TABLE 4. *Sources of Information for Job Descriptions in Manufacturing Management in 183 Companies (By Size of Company)*

| | | | NUMBER OF EMPLOYEES | | | | | | | | | | |
| SOURCE OF INFORMATION | TOTALS | | 1,000 OR LESS | | 1,001 TO 5,000 | | 5,001 TO 20,000 | | OVER 20,000 | | NO. NOT REPORTED | |
	No.	Per Cent	No.	Per Cent	No.	Per Cent	No.	Per Cent	No.	Per Cent	No.	Per Cent
Totals	*381*	*100.1*	*101*	*101.1*	*152*	*101.8*	*80*	*99.9*	*41*	*99.6*	*7*	*100.1*
Jobholder writes own description	67	17.6	22	21.8	19	12.8	17	21.2	9	21.0	0	0.0
Specialist gets information from:												
Interview with jobholder	107	28.1	25	24.7	46	30.0	24	30.0	9	21.0	3	42.9
Questionnaire filled out by jobholder	50	13.1	10	9.9	20	13.1	13	16.2	6	14.6	1	14.3
Observation of jobholder at work	75	19.7	22	21.8	31	20.2	11	13.7	8	22.0	3	42.9
Other	81	21.3	22	21.9	35	25.0	15	18.8	9	21.0	0	0.0
No answer	1	0.3	0	0.0	1	0.7	0	0.0	0	0.0	0	0.0

mining the cost of given projects. Few foremen and managers are regularly required to fill out such cards. Because of this, it is necessary to ask them to make out job logs well in advance of a description effort. Apparently, this method's lack of popularity can be ascribed, at least in part, to the feeling that asking managers to keep such a record would in some way diminish their status. Perhaps the respondents also feel that managerial work is not subject to accurate description in this way and that it would take too much valuable managerial time. One analyst, however, finds the job logs or time cards of blue-collar employees and clerical workers an invaluable source of information on the duties of the employees' superiors. In one program he managed, several foremen completely forgot to mention certain aspects of their work. The analyst picked up this information by examining time cards filled out by machinists and maintenance men under their supervision. When, in a subsequent follow-up interview, the foremen were questioned about their responsibility toward these activities, it became apparent that they had simply forgotten them.

The emphasis, in companies known to have good position descriptions, seems to be on flexibility in gathering data. One company which uses several methods of data gathering outlines its practices for foremen's descriptions as follows:

1. The foreman completes a questionnaire concerning his job.

2. The completed questionnaire is reviewed by the foreman's immediate supervisor and a member of the industrial relations staff.

3. The job description is written in draft form by the industrial relations staff.

4. The description is then reviewed by the foreman, the foreman's immediate supervisor, and the plant manager or one of his immediate staff.

5. The industrial relations department writes the final job description.

6. The description is reviewed and signed by the foreman's immediate supervisor and other line supervision to and including the plant manager. This usually consists of three or four levels of supervision. (No one from the personnel or industrial relations departments signs the descriptions.)

7. The foreman completes a questionnaire every six months indicating

any changes in his description. As a change is indicated, he will be interviewed by a member of the industrial relations department concerning the change.

This method of preparing job descriptions for foremen might well be used as a model for developing descriptions for higher management in that it provides for the two essentials: (1) adequate data-gathering methods; (2) ample opportunity for the incumbent and the superior, staff and line, to confer on content. No matter what specific methods are used, if these two essentials are taken care of, fair descriptions should result.

Another company includes an extended presentation of its procedures in a company manual. These are used for blue-collar employees as well as for supervisors and managers. The language of the document shows that it was prepared primarily with the non-exempt employee in mind, yet the company has found the methods embodied in it so flexible that they have been extended to describe exempt jobs. Again, adequate data-gathering methods are provided for, along with careful review of successive drafts:

. . . Preliminary data are often gathered on printed forms called "Individual's Job Questionnaire" and "Supervisor's Questionnaire," respectively. The purposes of these forms are to increase the degree of participation by employees and supervisors, and to provide preliminary information for the job analysts. However, they are not intended as substitutes for the interview with the employee at his workplace. Long experience with the use of questionnaires indicates that they aid the job analysts in the studies of new positions, but are not usually necessary for restudies of existing positions. In the latter cases, the existing job descriptions usually provide adequate preliminary data for the analysts.

I. The Individual's Job Questionnaire

This form is prepared by *every individual employee.* The information sought should represent each employee's own ideas concerning his job content and his opinions as to the qualifications required as well as the responsibility limits involved, and so forth. We realize that this may not be secured in all cases, particularly when there are a number of employees on the same job; in fact, some groups of employees prefer to appoint some one or more of their number to prepare a "community" answer to the questionnaire for their common job. While this may be permitted, as the choice of the group, it is not to be encouraged.

With a knowledge of the requirements of the completed job description, the job analyst should find the questions asked on the questionnaire self-explanatory. However, employees and supervisors frequently ask questions as to the meaning of sections of the questionnaire that are not clear to them. When and if the analyst may be called upon to answer such questions, he should apply, in his own mind, this test: "If I were writing a description from this questionnaire, what would I want to know, in answer to the question involved?" When this point has been settled in the analyst's mind, he should explain the *meaning* of the question to supervisor or employee but should avoid telling the inquirer *what* to enter in answer to the question.

Similar instructions should be passed on to supervisors. When their subordinates inquire concerning parts of the individual questionnaire, the supervisors should explain in detail the *meaning* of such parts, but should avoid any appearance of dictating what the employee should answer.

II. The Supervisor's Questionnaire

The immediate supervisor is required to fill in one of these questionnaires for each *job*, but not necessarily for each employee, under his jurisdiction. By "job" we mean a group of duties normally assigned to one person or group of persons. If assigned to more than one person, these duties must be similar in nature and of approximately equal complexity, requiring approximately equal minimum starting qualifications. The duties must be performed within the same responsibility limits and with equal authority. The conditions and surroundings of the workplace must be the same.

The job analyst may occasionally be called upon to advise the immediate supervisor about grouping a number of individuals on one questionnaire. The test setup in the preceding paragraph should be applied in answering such questions. In the case of new organization units never before studied, and of entirely new jobs, it is best to err on the side of too many supervisor's questionnaires than too few, as the analyst can, if advisable, combine them after the details have been developed and he is ready to write the specifications.

III. Use of Filled-in Questionnaires by the Analyst

Experienced analysts find that the completed questionnaires can be used as the basis of the interview with little detailed preparatory effort, other than perusal, on their part. Less experienced of new analysts will find some preliminary work with the questionnaires and a blank specification form helpful. The following instructions on the use of the questionnaires will apply only to the new analyst's study of his first few sets of questionnaires. As experience is acquired, the analyst will find less and less of his work along these lines going on a blank description form, and more and more showing as brief notes on the questionnaire or being stored in his mind to be covered during the interview. Inasmuch as the preparation of a pre-interview form is unnecessarily time-consuming, except from a training viewpoint, it should be discontinued by each new analyst as soon as possible.

Prior to attempting to study a job, the analyst-in-training should take a job folder (containing questionnaires, notes, and so forth) and, from the latest questionnaires, attempt to prepare a job description from questionnaire information only. This should be done in accordance with the instructions given [above]. . . . When this has been completed as far as the questionnaire information will allow, the analyst should secure the official description and the previous analysts' notes. Comparison of the hand-written description prepared from the questionnaire, the official description and the rough notes, as well as the analyst's own thoughts, will show what must be gotten during the interview.

The above process should be repeated several times with other recently studied jobs, except that the analyst-in-training should make notes as to additional information, not shown on the questionnaires, required for completion of an adequate description. Then the comparison of the new analyst's ideas and the previous analysts' work can be made, bringing out further information uncovered by the more experienced men.

Next comes the first assignment. The new analyst should attempt to complete it from the questionnaires. Notes may be made either on the questionnaire, or on separate paper, in connection with data to be secured or points to be cleared up. Such notes will be made on the basis of the training afforded by the practice method outlined in the preceding paragraphs.

IV. The Actual Interview

The job analyst's interview . . . is his primary way of getting information. . . . It enables the analyst to observe and discuss the work being done, and the conditions under which it is being done.

Arrangements for the interview should ideally be made with the . . . immediate supervisor. The time chosen should . . . be the earliest date mutually convenient. The analyst should resist undue postponements. . . . If the supervisor insists that changes are being made in the job content or methods, advise the section analyst [a supervisory employee in the personnel department].

Unless they know each other, the analyst should be introduced to the employee by the supervisor. Even if they do know each other, the analyst should not interview unless some member of the supervisory or executive force has first been advised.

Any attempt to set forth specific instructions on how to conduct an interview is hopeless.* The analyst is one man trying to get information from another. The reaction of different people to the different analysts cannot be predicted. . . .

During the interview, take notes of all significant points. Ask questions and guide discussions so that the facts required for the job description all come to light. In other words, attempt to visualize a complete description and record the details in such a way that your notes will become the description.

Obviously, the procedures outlined in this condensed version of one company's instructions are largely intended to foster reliance on the interview. This will be the case in any firm which relies heavily on the skills of a staff analyst rather than on the mutual give-and-take between superior and subordinate manager.

The forms used by this company in its questionnaire research are reproduced on the following pages. They were selected, because of their very complexity, from the numerous samples submitted in the course of the research. Few companies, except those of the largest size which have well-established programs, will require such elaborate forms. They embody practically every device that conceivably could be needed.

Exhibit 1. *Individual's Job Questionnaire*

			Section or
Name .... Dept. .... Location ....
Payroll	Time with	Time this	Name, Immediate
Title .... Company ...... position ...... Supervisor ....

PLEASE READ THE ENTIRE FORM BEFORE MAKING ANY ENTRIES.

DESCRIPTION OF DUTIES:

Supervisory Duties

(1) How many employees do you supervise? (List job names and number of people in each job.)
(2) Briefly, what is the general purpose of their work?

---

* See, however, *Defining the Manager's Job,* pp. 94–109, where a complete recorded interview is reproduced.

Personal Duties

  (3) What duties do you personally perform in the usual course of your work? (Please indicate the approximate percentages of your time spent on your major duties.)

  (4) What duties do you perform only at stated periods, such as weekly, monthly, etc.?

  (5) What occasional duties do you perform at irregular intervals?

MINIMUM STARTING REQUIREMENTS OF YOUR POSITION: (Note: Please do not enter your own personal education, experience, etc., unless it happens to agree with your opinion of *minimum* requirement.)

  (6) What is the lowest grade of grammar, high school, or college education that should be required of a person starting in your position?

  (7) If any special courses are needed, name them.

  (8) What previous experience should a new employee have had in order to meet the *minimum* starting requirements of your position?

    (*a*) What kind of experience is required?

    (*b*) Where can it be obtained?

    (*c*) What is the minimum length of time required to acquire it?

  (9) Given the above education and experience:

    (*a*) What *new factors,* not encountered in previous experience and training, would an employee starting in this position have to learn?

    (*b*) What would be the *minimum time* required to learn and practice these factors in order to perform the duties of this position?

(10) Please list any other requirements not covered above and any personal qualifications and characteristics which you believe should be present in a candidate for your position.

FACTORS CONCERNING YOUR DUTIES:

(11) How are you instructed, and by whom, as to what work is to be done?

(12) What instructions do you receive as to how the work is to be done?

(13) What decisions are you required to refer to higher authority?

(14) What parts of your work are checked by others?

(15) What machines or other equipment do you personally operate? Regularly or only occasionally?

(16) Roughly, what proportions of your time are spent in: Standing . . . . %; Sitting . . . . %; Climbing . . . . %; Lifting . . . . %; Walking . . . . %; Other . . . . %; . . . . %.

(17) What, in your opinion, is the most complex or difficult part of your work?

(18) What is the nature and extent of your responsibility for the employees under your supervision?

(19) What is your responsibility for materials processed, produced, handled, etc.? Please name the materials.

(20) What is your responsibility for equipment, if any? What is the equipment?

(21) What contacts with other people are you *required* to make, other than with your subordinates and your immediate superior? (Please list contacts within the Company and outside the Company.)

(22) What is your responsibility for cash and/or negotiable instruments?

(23) What, if any, is your responsibility for determination of methods to be used by yourself or others?
(24) What is your responsibility for records and reports?
(25) Describe any conditions present in the location and nature of your work, such as surroundings, dust, gases, temperature, etc., which you consider unfavorable, undesirable, or disagreeable.
(26) What dangers or accident hazards are present in your work?
(27) What are your regular working hours per day, and how many days per week do you work?
(28) Are you subject to call for emergency or other special work? If so, how frequently are you called?
(29) Does your work require traveling? If so, how often and for how long per trip?

Use this space and additional sheets of paper, if necessary, for any special features of your work not covered above, and for answers to questions for which more space is needed.

EXHIBIT 2. *Supervisor's Questionnaire*

Position ....Dept. ....Division ....
  Title and Name
Section ....Location ....Immed. Supervisor ....

Name (s) of employee (s) occupying this position:
1. Description of duties. (Please describe briefly the primary function or purpose of this position.)
2. Please enter below your opinion of the *minimum starting requirements* which would enable a candidate to qualify for this position. (Note: Do not enter the qualifications of the present incumbent unless they coincide with your opinions of the minimum requirements.)
   (a) What *minimum* formal education, or its equivalent, should be required of a candidate for the position?
   (b) What special courses or what specialized technical knowledge is required, if any?
   (c) What previous experience should the candidate have had in order to meet the *minimum* starting requirements of the work?
       (1) What kind of experience is required?
       (2) Where can it be obtained?
       (3) What is the minimum length of time required to acquire it?
   (d) Do any physical requirements of the work make it necessary to require certain physical qualifications of the candidate, such as height, weight, strength, etc.? If so, please list such qualifications.
   (e) Please list any other qualifications, not specifically covered above, that you consider necessary as starting requirements of this position.

3. Given the minimum starting requirements outlined in the preceding sections:
    (a) *What new factors,* not encountered in previous experience and training, would an employee starting in this position have to learn?
    (b) What would be the *minimum time* required to learn and practice these factors in order to perform the duties of this position at minimum acceptable proficiency?
4. How many employees are supervised by the incumbent of this position, and what is the nature and extent of this supervisory responsibility?
5. What are the primary responsibilities of the incumbent of this position?
6. What types of decisions can he make without reference to higher authority?
7. What are the types of decisions that the incumbent must refer to higher authority?
8. How frequently, and in what manner, are you in contact with the job to check progress, give further instructions, and answer questions?
9. What further checks are there on the effectiveness of the work?
10. What, in your opinion, is the most difficult part of the work?
11. From what positions within the Company could employees be promoted to this position?
12. For what higher positions in the Company should this work train an employee?
13. What are the regular working hours of the incumbent (s) of this position?
14. Is the nature of the assignment such that irregular, emergency, or overtime work is required? If so, how frequently?

5. Questions of Format and Content

M ANAGERIAL POSITION DESCRIPTIONS in manufacturing do not differ markedly from comparable descriptions in other functional areas. Examination of the collection in Part Two of this study will show that they usually contain much the same elements.

The staff specialist or production manager who is faced with the problem of carrying out a managerial position-description program in his firm ought, however, to familiarize himself carefully with the major sections of the job descriptions used in other company units so that his descriptions can be written in the same format—if the format already in use is adequate. Even though programs may begin here and there in the company with little over-all direction, some effort should be made to coordinate the contents of the descriptions so that the various departmental projects will culminate in a companywide set of descriptions for all managers.

If, on the other hand, the production or manufacturing department is the only unit in the firm with a managerial position-description program, it is obvious that the best possible format should be selected in the hope that other company units will adhere to it.

TITLE OF THE JOB

Normally, the first item to appear in any job description is the title of the job. Insofar as possible, most middle-management job titles are miniature job descriptions in themselves. For instance, "Manager, Production Control," certainly gives a basic, easily comprehended idea of the job's duties. "Maintenance Superintendent," "Works Manager," and "Director of Industrial Engineering," also are fairly clear. Yet numerous descriptions examined in the course of the research for this study have such titles as "Foreman," "Superintendent," and "Department Head." The weakness in using titles like these in job descriptions or organization charts is that they actually are only symbols of rank; they give the person who comes across them very little idea of the incumbents' duties.

In larger companies where there may be many managers working at the same level, it seems almost obligatory to use fuller titles. The usual custom is to state rank first. The familiar title "Vice President–Manufacturing" is quite clearly a statement first of rank and then of functional specialization. Equivalent titles in lower management are "Foreman–Sheet Metal Shop," and "Foreman–Equipment Maintenance."

Place and, to a certain extent, time at which work is done also enter into the question of adequate job titles if the company is geographically dispersed or operates more than one shift. We have, for example, "Night Superintendent, Sandusky Plant Maintenance"; "Works Manager, Canton, Ohio" (there are three shifts, but there is only one works manager in over-all charge); and "Tool Crib Manager, Plant A, Day Shift." Admittedly, there is little utility in including the man's shift unless the work performed differs markedly according to the time when it is performed, but in some jobs precisely this difference is apparent on reading the descriptions. To cite a case in point, maintenance people who work nights in plants which do not operate at night, and where the machinery is consequently shut down, have entirely different duties from those of maintenance crews in plants where the machinery is kept running around the clock.

Let us try to formulate a general rule. Job titles give rank, specialization, location, and time at which work is performed *if all these various designations are necessary to differentiate jobs clearly.* Of course, all kinds of abbreviations may be used when people are communicating verbally; but, in formal descriptions for a complex, interlocking series of jobs, clear, full titles are essential.

People who write job descriptions frequently report that it is difficult to keep this need for clear job titles in mind. Why? Simply because, in the process of working up a particular description, they become almost too familiar with all the details of the job. What they may overlook in this frame of mind is that a title developed in the course of a description program is often used in other company documents where the duties are not stated. The very fact that the title heading a written job description tends to become the official one may prevent the person using it elsewhere from adding explanatory words, even when using it rather informally.

The job analyst should remember that when the finally approved version of a description is put into use, the job's title is "frozen." In a series of descriptions, therefore, titles should be clear as to functional specialization and logically graded according to rank. One survey respondent remarked that job analysts in his company "test" titles by typing them on three-by-five cards and giving them to a person unfamiliar with the firm to grade in order of rank and organize into departments. If this process works out fairly well, they are sure that they have developed a set of clear titles.

A firm that makes machinery states its rules for developing titles in a job-description manual which reads in part as follows:

1. *Meaning and Purpose of Job Titles.* Webster tells us that, when used in reference to a person's occupation, a "title" is a *distinctive* appellation, especially one belonging to a person by right of rank, office, attainment, etc. Hence, in industry, a job title should be descriptive and unequivocal, not a combination of words whose connotation masks the actual work performed or magnifies duties out of their true proportions.

   Job titles serve many purposes. To some people they are status symbols with which to impress the Joneses, business associates, bankers, or credit investigators. When used for "calling-card purposes," a job title may signify prestige, authority, responsibility, educational background, glamour, or earnings potential.

   In their proper perspective, however, job titles should be *meaningful condensations of job descriptions.* To be useful tools, they should tell how and what is being done. For a uniform corporate pattern, job titles must be standardized within reasonable limits.

   The primary purpose of a job title is to designate the *organizational level* and *type of work performed* by the incumbent.

2. *Key to Good Titles.* To be descriptive and meaningful, job titles should be *brief, complete,* and *uniform.* With few exceptions,

EXHIBIT 3. *Examples of Good and Bad Job Titles*

GOOD TITLE	POOR TITLE	ERROR
Foreman–Product Painting	Foreman–Paint Shop	Location, not *what* is painted
Foreman–Tool Fabrication	Foreman–Tool Room	Location, not *what* is done to tools
Foreman–Parts Fabrication	Foreman–Press	Equipment used, not function performed
Foreman–Assembly	Foreman–D.90	Department number, not function performed
Foreman–General Maintenance	Foreman–Maintenance	Implies *both* electrical and mechanical maintenance
Foreman–Electrical Maintenance	Foreman–Maintenance	
Foreman–Mechanical Maintenance	Foreman–Maintenance	

this uniformity is obtained by denoting the organizational level before the "dash" and the function (what is done) after the "dash."

Good titles describe *what* is being done. Poor titles may describe *where* it is being done [when jobs do not differ according to location], type of equipment used, or imply more than what is being done [when an attempt is being made to "inflate" the job, usually in order to get a higher compensation rate].

The company also presents a set of good titles and poor titles, giving the reasons why the titles are poor. These appear in Exhibit 3.

The job-description manual then goes on to provide some guidance in setting up titles according to rank. The system is, of course, primarily appropriate for this particular company. No one will ever develop a set of standardized, ranked titles which will fit *all* businesses, but this set at least gives an example of orderly progression:

The term "Foreman" is used to designate men in charge of "blue-collar" workers. "Supervisor" is used for [those supervising] white-collar workers. The blue-collar job progression is: Foreman, General Foreman, Superintendent. The white-collar progression is: Supervisor, General Supervisor, and, when required, Manager. The number of titles required in any organizational unit will depend on its size, complexity, structure, and reporting relationships. To suggest all titles needed for a "typical" division would be difficult. Some are autonomous units which include all major industrial functions (manufacturing, quality control, personnel, accounting, procurement and production control, manufacturing engineering, research and product engineering, sales and sales service, and administration). Others are branch-type operations which do not include one or more of these functions, or are units supported solely by central services.

If the top divisional executive has all functions reporting to him, he is called "General Manager." If he does not have responsibility over sales or product engineering, his title is "Plant Manager." If he heads a service, rather than a product manufacturing division, he is a "Division Manager."

An *"Assistant to"* is someone in an administrative, coordinating, or specialist capacity. No one reports to him. On the other hand, the title *"Assistant General* (Division, or Plant) *Manager"* normally means that *all* divisional functions which report to the General Manager report *through* the Assistant General Manager.

Misnomers. Exaggeration, flattery, and glamour have little place in job titles. It may be good human relations to call a woman "pleasingly plump" or "stylishly stout," but it's not good practice to term her an "Administrative Assistant" when she's actually a Stenographer. Calling a Janitor a "Sanitary Engineer," or a Clerk–Personnel Records a "Personnel Assistant," or a Manager–Quality Control a "Technical Director" is just as ambiguous.

Words such as engineer, accountant, analyst, coordinator, editor, representative, assistant to, and so forth should generally be confined to non-supervisory positions whose incumbents are classified as exempt [from the provisions of the Fair Labor Standards Act requiring overtime compensation] but do *not* exercise bona fide supervisory responsibility over others (e.g., power to hire, fire or change pay status). The words "lead" or "lead man" should not be used for non-exempt jobs; they *imply* supervision over others. Rather, use the term "senior" to denote duties such as making routine work assignments, checking work . . . of lower-level employees, or other functional supervision.

Rule of Thumb. If a job title is not self-explanatory concerning organizational level and duties performed, it is not consistent with our functional system of titles.

IDENTIFYING DATA

Identifying data ordinarily do not appear in the position descriptions of smaller companies. Only quite large firms require such information, since it is only in firms with a large number of similar jobs that possibilities of confusion occur. Indeed, in some big companies, jobs are identified by a number system; a first digit perhaps identifies a position as exempt or non-exempt, and other, successive digits denote department and level in the organization. In smaller companies, much of this information appears under "Relationships."

The identifying data in a managerial position description usually follow the title, stating salary grade, department, division, section, location, title of supervisor, and, finally, date of document. This date is most important. Many job-description manuals state that it must be the day on which the description received official approval. Other companies simply instruct the analyst to date the description the day it is "completed." In any case, some statement of date is needed if the firm intends to review descriptions at periodic intervals.

A well-known oil refiner gives these instructions for completing this section of the position description:

A. *Name.* In this space enter the surname and initials of the jobholder. [In some firms this is *not* done, since the company does not wish to identify the job so closely with the man who is performing it. In such cases, the description carries only the title of the job.]

B. *Supervisor's Title.* Enter here the title of the jobholder's immediate supervisor. "Immediate" refers to the primary reporting relationship. Who the employee really reports to should be discovered by analysis. Special rules for this entry are: (*a*) In cases where the immediate supervisor's job is covered by the . . . program, simply copy the title appearing on his description; (*b*) if the supervisor is not covered . . . use his title in the records of the Industrial Relations Department; (*c*) to clarify the reporting relationship, the supervisor's name may also be shown (add it in parentheses after his title).

C. *Department.* Enter the jobholder's department's name, i.e., the name of the largest functional unit of which he is a part.

D. *Division.* Enter the name of the jobholder's unit next below the departmental level. [Note that this firm is not "divisionalized" in the ordinary sense of the word. The division is not the larger, more inclusive, unit but the smaller, subordinate unit.]

E. *Section.* Enter the name of the divisional sub-unit to which the jobholder belongs. . . .

F. *Location.* Enter here the physical site of the employee. However, this need only be done if the jobholder is placed away from the main location of his departmental, divisional, or sectional headquarters.

G. *Grade.* Enter the employee's numerical salary grade [if one is in effect and the job is not a new one or an altered one for which a grade is being determined]; i.e., a figure from 1 to 20. Obtain grades from Manager, Wage and Salary Administration.

H. Date. Note the month, day, and year on which the description was finished. For example: 11/8/60.

The sum of the identifying data should be enough to indicate the manager's position in the organization. A good test of whether or not this has been accomplished is to draw an organization chart of the unit being covered, using only the information from the job descriptions of all the managers in the department. If the chart is complete and clear, and is as accurate as the one in official use (or, perhaps, more accurate), the descriptions have been properly tagged and labeled.

JOB RELATIONSHIPS

A way to handle much of the information in an "Identifying Data" section is simply to write a brief outline of the important relationships of the job. Most commonly, this consists merely of a statement (1) of the jobs which report to the one being described; and (2) of the job to which the individual in the job reports. In addition, the description may describe "liaison" or staff contact relationships if these communication channels are important.

Another element which may appear in this section is a statement of the position's relationship to persons or agencies outside the company. For instance, one description examined states that the quality control manager in a large defense firm ". . . has extensive relationships with government inspectors for contracting agencies of the Armed Forces . . ." and ". . . must maintain intimate liaison with the inspection and quality control departments of firms supplying components and materials. . . ." When industry associations or contacts with universities, research organizations, and the like are important to the firm, they too are mentioned.

In fact, the chief difficulty in writing a good relationships section is to keep it short enough to be manageable. Only the important internal and external relationships are usually mentioned, often by devoting a single clear sentence to each. One company gives the following instructions for preparing the section relating to important contacts within the organization:

Indicate (*a*) the nature of the contact, i.e., to get information, to advise, to give information, to consult . . . ; (*b*) the subject matter involved, i.e., quality, safety, performance, material to be purchased, maintenance required . . . ; (*c*) estimate the frequency of contact. An example of such a list for a chief division inspector [follows].

> In discharging his responsibilities the Chief Inspector has the following relationships:
>
> *a.* *Project Engineers*—He coordinates his work with the Project Engineers or their delegates in regard to engineering specifications affecting quality control. Frequency: Often.
> *b.* *Chief Industrial Engineer*—He will maintain liaison with the Chief Industrial Engineering Manager or his delegates to assure a coordinated effort in the preparation of procedures needed to assure quality control. Frequency: Often.
> *c.* *Production Engineering Manager*—He will maintain liaison with the Production Engineering Manager or his delegates regarding tool and production planning. Frequency: Often.
> *d.* *Chief Inspectors of Other Sections and Divisions*—He will coordinate his activities with these when necessary to insure the best possible quality control throughout operations. Frequency: Occasional.

Another list, where individuals' titles are not named, is as follows:

> *a.* He (the Manager of Manufacturing) will cooperate with the executives of other divisional departments on all matters of mutual concern.
> *b.* He will cooperate with the executives of foreign affiliates on matters relating to their operations.
> *c.* He will cooperate with Administrative Staff executives, and will seek functional guidance from them in matters within their special provinces.

Sometimes the list of internal relations will specify membership on certain management committees—for example, the Division Operating Committee.

Descriptions which place relationships in a separate section often further segregate external or outside contacts. While these will vary widely with the job, certain typical areas tend to be stressed in manufacturing: relationships with vendors (normally conducted through the purchasing department), relationships with unions, and relationships with the community as a whole. The last category seems to be considered particularly important for plant managers located some distance away from headquarters.

Occasionally job descriptions will require technical employees to maintain membership in professional groups and attend their conventions and meetings.

PURPOSE, FUNCTION, OR OBJECTIVE

Except for the title of the position, we have been discussing parts of the job description that are usually regarded as optional. In smaller firms, where reporting relationships and external contacts have settled into a more or less understood pattern, job analysts usually forego these items. However, every managerial position description examined in the course of this research contains a section which briefly states the over-all purpose of the position. Sometimes it is labeled "Function," "Objective," "Over-all Duties,". but its purpose is to give the briefest possible description of the job. Companies may emphasize the "goal" aspect of the description in this section and head it "Goals," in which case it may consist merely of a listing. Yet even here the result is a short, over-all statement of the main duties of the position.

A job analyst for a metals fabricator stated in the survey that he always writes the objectives or goals section of his descriptions last, after having carefully listed or described the work content which follows in most descriptions. His system has the advantage of giving the analyst detailed knowledge on which to base his generalizations. This man, however, is working for a company whose organization is fairly settled. There are incumbents in every managerial slot, and job duties are reasonably well understood.

Other job description men, and many line managers who are running their own programs, are faced with quite a different situation. Their companies are newly organized, or their departments are setting up new sections with entirely new jobs. In such cases, they reported, it seems best to interview the highest line executive available in the company or unit and obtain a carefully considered statement of the job's objectives or goals. Then it is possible to work out the content of the job so that the duties contribute most efficiently to the attainment of the objectives. Of course, no job analyst would ever attempt to set down singlehanded the exact duties of a job which was not as yet in existence; but under the guidance of the line manager he can usually come up with a fair approximation, if only in general terms, which can be checked sometime later when an incumbent has been doing the work for a while. Moreover, if job descriptions for managerial jobs which as yet have no incumbent are carefully written to embody the ideas of line management, and if they conform to the general directives of company policy, they will be an invaluable aid to those faced with the job of recruiting the new man and orienting him to his work.

As one examines numerous job descriptions, there appears to be a very clear relationship between the objectives section of the description, with the more detailed list of job contents which follows, and the rank of the job. The higher the job in the hierarchy, the shorter and simpler the description of the work. This applies, usually, to the very top of the organization. In middle management, job descriptions tend to be quite complex, with both over-all and detailed sections; whereas, in the lower line echelons, foremen's job descriptions tend again to be shorter. One mistake which is often made is simply to repeat the main idea expressed in the title of the job. For instance, a senior design engineer's job description has an all-too-brief section reading: "Performs design engineering work of considerable complexity." Slightly more detailed but still perhaps too brief, especially in view of the vague nature of the job title, is this over-all statement of the work of a divisional superintendent in a manufacturing company: "Responsible for the management and direction of the Division's manufacturing activities, to produce its products at the lowest cost consistent with satisfactory quality."

Two examples of useful detail follow. For a supervisor of tools and tooling:

> Supervise (directly and through subordinate supervisors) the activities of the Tools and Tooling Department conducted in conjunction with the design, manufacture, inspection, maintenance, and storage of tools, tooling, and shop drawings utilized in the manufacture of the Division's products. Provide for the manufacture of tools, jigs, fixtures, etc., through subcontractors, and requisition standard and special tools and machine tool replacement parts. Maintain an inventory of all capital equipment in the Division. Responsible for: effective utilization of facilities, economical efficient tooling, quality and quantity of work

performed by personnel supervised, adherence to schȩdules, accurate estimates of tool costs and departmental operating expense.

For a production foreman:

> To manage, in an economical and efficient manner, the production activities of the Department, including material preparation and the packing, firing, unpacking, and cleaning of stock. To manage all non-process activities relative to the baking operation, or assigned to his Department, including the construction and maintenance of furnaces, periodic fire-hazard inspections as required by the insuring companies, and maintenance of the baked storage areas. To perform such other special assignments as may be delegated by the Assistant Production Superintendent.

Some rules for writing this general-purpose section of the description are given by one firm in a directive to its job analysts:

> This information is to be included immediately after the identifying information. . . . The purpose . . . is to state briefly the reason for the existence of the job. This should be done in such a fashion that those who are reasonably familiar with the over-all organization will be able to see its necessity and objective at a glance. The writer, when he summarizes this, should not try to present complete details but should rather state, in a few paragraphs, the major reason for the job's existence. It should be direct, not discursive; descriptive, not exhaustive; specific for the particular job, not general for the occupation of its holder. In sum, it should be differentiating, not standardizing.

BODY OF THE DESCRIPTION

This section has numerous titles: "Specific Responsibilities," "Duties," "Typical Duties," "Responsible for," "Accountable for," "Accountabilities," "Character of the Position," and many others. In lower-level descriptions, the favorite seems to be "Duties."

Little can be said about this section's nature. It should avoid unwieldy detail, but in some situations a very detailed description is needed—particularly when an effort is being made to differentiate two overlapping or conflicting jobs. There are, in short, two schools of thought on how all-inclusive the listing of responsibilities should be. One prescribes the briefest statements of the broadest duties;

its adherents, at their extreme, would be satisfied with only an expanded version of the over-all section which has already been discussed. They argue that it is unwise to become too specific about managerial jobs. A manager knows he is responsible for a certain sector of company affairs—completely and irrevocably accountable for everything that happens in his area. Therefore, as an active and alert man, he should not be hamstrung by a job description that is too confining.

The "more specific" school holds that managers need every possible guidance to show them what the company expects of them. These analysts make their descriptions as complete and as specific as they can. A good proportion of this group, however, feel there is some justice in the claim that incumbents may assume they have no obligations outside the formal list of duties embodied in the job description once it has been formally approved by the line superior. To guard against this, many job-description specialists add a sentence to the main body of the description which, for want of a better name, we shall call the "other duties" proviso. This clause, in its simplest form, reads: "The _____ is also responsible for the performance of such other duties as may from time to time be necessary to achieve his objectives." An examination of the descriptions reproduced in Part Two of this study will reveal many variations of this wording, but the intent seems always the same—blanket provision for duties of an important nature which may not have been identified in the job-description process or which may become necessary or desirable later on.

Two principal ways of organizing the material in the main body of the description are shown in the excerpts which follow. In the first, the duties of a general supervisor—forging research are simply listed without headings:

1. Consult with and advise Divisional and Works management in developing improved die- and forge-shop organizations.
2. Coordinate Works unification of forging methods, practices, equipment, and tooling, informing Works of noteworthy technical progress, following up, and reporting on results.
3. Furnish management with reports on comparative forging costs of the various Works.
4. Keep abreast of new forging developments through contacts with other industries, educational institutions, and technical societies.

5. Conduct research on forging problems, reporting on findings and results and arranging for distribution of such reports to management and interested Divisional and Works personnel.
6. Cooperate with the Patent Department concerning patent possibilities, copyrights, royalties, and related matters involving methods, techniques, tools, and tooling connected with the production of forgings which may be developed by Works or Manufacturing Research.
7. Make surveys and analyses of production-plant facilities involving equipment, tools, methods, techniques, and related items, recommending improvements which will effect economies in the production and processing of forgings.
8. Cooperate with Works and Product Engineering personnel, suggesting changes in design or redesign of forged parts.
9. Recommend improvements in die design and construction of related equipment employed in the processing of forgings, with a view to minimizing waste and assuring proper work flow.
10. Survey and study forging materials, recommending the most suitable materials, shapes, and sizes for economical usage.
11. Consult with and advise Works management on modernizing present forge shops or establishing new ones involving layouts, equipment, die designs, and methods of processing products.
12. Collaborate with the Purchasing Department in the procurement of forgings, recommending suitable suppliers and determining reasonable costs.

In the *second* typical variation, the main section of the job description is divided into one or more sub-sections. This is for a supervisor of tools and tooling.

Specific Responsibilities

The Supervisor of Tools and Tooling shall be accountable for the following broad responsibilities that he shall fulfill through delegation of responsibility and authority and by initiation and execution of action in keeping with the authority vested in his office and the applicable Corporation policies and procedures.

1. Analyze drawings of new or changed products scheduled for production and determine manufacturing requirements. Establish operations, sequence, and equipment. Follow up and clear away any difficulties that arise in manufacture or utilization of tooling.
2. Analyze products and recommend changes in manufacturing layouts based on anticipated quantities, available space, equipment, and so forth. Design and lay out tools for equipment in collaboration with Plant Engineering. Aid in the selection of manufacturing and test

equipment on the basis of the economics involved in collaboration with Plant Engineering. Obtain quotations through Purchasing Department from contractors for the purchase and installation of equipment. Plan and schedule installations in collaboration with Plant Engineering to assure minimum interference with current operations. All Division machine-shop installations to conform with specifications, including work done by outside contractors.

3. Collaborate with Methods and Standards in the analysis of existing methods and develop improvements where economically feasible. Prepare reports, recommending adoption of methods, equipment, design changes, and so forth, to effectuate cost reductions, outlining proposed change supported by substantiating cost data.

4. Maintain accurate and complete records of all capital equipment and tools to assure efficient storage and service and to provide the necessary control of capital-equipment inventory.

5. Serve (on request) as liaison with the manufacturers of new equipment or subcontractors engaged in tooling installation, service, or operation.

6. Furnish, ship, and arrange for return of any Company tools utilized on the Division's products by customers, subcontractors, and Service and Erection. Maintain records of all such transactions.

7. Furnish guidance and instructions to Machine Service and Maintenance on matters involving tools and equipment.

8. Arrange and schedule meetings of representatives of Engineering, Methods and Standards, Shop, and Inspection for the purpose of reviewing new or changed manufacturing drawings to reduce manufacturing costs and establish essential tooling requirements.

9. Keep abreast of developments in the field of tools and tool designs, materials, and manufacturing techniques by attending conferences and meetings, reading trade literature and bulletins, interviewing sales representatives, visiting other manufacturing plants, and similar activities; recommend adoption of innovations to effect improved efficiency, quality, or economy in the operation of the Division.

10. Train, instruct, and assign work to employees. Administer Company personnel policies, enforce safety and health regulations, and take prompt action on employee complaints to achieve good employee morale. Represent the Department at all stages of the grievance procedure and arbitration. Maintain current status with respect to employee morale. Keep management informed on status of employee morale. Maintain discipline. Check job performance of subordinates and advise them of good points and shortcomings; give counsel on individual growth potential.

11. Maintain equipment and tools in good working condition, machinery guards operating at all times, and working areas clear for safe, efficient operation.

12. Prepare budget statistics for normal Department operating expense for budget-determination purposes. Plan and schedule work and make effective use of employees' time. Keep Section operating expense within budget allowance.

Authority

The Supervisor of Tools and Tooling is vested with the following authority to be exercised in keeping with all established Corporation and Division policies and procedures in carrying out the responsibilities of the office.

1. To initiate the purchase requisitions for all perishable, semi-perishable, and capital tools and equipment for machine and allied departments in collaboration with Plant Engineering.
2. To recommend departmental layouts of machine tools, processing, and special equipment in collaboration with Plant Engineering.
3. To recommend the disposition of obsolete, scrap, or salable machine tools and equipment.
4. To make recommendations on matters involving cost and quality control.
5. To inspect and accept or reject all materials and supplies delivered to the Tools and Tooling Department.
6. To hire authorized personnel, recommend salary rates or personnel-status changes in the Tools and Tooling Department. To penalize or discharge any employee in the Department guilty of an infraction of Company rules calling for such penalty.
7. To settle any grievance or complaint in the Department within the limits of Company policy and Union contracts.
8. To approve movement of all capital equipment to assure an accurate inventory for control purposes.

A somewhat different organization for the body of the description is illustrated below. Here, following the statement of "scope" (over-all view of the job), the main section is divided into three units: "Character of the Position," "Principal Functions," and "Account-ability." The job is that of a corporate director of engineering.

Character of the Position. This position has two broad but interdepend-ent areas of responsibility. These are best defined by an explanation of the role of Corporate Staff Engineering in the total engineering effort of the Corporation.

The engineering philosophy of the Company is to deploy principal engineering talent and effort at the plant operating level, with functional guidance from the Division Director of Engineering. The underlying concept is that Plant Engineering should be essentially self-sufficient in respect to the existing technological requirements of its operations. The role, then, of Corporate Engineering becomes broad in perspective, de-emphasizing the day-to-day engineering service of Staff Engineering and emphasizing the more creative and planning aspects. The Corporate Engineering staff seeks to encourage a positive attitude and perspective within the various Engineering Departments, focusing on broader objec-tives of better utilization of plant and equipment and greater profita-bility.

The principal organization by which these concepts are conveyed to Division and Plant Engineering groups is the Central Engineering De-partment. The Department is composed of specialists in specific engineer-ing areas such as utilities, standards, instrumentation, and so forth. The Department provides expert consulting assistance as requested and initiates its own continuing involvement in Division and Plant Engineer-ing activities through regular contacts with engineering personnel. In fulfilling its corporate responsibilities it encourages and assists in the engineering planning by plants and laboratories and seeks to develop an acceptance and understanding of the responsibilities of engineering. Through its corporate-wide involvement it is able to circulate engineer-ing ideas and information and contribute to the coordination of per-sonnel planning of engineering manpower.

As the principal staff assistant for engineering, the incumbent has the broad responsibility of developing and recommending engineering plans and objectives which will contribute to the increased efficiency and profitability of plant facilities. He is continually concerned with the progress of technology as it may be applied to operations, encouraging changes and adaptations where feasible. He is additionally concerned with assuring throughout the Corporation a high degree of engineering capability.

In assisting the Vice President, a major emphasis of this position is in coordinating engineering objectives with Corporate long-range objectives, assuring the integration of existing and proposed facilities with Corporate growth objectives. With the addition of new plant facilities and processes, it is the incumbent's responsibility to assure that facilities are properly integrated and efficiently coordinated with existing operations.

Principal Functions

1. Directs and plans the activities of Central Engineering.
2. Advises Corporate management, operating companies, plants, and foreign affiliates on specialized engineering questions through Cen-tral Engineering staff or outside consultants.
3. Assists respective managements in the selection of outside consult-ants.
4. Assures through personal influence or departmental contact the

development and use of engineering standards and specifications; assures engineering planning throughout the Corporation.

5. Completes special engineering studies for the Vice President–Manufacturing and Engineering; initiates routine engineering reports and studies by engineering staff.

6. Appraises engineering personnel in various areas of the Corporation; recommends transfer and promotion to assure development of adequate engineering resources. Recommends staffing of various facilities to achieve established objectives.

7. Reviews major requests for appropriations for engineering projects; recommends disposition to Vice President.

8. Participates in major construction projects; advises on the selection of contractors and the formulation of plans and schedules.

9. Reviews all agreements with outside consultants and agencies prior to review by the Legal Department and approval by the Vice President–Manufacturing and Engineering.

10. Advises Corporate and Company management on the selection and acquisition of plant sites and other property.

Accountability. Has indirect accountability for total engineering activities of the Corporation, which includes the aggregate of plant and Division engineering budgets approximating $30 million annually and total capital expenditures for addition and replacement of plant and equipment totaling approximately $25 million annually.

Has primary accountability for the effective utilization of the Central Engineering budget, approximating $225 thousand annually.

It is noticeable from these two examples that the treatment of the contents section of a job description may vary from company to company. Where, for instance, fairly tight supervision is emphasized, there will usually be an accountability statement in this major part of the description. Some firms also include the authority statement here, yet it seems apparent that the essence of the contents section is a fairly detailed listing of job duties.

JOB SPECIFICATIONS

Job or man specifications usually give minimum hiring or promotion requirements; that is, they state the education and experience a job candidate must have to be acceptable to the company. Out of 217 companies surveyed, 47.7 per cent said they used such statements. A very small percentage used only specifications, not descriptions. Most, however, used both.

The survey returns indicated that job specifications are very seldom included in written descriptions formulated for managerial jobs in manufacturing. In the course of the basic research, several hundred such descriptions were examined, very few of which included any statement of qualifications for the job. Moreover, this large sample of descriptions shows that written specifications almost always occur at the level of the first-line supervisor. The higher one goes in the company hierarchy, the rarer they become.

The respondents to this survey were asked to submit any written specifications they might have for managerial production jobs *whether or not* these specifications appear as part of job descriptions. Though a few were received for first-line supervisors and salaried professionals, none of the companies offered such specifications for a vice president of manufacturing or for anyone with a comparable title. In most cases the specifications made available to the researchers were bare statements of the educational level required and the previous experience necessary to be considered for the job.

A reason for the scarcity of managerial job specifications may be the really difficult problem of pinning down precise educational and personal qualifications. It is easy to say that a salesman must be "outgoing," "social," "interested in people"; but, when it comes to the manager of manufacturing research, these qualities may be much less desirable or may, in fact, interfere with good performance. What are the essential qualities of a successful manager? So far no one is sure. Almost every college textbook on management dwells on them at some length, and the list seems to differ in every case.

Companies may simply find that written specifications for managerial jobs are so difficult to formulate and keep up to date that they do not bother to include them in position descriptions.

USE OF LANGUAGE

The essence of good writing in job descriptions is clarity and terseness—qualities which are the mark of any good writing. Many companies gave AMA examples of written instructions for preparing job descriptions. Of them all, the following seems to exhibit in the highest degree the two qualities most often prescribed for proper job-description style. After enjoining the writer to use accepted usage for capitalization and punctuation, the procedure statement continues:

- Use the singular, regardless of the number of individuals working on a job. (Not, "Incumbents oversee six men," but, "Incumbent oversees six men.")

- Use the active, not the passive voice. (Not, "Routine pumping and maintenance operations are checked," but, "Checks routine pumping and maintenance operations.")

- Omit the subject of the sentence when the subject is the same as the title of the job. Thus, in describing the duties of a Field Foreman, say only, "Checks pumping and maintenance operations," and not, "Field Foreman checks pumping and maintenance operations." However, if in describing the work of a Field Foreman it is necessary to mention work done by another occupation, then use the subject of the sentence.

- To summarize rules 2, 3, and 4, use the *active voice, indicative mood, present tense, third person,* and *singular number* of all verbs and omit the subject when it is identical with the job title.

- Omit all articles (a, an, the) unnecessary to sense.

- The various duties of the position should be grouped under numbered paragraphs. Each of these should cover one major division of the work. Each paragraph should begin with a statement briefly outlining the duty performed and should be followed by all data pertinent to giving a clear conception of the job. Scattering information haphazardly throughout the description not only brings confusion to the reader but often indicates that the writer has not analyzed the job with sufficient care to gain a clear idea of its duties and their interrelationships. When the data may be obtained, the approximate percentages of time spent on major duties should be entered.

6. Flexibility: Provision for Review And Restudy

CLEARLY THE JOB-DESCRIPTION effort will be limited in value unless the resulting descriptions are kept up to date. Descriptions ought to be revised when jobs are changed substantially or when new men enter established positions. Some firms make it a policy to review them upon the request of either the job incumbent or his immediate superior. A few firms survey all jobs at periodic intervals with an eye to possible review and alteration of existing descriptions to make sure that they still represent the appropriate positions as the work is currently being performed.

Table 5 gives the responses of 183 companies on this matter of review and restudy. By far the most common reason for re-examination is that a major change has occurred in the position.

The following procedure from the instructions of a manufacturing company may be helpful to the company that would like to have a better idea of exactly what is involved in reviewing job descriptions; that is, when and how it should be done.

Proper management of the job analysis and evaluation program requires that job studies be made *as new jobs are added or as existing jobs are materially changed*. There are four ways by which jobs are selected for study.

TABLE 5. *Frequency with Which Job Descriptions Are Reviewed in 183 Companies*

PERSON WHO WRITES JOB DESCRIPTION

FREQUENCY OF REVIEW	TOTAL		JOBHOLDER HIMSELF		HIS IMMEDIATE SUPERVISOR		COMPANY SPECIALIST		CONSULTANT		OTHER		NOT GIVEN	
	No.²	Per Cent	No.	Per Cent	No.	Per Cent	No.	Per Cent	No.	Per Cent	No.	Per Cent	No.	Per Cent
Total¹	330	99.9	99	99.9	142	100.0	187	100.2	13	100.0	72	99.9	4	100.0
Rarely	9	2.7	3	3.0	2	1.4	4	2.1	1	7.7	5	6.9	0	0.0
At regular intervals	49	14.9	13	13.1	17	12.0	28	15.0	2	15.4	10	13.9	0	0.0
When job changes	144	43.6	51	51.5	82	57.7	82	44.0	7	53.8	31	43.0	1	25.0
When jobholder changes	35	10.6	11	11.1	13	9.2	17	9.1	1	7.7	8	11.1	1	25.0
When jobholder asks for review	48	14.5	14	14.1	19	13.4	28	15.0	0	0.0	9	12.5	1	25.0
Other	42	12.7	7	7.1	8	5.6	26	13.9	1	7.7	8	11.1	1	25.0
Not given	3	0.9	0	0.0	1	0.7	2	1.1	1	7.7	1	1.4	0	0.0

¹ Total answers exceed total number of companies because many companies gave more than one answer.
² Totals in this column represent the total number of companies that gave this answer. They do not represent the total of the horizontal line because many companies indicated more than one person who writes job descriptions.

I. *The New Job*
   A. When a new job is added, the supervisor gives' the Personnel Department a description of its duties and his estimate of the qualifications needed to fill it.
   B. The Personnel Department (in cooperation with the Job Evaluation Section) establishes a preliminary grade for the new job.
   C. The Job Evaluation Section must make a study of the job within six months of the employee's assignment. Deferment beyond this period requires the approval of the Salary Committee.

II. *Supervisor's Request for Restudy of Existing Job*
   A. A supervisor may request restudy of an existing job when its duties and responsibilities have changed materially or when he believes an inequity in grade exists.
   B. The Job Evaluation Section is required to make a study of the job within three months. Deferment beyond this time must be approved by the Salary Committee.

III. *Employee's Request for Restudy of an Existing Job*
   A. An employee may request a restudy of his job from his supervisor.
   B. Supervisors should, when asked to do so, discuss job description and grade with the employee.
   C. If the supervisor agrees that a job restudy is indicated, he should ask for one.
   D. If an employee does not agree with his supervisor's decision, he may discuss the matter with the Personnel Department.

IV. *Request for Restudy Resulting from Periodic Reviews of Descriptions*
   A. Supervisors receive a "Periodic Job Review Form" listing jobs under them scheduled for review.
   B. Supervisors should carefully review the description and classification of each job listed to see whether or not the duties and responsibilities have changed significantly since it was last studied.
   C. On the "Periodic Job Review Form," supervisors should indicate whether or not they believe the job requires restudy.
   D. When practical, supervisors should give each employee an opportunity to review his job description.

PART TWO

A Handbook of Managerial Job Descriptions
In Manufacturing

1. General Responsibilities

As a beginning we present two generalized statements of responsibility: one for managers, the other for supervisors. Companies often preface their organizational manuals with such a statement in order to avoid repetition in particular descriptions.

GENERAL RESPONSIBILITIES OF MANAGEMENT POSITIONS

Policies and Procedures: To recommend policies and procedures to govern the activities directly supervised, and to insure that subordinates understand and adhere to approved standard practices.

Planning: To continually plan and schedule own activities and those of subordinates so that the work is carried out effectively.

Organization: To recommend for approval the appropriate organization to carry out the necessary activities with efficiency and speed. To insure that the number of employees on the payroll is held to the minimum necessary to meet requirements.

Delegation of Responsibility and Authority: To delegate appropriate responsibilities and commensurate authority to the lowest level of the organization at which all facts necessary for an intelligent decision are available; to retain over-all repsonsibility and accountability for results. To delegate authority and responsibility during own absence or unavailability, and to inform those concerned. To adhere to approved lines of authority and communication, by issuing orders only to immediate subordinates.

Employee Status: To cooperate with the personnel manager in the selection and hiring of hourly employees. To consult with the personnel manager before action is taken on the promotion, transfer, or discharge of hourly employees. On the hiring of salaried employees, to consult with the personnel manager and secure the approval of the president and the vice president concerned.

Employee Training and Development: To cooperate with the personnel manager in the orientation of all new employees. To provide employees with the information and tools necessary to carry out their responsibilities. To maintain an adequate training system to develop technical and management skills of immediate subordinates.

Supervision: To provide adequate direction for the employees directly supervised. This involves maintaining clarity of work assignments; coordinating subordinates' duties; providing help when needed; inspecting finished work for quality and quantity; and making fair and objective decisions, within policy, when changing employee status or compensation.

Work Simplification: To simplify all activities; to consolidate similar activities and eliminate those which are not essential.

Facilities: To preserve and make effective use of the company's physical assets. To keep superiors informed of needs and any shortage or excess of supplies so as to insure efficient and economical operation.

Budgets: To recommend budgets for activities supervised and to insure adherence to approved budgets.

Progress Reports: To keep superior fully informed of the progress of the activities supervised.

Maintenance, Safety, and Security: To make sure that work areas within own jurisdiction are kept in good condition and that proper safety and security measures are established and followed.

Customer and Public Relations: To promote and maintain company goodwill in interdepartmental and personal contacts.

Files: To maintain complete and easily available records and files of information of future reference value which are not kept elsewhere, and to dispose of such records and files after they have ceased to be of value.

GENERAL RESPONSIBILITIES OF SUPERVISORS

Function: Each supervisor will supervise and control workers under his jurisdiction so as to accomplish his assigned work most effectively.

Reports to: His senior supervisor or general supervisor.

Primary Authority and Responsibility: To complete his work assignments efficiently by using his authority to direct, discipline, and instruct the workforce under his jurisdiction. He will refer variant or questionable cases to the senior supervisor or general supervisor.

COMMON MANAGEMENT RESPONSIBILITIES

1. To make or recommend such adjustments in the basic organization of his activity as may be necessary to accomplish assigned objectives.
2. To interpret and apply within his area of activity approved policies and procedures concerning company personnel, labor relations, and salary and wage control.
3. To promote good supervisor/employee relations and endeavor to maintain a high level of employee morale.
4. To train and develop the skills of employees in accordance with company policies and procedures, and to take or recommend such other action as may be necessary to prepare subordinates for performance of assigned duties.
5. To review periodically the performance of immediate subordinates; to counsel and advise them on their responsibilities and their manner of discharging them.
6. To develop and apply internal policies and procedures within the limits of policies received from higher management.
7. To maintain surveillance over operations and keep superiors informed of trends and problems.
8. To coordinate the operations of his unit with those of other members of management on matters of mutual or companywide concern.
9. To continually review factors affecting the administrative and operating costs of his activity and take or recommend action necessary to keep costs consistent with objectives.
10. To administer company safety programs and policies and take or recommend other such action as may appear desirable to prevent physical injury to subordinates or company property.

OTHER GENERAL RESPONSIBILITIES

1. To assume responsibility for total and efficient completion of assigned work package in accordance with established manufacturing schedules and required quality and at minimum expense. This includes obtaining the required support of other organizations.

2. To assume responsibility for the reliability of that portion of the product which he controls directly. To notify superiors of any defective components or materials directly related to his assigned work.

3. To assure proper orientation of employees new to his organization.

4. To thoroughly understand and uniformly and correctly apply a performance-analysis program in rating the performance of assigned employees, having in mind, where applicable, the provisions of collective bargaining.

5. To assign work to subordinates, giving due consideration to the individual classifications and capabilities of the employees, the company's obligations under the labor relations agreement, and the efficient completion of the work.

6. To issue sufficiently clear instructions to employees and follow up on such instructions to assure optimum performance.

7. To coordinate and cooperate with shifts or organizations as required.

8. To take appropriate action concerning the employment, release, transfer, upgrading, and utilization of assigned employees.

9. To take appropriate disciplinary action when required.

10. To adjust appropriately any grievances affecting assigned employees, using independent judgment when such cases are routine or standard and conferring with the general supervisor or senior supervisor on other cases.

11. To know the name, personality, experience, capability, and ambitions of each of his subordinates in order to utilize their skills most effectively and help them attain the greatest possible personal satisfaction.

12. To exercise effective leadership by stimulating and encouraging workers to increase and develop their personal talents and capabilities and to give their wholehearted cooperation to improvement of the company's methods and products.

13. To make recommendations concerning policies, procedures, techniques, facilities, production planning, and any other matter relative to the effective operation of the individual section or of the company as a whole.

14. To carry out all these responsibilities in conformance with company policies, procedures, directives, and other information available for his guidance in addition to verbal instructions from his immediate supervisor.

2. The Manufacturing Line

For CONVENIENCE the positions described in the following pages have been divided between line and staff. The line has been subdivided into senior manufacturing management, intermediate manufacturing management, and first-line supervision. The staff has been subdivided into the traditional functions of quality control, maintenance, production control, and so forth. Editorial details have been altered in some cases for uniformity of appearance, but the descriptions are substantially as used in the companies named.

Senior Manufacturing Management

Included in this classification are a variety of positions ranging from vice president through general manufacturing manager (or superintendent) to manufacturing (or production) manager (or director).

VICE PRESIDENT FOR PRODUCTION OPERATIONS

Olin Mathieson Chemical Corporation

REPORTS TO: Vice President and General Manager, _____ Division.

MAJOR FUNCTIONS: Under the general direction of the Vice President and General Manager, _____ Division, develops, recommends, and imple-

79

ments policies, procedures, and operating objectives for the manufacture of all products produced by the Division. Provides and directs all manufacturing, production planning and control, purchasing and transportation, and production and plant engineering activities required for introduction of new and/or improved products and processes and for continuing manufacture of existing products.

RESPONSIBILITIES INCLUDED

1. Directing and approving the establishment of manufacturing methods, standards, techniques, and plans so as to insure the production of all products of the Division at the lowest cost consistent with established specifications as to quality and quantity.

2. Directing, and coordinating with the Vice President for Marketing, the development of production schedules, economic inventory levels, and control procedures in order to meet approved sales forecasts.

3. Directing, and coordinating with the Vice President for Research and Development as required, the development and establishment of adequate process, industrial, design, and plant engineering activities for the introduction of new and/or improved products, processes, and facilities, as well as the continued manufacture of existing products.

4. Directing, and coordinating with appropriate authorities outside the Division, the development and establishment of policies and procedures necessary to insure the maximum utilization and control of corporate facilities. Providing the necessary utilities, ground and facilities maintenance, plant engineering, and mechanical services to all parts of the New Haven operations.

5. Directing the establishment and implementation of all purchasing and transportation activities at _____ in order to insure that parts, materials, supplies, services, and subcontracting work are purchased at the lowest possible cost consistent with predetermined standards for quality, quantity, and service, and that finished products are shipped expeditiously and economically.

6. Reviewing and recommending approval of proposed product design changes and major manufacturing process changes where a change in product is apparent. Reviewing proposed changes that may affect product functioning, or vice versa.

7. Administering, in cooperation with other Division managements, the coordination of approved plans for Division growth and development; informing the Vice President and General Manager and others concerned on progress being made in comparison with established budgets and schedules for various programs and projects.

8. Providing the Military Sales Department with technical personnel for soliciting new business and advising on the availability of manpower, facilities, and capabilities to perform successfully on a proposed contract. Insuring the production of military items in sufficient quantity to meet predetermined requirements of military production contracts.

9. Obtaining pertinent information for the preparation of estimates, forecasts, reports, and technical data relating to production matters in order to evaluate and/or make policy recommendations to the Vice President and General Manager of the Division.

10. Developing, in collaboration with the Financial Officer and plant management, and recommending for approval the annual budgets for production and related operations. Administering the budgetary program in accordance with established policies and procedures.

11. Reviewing and recommending action to be taken by the Vice President and General Manager of capital appropriation requests which exceed the limits of his own approving authority.

12. Participating in Division staff meetings to plan and review progress on over-all policies, programs, and operations of the Division; conferring with other Division or corporate management personnel to obtain and/or supply information of mutual interest.

13. Appraising and evaluating the performance of the immediate staff and recommending changes in status in accordance with established policies. Approving proposed organization and manpower plans for assigned areas of responsibility.

SUPERVISION EXERCISED: Directly, 5. Indirectly, 4,000-4,500.

EDUCATION REQUIRED: A college degree in engineering, including courses in labor relations and business administration.

PREVIOUS EXPERIENCE PREFERRED: A minimum of 15 years in manufacturing, production control, or related operations at a lesser level, either within or outside the Corporation.

RELATED EXPERIENCE ACCEPTABLE: Experience in plant administration, manufacturing processes, and/or machine shop practices; or work as a consultant in engineering, manufacturing, and/or management fields.

VICE PRESIDENT, PRODUCTION

New York Trap Rock Corporation

MAJOR FUNCTION: Is responsible for the direction of production planning, and for the manufacture of all Company products, at the lowest possible cost consistent with established specifications as to quantity and quality, within the framework of Company policy.

SPECIFIC RESPONSIBILITIES

1. Develops company production policy.

2. Defines and recommends Production Department objectives; develops, with supporting budget requests and financial estimates, specific short-term and long-range plans and programs, taking advantage of modernization, standardization, and automation wherever feasible.

3. Develops and maintains an effective plan of organization for the Production Department.

4. Is responsible for the staffing of the Production Department, including the engineering and purchasing functions, with an adequate number of qualified personnel; also, is responsible for over-all development, training, and performance throughout the Department.

5. Participates in the development of labor relations policy and is responsible for its administration in the Production Department.

6. Is responsible for the personal safety of all Production Department employees; participates in the development of safety policy.

7. Is responsible for the safeguarding of all properties, plants, and equipment under the jurisdiction of the Department.

8. Is responsible for the preparation of reports and memoranda required to insure the continuous flow of necessary information concerning the Department to all levels of management.

9. Is responsible for the operation of production facilities in conformity with Company public relations policy.

10. Keeps informed of real estate matters in regard to Company holdings and to property containing additional available stone reserves; is responsible for seeing that the stone reserves are adequate.

11. Maintains close liaison with the Sales, Transportation, and Marine Departments, keeping them fully informed of changes and contemplated changes in production procedures.

12. Maintains close liaison with the Finance Department regarding costs and expenditures in the Production Department; and, as a member

of the Expenditures Committee, participates in companywide cost control.

13. Assists in diversification studies relating to production of materials.

14. Participates in over-all development of Company policy.

15. Keeps abreast of state and national matters affecting the stone industry through close contact with trade associations and with professional and industrial groups.

16. In accordance with the bylaws of the Corporation as adopted by the Board of Directors, acts as the chief executive officer of the Corporation in the absence of the President and Executive Vice President.

RELATIONSHIPS

1. The Vice President, Production, is elected by the Board of Directors and is responsible to the President or Executive Vice President, as detailed in the "Preamble to Specific Responsibilities and Authority" contained in their respective job descriptions.

2. Directly supervises:
    Chief Engineer.
    Production Manager.
    Director of Purchasing and Stores.
    General Mechanical and Electrical Superintendent.

3. Serves on the following committees and boards:
    Expenditures Committee.
    Salary Committee.
    Hurricane Committee.
    Research and Technical Committee.
    Hourly-Paid Employees' Pension Administrative Committee.
    Labor Negotiating Team.
    Budget Accounting Committee.

GENERAL MANUFACTURING MANAGER

A Business Forms Manufacturer

REPORTS TO: Vice President–Operations.

PRIMARY FUNCTION: To effectively direct and supervise manufacturing and sales service activities as assigned; to produce at established quality levels and at costs within manufacturing labor and overhead budgets.

SPECIAL DUTIES AND RESPONSIBILITIES

1. To know, to fully understand, and to comply with the several duties and responsibilities separately stated in "General Responsibilities of Management Positions."

2. To provide and maintain services and procedures which will result in prompt and reliable shipments to customers. This is to be a continuing effort with improvement as a constant goal.

3. To arrange for the efficient receiving and safe warehousing of incoming materials, for the safe and efficient warehousing of finished goods inventory, and for the efficient shipment of products in the most economical manner possible.

4. To arrange for purchasing, as it relates to manufacturing, at the lowest cost commensurate with all considerations; to confine raw materials inventories to the lowest reasonable levels.

5. To correctly administer established personnel policies; to staff efficiently and adequately all required activities and to supervise, direct, and control the hiring, training, promotion, or separation of all personnel acquired or assigned.

6. To maintain all equipment and facilities in first-class condition and to provide engineering and maintenance services for that purpose.

7. To assist in the preparation of manufacturing cost center budgets, continuously review the performance of such cost centers (actual vs. budget) and improve or maintain the operating-cost levels established by such budgets.

8. To maintain efficiently functioning sales service groups as directed, insuring their effective integration with manufacturing personnel and achieving coordinated sales/manufacturing action which will satisfy customer expectations to the greatest degree consistent with balanced consideration of good operating practices and good customer relations.

9. According to policies determined, to implement and supervise the functions of estimating and pricing for products assigned.

10. On the basis of sales goals or market research information offered by or requested from the Director of Marketing, to investigate and recommend all new equipment purchases or revisions of existing equipment.

11. To perform such special assignments as may be requested.

12. To keep the Vice President, Operations, fully informed of all happenings or conditions which affect or may affect, directly or indirectly, efficient and economical operations or relations with customers or personnel.

GENERAL MANUFACTURING SUPERINTENDENT

The Morgan Engineering Company

BASIC FUNCTION: To be responsible to the Vice President of Manufacturing for production operations required to manufacture Company products as designed by the Engineering Division and scheduled by the Production Planning Department, with services provided by the Plant Engineer, Chief Inspector, and Material Control Superintendent.

BASIC OBJECTIVE: To see that the men, material, and equipment constituting the Production Department are directed and supervised so that production is maintained within budgeted costs and in accordance with planned schedules and quality standards.

MAJOR DUTIES AND RESPONSIBILITIES

1. *Organization and Personnel*

   a. To maintain and administer an organization which is adequate for the performance of production operations.

   b. To insure that the duties and responsibilities of subordinates are clearly defined and fixed and to approve the position descriptions of immediate subordinates.

   c. To recommend to the Vice President of Manufacturing major changes in the form and size of the Production organization as required to meet changed conditions.

   d. To see that personnel in the Production organization are kept fully and currently informed of all pertinent Company policies and that such policies are followed in the organization.

   e. To direct the Company's personnel policies within the Production Department.

   f. To recommend to the Vice President of Manufacturing the employment, promotion, dismissal, or change in compensation of immediate subordinates and of personnel reporting directly to these subordinates.

   g. To review and appraise the qualifications of each subordinate periodically as prescribed by Industrial Relations policies.

   h. To receive and process employee grievances originating within the Production Department, as directed by the Company contract with the union; and to adhere to all other Company/union contractual agreements.

2. *Production*: To direct supervisory personnel in such a manner that maximum effectiveness is obtained from the men, materials, and

equipment available to accomplish the basic goal of meeting production schedules.

3. *Quality*: To see that men and machines are so directed and supervised that products manufactured conform to the tolerances and specifications established by the Inspection Department and the Engineering Division.

4. *Budgets*

   a. To prepare the annual budget for the Production Department and submit it to the Vice President of Manufacturing.

   b. To operate the Production Department within the approved budget.

   c. To review and approve the annual budgets covering operating expenses as submitted by the departmental superintendents.

   d. To review periodically, with the superintendents reporting to him, actual operating performance in relation to budget.

5. *Costs*

   a. To assist and confer with the Plant Engineering Department, as required, to analyze facilities, equipment, and methods for improvement or replacement.

   b. To assist and confer with the Plant Engineering Department, to locate and correct improper or ineffective operations.

   c. To see that the methods, tools, equipment, standard practices, and production techniques developed by the Plant Engineering Department and approved for installation are followed as recommended.

6. *Maintenance*

   a. To see that maintenance controls established by the Plant Engineer are followed as they relate to production operations.

   b. To review the preventive maintenance program developed by the Plant Engineer and to make necessary adjustments in personnel to eliminate lost time caused by that program.

7. *Material Flow*: To see that in-process materials are moved to successive operations by the Material Handling Supervisor according to schedules established by the Production Planning Department.

8. *Traffic and Transportation*: To see that shipping and transportation services are provided by the Traffic and Transportation Supervisor.

9. *General*

   a. To confer with the Director of Industrial Relations with respect to the orientation and training of personnel within the Production Department.

b. To confer with the Director of Industrial Relations with respect to the development and operation of the Company safety program within the Production Department.

c. To approve the expense accounts of personnel reporting directly to him.

d. To approve requisitions within the Production Department for equipment, supplies, services, or any other expenditures except budgeted capital equipment as authorized in the purchase requisition procedure; to recommend, to the Vice President of Manufacturing, amounts in excess of authorized limits.

e. To approve, in conjunction with the Plant Engineer, requisitions within the Production Department for budgeted capital equipment expenditures as authorized in purchase requisition procedure; to recommend, to the Vice President of Manufacturing, amounts in excess of authorized limits.

f. To perform any additional duties requested by the Vice President of Manufacturing.

DIRECTOR OF MANUFACTURING

Olin Mathieson Chemical Corporation

REPORTS TO: Vice President for Production Operations.

MAJOR FUNCTIONS: Under the general guidance of the Vice President for Production Operations as to the objectives to be accomplished, directs all manufacturing operations of the _____ Division, including production planning and control and the purchase of all materials, services, and subcontracted parts. Insures that all manufacturing operations are conducted in an efficient and profitable manner consistent with production and quality requirements or specifications and established policies. Controls and directs activities relating to internal material handling, warehousing, and external transportation required in connection with materials and products. Performs special assignments as required.

RESPONSIBILITIES INCLUDED

1. Directing the manufacture of all Division products in accordance with established process and product specifications, quality stand-

ards, delivery schedules, and standard costs, so as continually to improve the efficiency, economy, and safety of operations. Developing and recommending plans and programs to meet improved manufacturing objectives for the production of Division products.

2. Directing the development, establishment, and implementation of production schedules, economic inventory levels, and control procedures for all products in order to meet approved sales procedures and forecasts for all products and to insure maximum utilization of personnel and facilities.

3. Maintaining strict appraisal, in conjunction with the Director of Development Engineering and Control, of production quality and making any changes necessary to achieve established quality standards.

4. Assisting the Director of Engineering with activities necessary to the introduction of new and/or improved processes and products, such as selection of equipment and facilities, time studies, tool tryouts, plant layout, and pilot runs. Directing plant engineering, maintenance, and utilities activities at _____, under the functional guidance of the Director of Engineering, in order to provide required services to the divisions at that location.

5. Directing the development and establishment of policies and procedures designed to effect the purchase of all materials, services, and substantial parts at the lowest possible cost consistent with predetermined standards for quality, quantity, and service. Directing the arrangement and control of transportation required for inbound and outbound materials and products.

6. Providing for the establishment and staffing of an organization of skilled craftsmen engaged in the building and maintenance of tools, fixtures, gauges, and other in-plant equipment as required by the needs of the divisions located at _____ and _____.

7. Assisting in the preparation of bids and proposals to civil or government organizations on items of procurement which have been determined profitable for Division manufacture. Insuring that work on civilian and/or military production contracts accepted by the Division is performed in accordance with the provisions and requirements of the contracts.

8. Developing and establishing adequate controls and reporting systems to provide himself and management with sufficient information as to the accomplishments, progress, capabilities, and/or problems of the manufacturing organization.

9. Directing the preparation of the annual operating budget for his various manufacturing units and submitting it for review and approval to the Vice President for Production Operations. Insuring the

proper expenditure of approved funds by establishing and adhering to standard budgetary control and limitation procedures and techniques. Reviewing and recommending action to be taken by the Vice President on capital appropriation proposals that exceed the limits of his approving authority.

10. Insuring the establishment and maintenance of safe and healthful working conditions and areas for manufacturing employees. Enforcing safety rules and regulations designed to create and maintain safe working habits in order to reduce the frequency and/or seriousness of industrial accidents.

11. Establishing and maintaining an effective organization within his area of responsibility by recommending and/or approving the selection, hiring, change in status, or termination of assigned employees. Participating in the over-all implementation and administration of Division and corporate personnel management and employee relations programs.

SUPERVISION EXERCISED: Directly, 6. Indirectly, 3,500-3,800.

EDUCATION REQUIRED: A college degree in engineering or industrial administration.

PREVIOUS EXPERIENCE PREFERRED: A minimum of 15 years in manufacturing activities, with demonstrated executive ability in a succession of responsible managerial positions.

RELATED EXPERIENCE ACCEPTABLE: Experience in process engineering, production engineering, purchasing and traffic, and/or machine shop practices.

MANUFACTURING MANAGER, ALL DIVISIONS

A Large Oil Company

FUNCTIONS: The Division Manufacturing Manager has the basic function of supervising and coordinating the Division's manufacturing activities, including construction, operation, and maintenance of refinery equipment, and storage and shipping of petroleum products. He also studies and effects changes in product yields to fulfill sales requirements and improve realizations.

RESPONSIBILITIES

1. Develops and recommends policies, plans, and methods covering manufacturing operations designed to produce the largest volume of products that can be sold profitably.

2. Keeps informed on over-all policies and objectives and interprets them to his staff and organization.

3. Prepares budgets and forecasts of capital requirements, operating programs, and operating expenses for manufacturing activities, including long-term plans and trends.

4. Reviews actual performance as compared with operating and capital budgets and recommends such modifications as he believes are necessary and reasonable.

5. Analyzes operations and expenses to insure the maintenance of operating efficiency and low costs.

6. Makes sure that his staff is adequate for the workload and also represents an efficient use of manpower.

7. Promotes harmonious working relations between supervisors and employees, encourages proper communication throughout his organization, and maintains adequate training programs.

8. Is primarily responsible for the following specific activities within the limits of approved budgets or programs and established policy:

   a. Determining which raw materials (for processing) will produce the highest profit margins.

   b. Planning and scheduling operating programs.

   c. Coordinating operating programs with receipt of raw materials.

   d. Determining and recommending for approval the optimum levels for refinery inventories of raw materials and finished and unfinished products.

   e. Constructing, operating, and maintaining processing units and auxiliary equipment, including the planning of shutdowns for major repairs.

   f. Operating and maintaining receiving, storage, and shipping facilities.

   g. Studying and improving product yields for highest realizations.

   h. Carrying on continuous studies of unit operations and equipment efficiency.

   i. Operating laboratories for controlling product specifications and improving production.

   j. Studying and developing joint operations with chemical companies for the purpose of manufacturing petrochemicals.

9. Keeps informed on new techniques and developments, conducting engineering tests of new equipment and methods and setting equipment standards.

10. Assures compliance with provisions of agreements and contracts.

11. Establishes controls for maintaining economical stocks of materials and supplies; reviews over-all requirements for ordering and stocking important categories.

12. Studies means of increasing volume by enlarging operating units and adding new processing units and equipment that will improve yields and quality and will lower costs.

13. Recommends the abandonment of uneconomical methods and equipment and the disposal of obsolete or surplus equipment.

14. With the guidance of the Employee Relations Department, is responsible for negotiating collective bargaining agreements with labor organizations (where such exist) and assures compliance with terms of contracts.

15. Sees that supervisors keep employees continually aware of the Company's safety regulations.

16. Assures compliance with governmental regulations.

17. Keeps informed on developments in the industry.

18. Maintains operating records necessary to control and analyze activities.

RELATIONSHIPS

1. Reports to the Division General Manager and keeps him informed on manufacturing developments within the Division and the industry.

2. Cooperates with the Oil Purchase and Exchange, Transportation, and Marketing Departments to provide desirable raw materials, establish product requirements, and balance refinery production and product yields.

3. Collaborates with the Marketing Department on product specifications and the development of new products.

4. Obtains advice from the Employee Relations Department in carrying out the Company's policies covering employment, safety, employee relations, and benefits.

5. Seeks advice from and consults with his counterpart Home Office Department Manager on forward planning and operating and technical problems.

DIRECTOR OF MANUFACTURING

A Manufacturer of Proprietary Products

BASIC FUNCTION: The Director of Manufacturing is responsible for producing economically the Company's products in the quantity and quality required and for meeting delivery schedules.

ORGANIZATIONAL RELATIONSHIPS

Reports to: Vice President of Manufacturing.

Supervises: Manager of Industrial Engineering.
            Manager of Quality Control.
            Traffic Manager.
            Manager of Production Planning.
            Plant Managers (4).

PRINCIPAL ACTIVITIES

1. To direct the Manager–Production Planning in the preparation of annual and quarterly production budgets for each plant. These budgets will be based on the forecast of shipments (established by the Directors of Marketing), which will be detailed by sizes, deal packs, geographical areas, and other specifics so that realistic and stable manufacturing schedules can be prepared. The periodic production budgets will be expressed in terms of "take away" from each plant or plant area and will reflect adjustments from the forecast for the purpose of transshipment of goods among plant areas to meet production requirements and balance of inventories.

2. To direct Plant Managers in translating the annual and quarterly production budgets into firm manufacturing schedules.

3. To control total plant inventory investment in accordance with objectives defined by corporate policy on inventory. To explain to the Vice President of Manufacturing any variances from these inventory objectives and to proceed in either of the following ways:

   a. Take corrective action in these cases within the scope of authority of the Director of Manufacturing.

   b. Recommend to the Vice President of Manufacturing any needed corrective action that is outside the scope of the Director's authority.

4. To direct Plant Managers in fulfilling established production budgets, maintaining close control of shipments to insure that needed quantities are supplied and providing adequate customer service.

5. To review operating reports to determine that established objectives of cost, quality, and on-time delivery are met at all plants. To investigate any important variances, plan corrective action, and inform the Vice President of Manufacturing of the variances, their cause, and the action taken to rectify them.

6. To direct the Manager–Quality Control in establishing test and inspection procedures and controls to insure that raw materials and finished goods meet approved specifications and that standard practice instructions issued by the Research and Development Department are observed by the plants.

   When temporary deviations from standards are required by Plant Managers, owing to limitations of equipment or materials, to grant such deviations by written authorization only, this to be secured, in writing, from the Director of Research and Development.

7. To direct the Manager of Industrial Engineering in evaluating new manufacturing methods, layouts, equipment, and techniques and in preparing recommendations on their adoption by the plants.

8. To initiate and continue a program of cost reduction in manufacturing, accounting, and allied services under the coordination of the Manager of Industrial Engineering. To take the lead in recommending action to the Vice President of Manufacturing on cost reduction opportunities that are dependent on decisions in other functions (e.g., Marketing) and thus require such executive action.

9. To plan and administer the annual capital budget for improvement, re-equipment, and expansion of plants and offices.

   To recommend, to the Vice President of Manufacturing, investments in plant production facilities that will reduce operating costs, improve product quality, or improve the ability of the plants to fulfill the production requirements of Marketing.

10. To provide information to the Marketing Department on feasibility, cost, estimated time of delivery, or other manufacturing considerations bearing on plans of the Marketing Department. The Company Manufacturing Office will be the point of inquiry for the Marketing Department; inquiries will not be made directly to Plant Managers. Inquiries requiring extensive analysis, such as those to ascertain costs of proposed deals, will be approved by the Director of Marketing before transmission to Manufacturing.

    These relationships between Marketing and Manufacturing go beyond supply of information on specific topics. One of the major aims is to provide, at the operating level, a close coordination of marketing plans with manufacturing operations so that sufficient lead time is allowed Manufacturing in meeting unusual demands and Marketing can exploit to the fullest any unusual manufacturing capabilities. This objective requires that the Directors of Marketing and Manufacturing have a good understanding of what is taking place and what is in prospect in each other's functions and that both are motivated by a common aim—securing the maximum profitable share of market.

11. To participate in planning the labor relations program of the Company and in bargaining with the unions.

12. To meet as necessary with the Vice President of Manuafcturing, the Vice President of Research, and the Research and Development executives to exchange information on current and prospective technical developments and to coordinate the planning of engineering and research studies, projects, and programs.

13. To direct the Manufacturing staff in providing technical assistance to the Plant Managers as necessary. This assistance will take the form of periodic appraisals of plant operations (to supplement the audits by the Research and Development staff) and will provide aid on specific problems at the request of the Plant Managers or at the direction of the Director of Manufacturing.

14. To participate in planning and directing the program for recruiting technical and supervisory personnel into the Company under the leadership of the Vice President of Employee Relations.

To cooperate with the Vice President of Manufacturing and the other Directors in providing job rotation opportunities to develop technical and supervisory personnel.

GENERAL MANAGER,
MANUFACTURING AND MANUFACTURING SERVICES

A. O. Smith Corporation

REPORTS TO: General Manager.

SUPERVISES: General Foreman, Parts Fabrication.
General Foreman, Assembly.
General Supervisor, Industrial Engineering.
General Foreman, Receiving, Material Handling, and Warehousing.

General Supervisor, Traffic Services.
Foremen (17).
Supervisor, Industrial Engineering.
Industrial Engineers (8).
Senior Tool Designer.
Non-exempt salaried employee.
Hourly-paid shop employees (425-475).

PRIMARY FUNCTION: Directs, through Department Heads, the Department operations necessary to convert raw materials and vendor-produced parts and assemblies into a product ready for shipment. This includes tool and parts processing, tool and equipment procurement, cost estimating, establishment of work standards, tool design, tool fabrication, general maintenance, parts fabrication and finishing, assembly, testing for functional operation and product repair, shipping and traffic, material handling, and parts storage. Plant-produced products include S. S. pumps; hand pumps; submersible pumps; tank units; commercial, farm, marine, and airport pumps; Smithway Marketing System; liquid meters and accessories; liquid flow control valves; tank truck valves and fittings; liquid filters; and filter separators.

DUTIES AND RESPONSIBILITIES

1. Defines and develops organizational structure and functional responsibilities of the departments under his jurisdiction. Staffs departments with qualified employees, delegates authority without relinquishing accountability, and holds department heads responsible for meeting their functional responsibilities.

2. Assists Division Manager in the establishment of manufacturing policies and Industrial Engineering programs and in making major decisions as necessary in the best interests of the Company.

3. Coordinates manufacturing schedules with schedules established by the Service Planning Department in order to fulfill sales commitments.

4. Directs and establishes controls necessary to product quality in accordance with Company-accepted standards.

5. Directs the application of facilities, material, and manpower in the fabrication of parts and the assembly of subassemblies into product systems, on schedule and at minimum cost, consistent with operating levels and established quality standards.

6. Analyzes Industrial Engineering problems with reference to manufacturing processes, make-or-buy decisions, work-standard policies,

cost estimating, tool design, and procurement. Analyzes special machine requests with particular emphasis on major cost items such as capital equipment changes, plant layout, and material handling equipment and determines the appropriate action to solve these problems.

7. Establishes and directs test facilities and equipment that may be necessary to assure functional performance of established products in accordance with Company standards and regulatory requirements.

8. Correlates tool design with parts, subassemblies, and systems design with respect to tooling and production costs in accordance with anticipated requirements.

9. Directs the design and/or procurement of tooling required for new and revised parts.

10. Coordinates activities between Manufacturing Departments and also coordinates their activities with those of other departments within both the plant and the Company in order to obtain maximum overall efficiency of operations in conformance with Company policy.

11. Recommends procurement from vendors of parts and capital equipment not available at the most economical rates when using plant facilities. Provides such technical assistance as may be necessary to vendors producing parts to A. O. Smith specifications in order to assure uninterrupted production; authorizes emergency expenditures as necessary for the fulfillment of this objective.

12. Establishes an efficient preventive maintenance program for manufacturing facilities and the plant proper in order to assure uninterrupted production; authorizes emergency expenditures as necessary for the fulfillment of this objective.

13. Controls cost of Departments under his jurisdiction by reviewing quarterly a comparison of current operating costs with past costs (adjusted according to comparable operating levels). Directs measures to prevent recurrence of controllable high costs.

14. Coordinates activities between Manufacturing Departments and the Material Handling, Parts Storage, Shipping, and Receiving Departments.

15. Administers Company personnel policies as they apply to employees under his direction with reference to training, vacations, merit increases, promotions, safety and housekeeping, disciplinary action, etc. Gives final approval in the hiring of non-exempt and first-line, exempt, salaried employees.

PRODUCTION MANAGER

A Paper Manufacturer

FUNCTION: To direct the activities of all specialty packaging plants so as to achieve specified quality at lowest cost in keeping with established production plans, profit objectives, and customer requirements. To participate in the development of over-all plans and objectives for the Division and to provide for their coordination with production facilities. To serve as chief production executive on the Division Director's staff.

RESPONSIBILITIES

1. Reviews and approves plant organizational structure. Recommends plant organizational changes and revisions as necessary.

2. Is responsible for selection of Plant Managers. Consults with Division Director and other appropriate members of management to arrive at final selection of Plant Managers.

3. Confers with Plant Managers concerning selection of key staff members for plant assignments.

4. Evaluates performance of Plant Managers and employees assigned to Production Manager's staff. Arranges for periodic discussions with employees reporting directly to him in order to review evaluation of their performance and potential.

5. Participates, with the Division Director and the Personnel Department, in planning and executing programs designed to employ, develop, and train employees for production areas.

6. Determines that adequate training programs for hourly-paid employees are carried on in all plants. Suggests areas in which training is required and recommends techniques for achieving the desired level of training.

7. Participates in annual negotiations with labor unions, representing plants under his supervision. Confers with Vice President of Industrial Relations and representatives of Labor Relations Department before negotiation time in order to highlight key issues as related to manufacturing; also assists in formulating Company's basic labor policy.

8. Represents management in fourth-stage labor grievances. Makes himself familiar with facts of each case and the related portions of the labor contract to insure a sound, equitable decision which does not violate provisions of the contract.

9. Approves recommendations from Plant Managers concerning the

salary, transfer, termination, demotion, promotion, and grade classification of employees under their supervision. Advises Plant Managers of changes in the recommendations as deemed necessary.

10. Participates in formulation of over-all Company policies and procedures related to manufacturing operations. Determines that such policies and procedures are understood and enforced by Plant Managers.

11. Supervises the Division Production Planner in developing over-all production plans for the Division.

12. Develops and fosters liaison between specialty packaging plants and all other organizational units of specialty packaging.

13. Develops and fosters liaison between specialty packaging plants and the production areas of other operating divisions. Assists in resolving manufacturing problems of an interdivisional nature and makes recommendations concerning procedures related to products manufactured on an interdivisional basis.

14. Reviews, and recommends for approval, plant capital expenditure projections. Approves requests for capital expenditures within the limits of his authority and insures plant compliance with Company capital expenditure policy.

15. Makes himself familiar with the operation of all staff areas within manufacturing plants and determines that all such areas are functioning in a manner that will achieve objectives. Acquaints himself with trends and developments in each of these fields, particularly as related to the paper industry. Such areas include:

    a. Industrial Accounting.
    b. Industrial Relations.
    c. Industrial Engineering.
    d. Plant Engineering.
    e. Production Services.
    f. Customer Service.
    g. Technical Services.

16. Maintains knowledge of customer requirements and keeps informed on trends and developments in the packaging field.

17. Keeps informed of competitive activity, particularly as related to competitors' production facilities.

18. Evaluates the performance of each plant, giving due consideration to such factors as total production, efficiency, costs, and manning. Makes recommendations on methods for reducing operating costs, increasing efficiencies, and so forth.

19. Reviews plant inventories to assure their maintenance at a level consistent with operating requirements and profitable operations.

20. Supervises the Division Technical Services Supervisor in establishing quality standards for all plants. Ascertains that such quality standards are met.

21. Keeps abreast of machine developments or modifications that are applicable to his production operations. Recommends the acquisition of necessary equipment.

22. Reviews or initiates recommendations for expansion of production facilities. Assists the Division Director in preparing recommendations of this nature which require higher management approval.

23. Makes recommendations and participates in decisions related to selection of plant sites.

24. Approves the production of experimental products being considered for commercial production. After the necessary period of experimentation, indicates whether such products can be produced commercially in keeping with Company manufacturing and profit objectives.

25. Utilizes Central Staff Service Departments and determines that proper relationships exist between such Departments and his manufacturing plants.

26. Determines that satisfactory community and public relations are developed in all communities where plants are located.

27. Attends a representative number of his plants' sales meetings. Speaks at formal meetings as requested.

28. Attends a representative number of association meetings, trade shows, and similar events of interest to the Company.

29. Greets customer representatives, and visits customer locations as requested. Confers with customers on matters related to manufacturing.

30. Carries out special assignments from the Division Director. Serves as a member of regular or special management committees as requested.

31. Determines that required maintenance and protection of plant equipment and buildings are in keeping with Company policies.

MANAGER, MANUFACTURING BRANCH

The Carborundum Company

I. GENERAL RESPONSIBILITY: Responsible for directing all activities of the Manufacturing Branch of the Division, including manufacture of products, product inspection, industrial and maintenance engineering, maintenance of plant and equipment, purchasing, order processing, inventory and production control, receiving, warehousing, and shipping; for preparing and recommending annual programs and controlling expenses and operations within such programs; for improving manufacturing efficiency through improved methods, processes, manpower utilization, and loss reduction; for coordinating line and staff activities within the Manufacturing Branch; and, in cooperation with the Manager of the Personnel Branch, for administering the union–management collective bargaining agreement, including the hourly group incentive plan, and other personnel policies related to Manufacturing Branch personnel.

II. ORGANIZATIONAL RELATIONSHIPS

A. *Line:* Responsible to: Vice President and General Manager, Coated Abrasives Division. Supervises:
Superintendent, Coating.
Superintendent, Finishing.
Manager, Manufacturing Services.
Manager, Production Control.
Division Purchasing Agent.

B. *Staff:* Advises and receives advice from heads of other branches in Coated Abrasives Division Staff and Operating Division Heads and their subordinates.

III. SPECIFIC DUTIES

KIND OF ACTIVITY	SCOPE	TYPE OF ACTION
A. *Line or Operational*		
1. Production operations: Coating, finishing, product inspection.	Manufacturing Branch, Coated Abrasives Division.	Directs line organization in the production of products and the inspection of in-process and finished products; develops programs, plans, methods, and processes for improved manufacturing efficiency, manpower utilization, and loss reduction.
2. Industrial engineering: Preparation of hourly job descriptions,	Manufacturing Branch, Coated Abrasives Division.	Directs the preparation of job descriptions, job evaluations, and time studies.

III. SPECIFIC DUTIES (cont'd)

KIND OF ACTIVITY	SCOPE	TYPE OF ACTION

A. *Line or Operational*
   (cont'd)

   job evalua-
   tion, time
   study.

3. Mainte-   Manufac-   Directs all maintenance work
   nance of   turing   on plant buildings and equip-
   plant and   Branch,   ment, including the planning
   equipment: Coated   of major shutdowns for over-
   Mainte-   Abrasives   haul or replacement of ma-
   nance of   Division.   chines and major building
   buildings   repairs.
   and equip-
   ment; major
   shutdowns
   for repair.

4. Purchasing: Manufac-   Directs the purchasing function
   Buying all   turing   of the Division, including
   raw   Branch,   purchase of all raw materials,
   materials,   Coated   supplies, equipment, and
   supplies,   Abrasives   services; investigation of new
   equipment,   Division.   sources of raw materials;
   and   maintenance of purchasing
   services.   records; and preparation of
   periodic reports on market
   conditions.

5. Order   Manufac-   Directs the processing of cus-
   processing: turing   tomer and district stock re-
   Preparation   Branch,   plenishment orders, including
   of sales   Coated   censoring, pricing, prepara-
   orders,   Abrasives   tion of plant papers, discard-
   customer   Division.   ing from inventory records,
   service, and   preparation of labels and
   order   sleeves, processing of order
   expediting.   changes and cancellations, expediting, and the answering
   of customer and district inquiries on order status.

6. Inventory   Manufac-   Directs establishment of inven-
   and pro-   turing   tory levels and maintenance
   duction   Branch,   of records on raw materials,

III. Specific Duties (cont'd)

KIND OF ACTIVITY	SCOPE	TYPE OF ACTION
A. *Line or Operational* (cont'd) control: Control of all raw materials, in-process stock, finished stock, supplies, plant levels of operation, scheduling, order promising.	Coated Abrasives Division.	in-process stock, finished stock, and supplies, including write-off and salvage procedures, in compliance with Company policies and directives; directs plant production control activities, including establishment of plant operation levels, scheduling of machines, preparation of reports on plant performance, workload, and backlog, and promising of customer order delivery dates.
7. Receiving, warehousing, and shipping: Handling and storage of raw materials, in-process stock, finished stock, supplies, returned merchandise.	Manufacturing Branch, Coated Abrasives Division.	Directs the receiving, storing, and issuing of raw material, in-process stock, and finished stock; receiving, checking, and disposal of returned merchandise; assembly and loading of finished stock; determination of routings and carriers; and follow-up on emergency shipments.
8. Preparation of annual programs and control of expenses: Analyzes annual requirements,	Manufacturing Branch, Coated Abrasives Division.	In cooperation with Sales and Accounting Branches, sets up annual production program; prepares departmental programs and operates within the limits of those programs; directs preparation of operating records and reports; coordinates operations of the vari-

III. Specific Duties (cont'd)

KIND OF ACTIVITY	SCOPE	TYPE OF ACTION
A. Line or Operational (cont'd)		
sets plant levels, and operates within levels.		ous Departments of the Branch.
9. Employee relations: Assignment, increases and decreases, grievance procedure, salary administration.	Manufacturing Branch, Coated Abrasives Division.	Directs the assignment and training of personnel, as well as increases and decreases in the workforce; authorizes the hiring, compensation, promotion, and discharge of hourly and office and laboratory salaried employees and recommends such action in the care of supervisory and professional employees. In cooperation with the Manager of the Personnel Branch, administers the union contract; grievance procedure; employee progress review, appraisal, safety, plant protection, and health programs; and other personnel policies related to Manufacturing personnel.
10. Hourly group incentive plan	Manufacturing Branch, Coated Abrasives Division.	Acts as permanent chairman of the Divisional Committee and has line responsibility for the operation of the hourly group incentive plan. In cooperation with the Personnel Branch, develops and directs programs to reduce labor and material costs and to improve operating efficiency.
B. Staff or Functional		
1. Production operations: Product de-	Coated Abrasives Division.	Consults with and advises the Coated Abrasives Division General Manager and Branch

III. SPECIFIC DUTIES (cont'd)

KIND OF ACTIVITY	SCOPE	TYPE OF ACTION
B. Staff or Functional (cont'd)		
velopment and specifications, inventories, customer service, district activities.		Heads on problems concerning product development, product specifications, quality control, inventory content, inventory levels and accounting, customer delivery service, and district warehouse inventory control.
2. Industrial relations, traffic, and purchasing.	Functional Staff.	Consults with and advises heads of Functional Staff Branches on industrial relations, traffic, and purchasing matters as applicable to manufacturing operations.

MANAGER OF MANUFACTURING

A Machinery Company

FUNCTION: To supervise, directly and through subordinate supervisors, all aspects of the activities involved in planning, scheduling, and manufacture; to inspect, test, and ship the Division's products; to service and maintain the buildings and equipment; to control inventory, quality, and costs; to maintain satisfactory labor relations. To coordinate the various operating phases to insure the proper flow of work. To be responsible for operating costs, quality and quantity of work, and performance against delivery commitments.

ORGANIZATIONAL RELATIONSHIPS

1.   Manager of Manufacturing

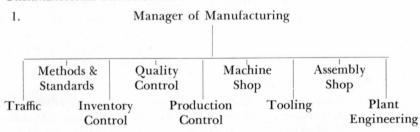

2. The Manager of Manufacturing reports to the General Manager. His duties require close collaboration with Sales and Engineering on customer-relations problems to achieve efficiency and economy in the over-all operation of the Division.

SPECIFIC RESPONSIBILITIES: The Manager of Manufacturing shall be accountable for the following broad responsibilities that he shall fulfill through delegation of responsibility and authority and by initiation and execution of action in keeping with the authority vested in his office and the applicable Company policies and procedures.

1. To maintain a current knowledge of developments in the field of the Company's products, materials, and manufacturing techniques by attending trade conferences and meetings; reviewing trade literature and bulletins; witnessing equipment in operation in the field; interviewing equipment manufacturers' representatives; and other activities which will enable him to recommend innovations to improve the quality, efficiency, and economy of the Company's operations.

2. To plan and schedule all manufacturing operations so as to meet scheduled delivery dates with the minimum work-in-process time consistent with proper utilization of facilities.

3. To machine, assemble, and test all products of the Company at the most economical costs consistent with prescribed quality, accuracy, and performance standards.

4. To maintain inventory controls so as to keep inventories at the optimum required by manufacturing time cycles; to maintain minimum-quantity economical production runs of standard parts; and to provide appropriate service for equipment in the field.

5. To submit periodic reports to management on current status of various responsibilities; to make recommendations in cases of unsatisfactory results and achieve improved efficiency and effectiveness.

6. To keep management informed with respect to obsolescence of equipment and facilities and to submit recommendations regarding replacements, including cost data on return on capital outlay.

7. To administer the hourly wage incentive system in conformance with the Corporation's incentive policy manual and the applicable practices, procedures, and labor contract obligations.

8. To maintain plant property in good repair and appearance as economically as possible; to submit recommendations with respect to improvements essential to effective operations.

9. To procure, develop, and maintain competent employees and adequate facilities to fulfill the requirements of the Manufacturing

Division. To delegate responsibility and authority so as to permit employees to develop and assume greater responsibility. To maintain an open mind at all times and encourage individual initiative and creativity. Within the Department, to administer Company personnel policies, enforce safety and health regulations, and take prompt action on employee complaints so as to encourage high morale. To review subordinates' job performance and advise them on their good points and shortcomings, give counsel on growth potential, and plan and implement individual development programs. To recognize and commend individual merit and correct laxity or breach of discipline.

10. To participate in organizations engaged in industry and public relations activities by serving on committees; to make speeches with a view to improving the Company's standing in industry and the communities where it conducts business.

11. To participate in fourth-step grievances and arbitration.

12. To compile statistics of anticipated operating expense as the basis for determination of operating expense budget.

13. To keep informed on the status of production schedules and to direct action to clear away any difficulties that are creating delays.

14. To keep up with current general business trends and management philosophy, practices, and procedures through selected reading and study, and to apply this knowledge to the improvement of Manufacturing Department management.

15. To develop and maintain active cost, scrap, and extra-work reduction programs to improve the profit position.

16. To maintain the appropriate ratio of direct to indirect labor.

17. To develop and maintain effective two-way communication internally and with other concerned divisions and/or departments of the Company so as to assure adequate dissemination of information concerning plans and new developments.

AUTHORITY: The Manager of Manufacturing is vested with the following authority to be exercised in keeping with all established Company policies and procedures in carrying out the responsibilities of the office.

1. To initiate, for approval of the Division General Manager, requests for machines, tools, and equipment requiring capital appropriations.

2. To initiate purchase requisitions for machines, tools, and supplies.

3. To hire authorized personnel and discharge, promote, or downgrade employees within the limitations imposed by personnel policies and labor contract obligations.

4. To approve wage and salary changes up to the limits established by the Division Manager.

5. To reject substandard work and material.

6. To adjudicate any issues, including those concerning standards, that develop within departments (within the limits of the policy and practice of the incentive system).

ASSISTANT GENERAL MANUFACTURING SUPERINTENDENT

The Morgan Engineering Company

BASIC FUNCTION: Is responsible to the General Manufacturing Superintendent for coordinating the activities of Production Department Superintendents and Foremen; for liaison between the Production Department and other Company Divisions and Departments; for coordinating the subcontracting of fabricating, machining, and assembly work on Company products; and for coordinating such special projects, surveys, and analyses as may be assigned or directed by the General Manufacturing Superintendent.

BASIC OBJECTIVE: To provide assistance to the General Manufacturing Superintendent in the administration of his functions for the attainment of Production Department objectives.

MAJOR DUTIES AND RESPONSIBILITIES

1. Organization and Personnel

   a. To see that personnel in the Production Department are kept fully and currently informed of all pertinent Company policies and that such policies are followed in the Production Department.

   b. To recommend, to the General Manufacturing Superintendent, major changes in the form and size of the various sections of the Production Department as required to meet changed conditions.

   c. To see that the various sections of the Production Department are supervised in a manner which enables them to perform their functions most efficiently.

2. *Production*

   a. To coordinate the activities of the various Shop Superintendents and Foremen in such a manner that maximum effectiveness is obtained for the production of quality products within anticipated costs and planned schedules.

   b. To act as liaison between the Production Department and various Company Divisions and Departments in the resolution of manufacturing and production problems.

   c. To coordinate the subcontracting of fabricating, machining, and/or assembly work on various Company products; to determine the subcontractors' facilities and ability to meet specifications and deliveries; and to negotiate prices and schedules.

   d. To act as liaison between the Production Department and the Sales Division in the sale of the Company's facilities and services.

3. *Quality*: To act as liaison between the Production Department and various Company Divisions and Departments, such as Engineering, Inspection, Purchasing, Processing, and Plant Engineering, in the resolution of problems concerning tolerances and specifications.

4. *Budgets*

   a. To assist the General Manufacturing Superintendent in developing the annual budget for the Production Department.

   b. To review the annual budgets covering operating expenses, as submitted by the Department Superintendents, and recommend their approval to the General Manufacturing Superintendent.

5. *Material Handling*

   a. To see that in-process materials are moved to successive operations by material handling personnel according to schedules established by the Production Planning Department.

   b. To see that finished material is shipped according to schedules established by the Production Planning Department.

6. *General*

   a. To assume the duties and responsibilities of the General Manufacturing Superintendent in his absence.

   b. To perform any additional duties requested by the General Manufacturing Superintendent.

ADMINISTRATIVE ASSISTANT
TO MANUFACTURING MANAGER*

An Aircraft Company

OCCUPATIONAL SUMMARY: It is the responsibility of the Administrative Assistant to the Manufacturing Manager to perform specialized and administrative duties for the Manager; to develop, coordinate, and review the status of budgets and manpower forecasts; to coordinate and develop systems to measure departmental performance; to study and recommend solutions to administrative problems; to represent the Manager in Industrial Relations; to develop systems to maintain uniformity in administration, systems, reports, policies, and programs.

DUTIES

1. To develop, follow up, negotiate, and review the status of budgets and manpower forecasts for the Manager. To establish and maintain control systems and forms that will reflect accurately the current status of such items as budget, quality control, schedule, workload, labor requirements, organization, and personnel. To coordinate for the entire Manufacturing organization the safety, security, and housekeeping programs, including investigation and corrective action, as required. To represent the Manager in activities related to Industrial Relations and Personnel.

2. To coordinate administrative problems in manufacturing operations within the Manufacturing Manager's organization and with other affected organizational units, insuring standardization of all reporting and administrative functions. To assist Manager as needed.

3. To screen correspondence, documents, and reports; to conduct required interviews; to make digests of information so as to conserve the time and lighten the workload of the Manager. To review and approve changes of status, merit reviews, and labor requisitions.

4. To initiate and conduct surveys and audits whenever analysis of records or reports suggests the need for corrective or remedial policy action by the Manager. To submit completed recommendations for final affirmative or negative action by the Manufacturing Manager.

5. To determine the validity of capital expenditure requests submitted

---

* An "assistant to" title normally implies a staff position. However, because the job described here requires the incumbent to represent senior manufacturing management and work closely with it, the description has been placed in the line category.

by the Manufacturing organization; maintain records; and follow up to assure prompt fulfillment of requirements.

6. To advise affected personnel in the Manufacturing organization of policies and decisions made by the Manager and by executive management; interpret procedures, directives, and reporting requirements for them. To prepare written communications on policy and procedural matters, special operating instructions, and organizational problems.

7. To collaborate with the Manager in maintaining the greatest possible uniformity in administration, responsibility, systems, policies, and programs within the Manufacturing organization.

8. To coordinate and summarize program reports and annual objectives.

KNOWLEDGE AND ABILITY REQUIRED: A degree in business administration, economics, accounting, or the equivalent and a minimum of eight years' heavy experience in responsible staff administrative assignments, scheduling, budgeting, and report preparation. Demonstrated knowledge and familiarity with all organizational segments, administrative procedures, and technical operations. Demonstrated ability to deal effectively and harmoniously with all levels of personnel and act as representative for organization on administrative matters.

Intermediate Manufacturing Management

In the intermediate category are the jobs of plant or works manager, shop superintendent, production superintendent, and others at the same general level.

PLANT MANAGER

Burroughs Corporation

PURPOSE: Under the guidance of the Division General Manager, the Plant Manager administers and directs the plant production activities, including the manufacture of all product parts for his plant and some for other plants; the assembly of commercial and defense products; the control of production and quality standards; and the maintenance and improvement of plant facilities.

TYPICAL RESPONSIBILITIES

1. To develop and administer plans and programs to meet manufacturing objectives of the plant in accordance with Division policies, approved marketing forecasts, quality requirements, and budget limitations by establishing operating objectives and determining staffing and facility requirements for the manufacturing activity.

2. To direct the manufacture of product parts and the assembly of commercial and defense products within quality and quantity requirements.

3. To direct the development and control of production schedules for parts and products to (a) meet approved sales forecasts and requirements for inventory and interdivisional transfers and (b) economically utilize facilities and personnel. To direct the requisitioning of raw materials and equipment requirements. To direct supporting activities, including storage, internal and external traffic, packing, and shipping.

4. To direct the control of quality standards to insure that materials received from vendors, in-process parts, and finished products conform to product engineering specifications and also to insure that fabricated parts transferred to other divisions conform to specifications established by the serviced divisions.

5. To direct Industrial Engineering services which provide for the development and improvement of plant manufacturing tools, equipment, and processes; and for the construction, maintenance, and repair of building facilities and equipment. To direct the establishment and maintenance of production time standards and methods within the manufacturing activity.

6. To review manufacturing activity objectives, budgets, processes, and facilities to determine effectiveness. To initiate studies designed to develop short-term and long-range alternative plans and programs. To evaluate findings and present program recommendations, with supporting estimates of costs and planned savings, to Division management.

7. To collaborate and coordinate with Product Engineering in (a) the formulation of new or modified commercial or defense product proposals by providing cost estimates for manufactured parts, assemblies, tooling, equipment, manpower, and time requirements; and (b) the maintenance or modification of existing products or the effective installation of approved new products by furnishing technical assist-

ance on manufacturing tooling and process requirements during the developmental stages.

8. To utilize supporting staff functions to study and advise in resolving problems and to develop and install programs in areas such as training, budgets, employment, safety, and inventory.

9. To develop and maintain an organization plan for the manufacturing activity by reviewing and appraising staffing and productive effectiveness. To initiate studies or direct changes.

10. To insure the maintenance and development of manufacturing records and statistical data. To discuss status reports with Division management.

SCOPE AND INFLUENCE

1. The manufacturing activity of the plant is assigned 750,000 square feet of floor space located in a multifloored structure. The total book value of plant and equipment represents $10 million with an original cost of $28 million. The average book value of assigned inventory is $18 million.

2. As a member of the Division Production Planning Committee, the Plant Manager participates in the review, recommended revisions, and/or Division approval of the preliminary marketing forecast (production schedule). Upon Corporate concurrence in the preliminary schedule, the detailed plant production schedule is formulated by the plant production-control staff and submitted to the incumbent for evaluation, revisions, and approval before submission to the Division General Manager.

3. Upon corporate approval of the final production schedule, incumbent makes daily operating decisions, including the authorization of capital expenditures within budgeted allocations. However, when scheduled production deviates for reasons including engineering changes, revised sales forecasts, quality problems, equipment or materials shortages, and work stoppages, corrective action may be directed as indicated:

   a. Layoff: More than one day requires General Manager and Industrial Relations Manager concurrence.

   b. Overtime: May be authorized for hourly and non-exempt personnel, but exempt personnel authorization requires General Manager's concurrence.

   c. Hiring: May hire direct labor. Indirect labor hiring requires concurrence of General Manager if the addition exceeds approved manning tables.

d. Emergency purchase of materials and repairs: Approves requisitions to purchase.

e. Contracting for outside manufacturing: Approves requisitions for contracting services.

f. Transfer of production when capacity exists: Generally discussed and agreed upon informally among the Plant Managers.

PLANT MANAGER

A Proprietary Products Manufacturer

BASIC FUNCTION: The Plant Manager is responsible for the economical manufacture and shipment of products according to the approved production budgets; for meeting quality standards; and for local credit, collection, and customer accounting activities. He must also preserve the safety and welfare of the personnel and properly maintain the facilities in his charge. He is responsible for an estimated $_____ million of annual production.

ORGANIZATIONAL RELATIONSHIPS

Reports to: Director of Manufacturing.

Supervises: Supervisor–Quality Control.
Supervisor–Employee Relations.
Supervisor–Industrial Engineering.
Supervisor–Planning and Procurement.
Supervisor–Printing.
Supervisors–Production (3).
Supervisor–Receiving, Shipping, and Warehousing.
Plant Engineer.
Plant Doctor.
Plant Controller.

PRINCIPAL ACTIVITIES

1. To manufacture products to meet the requirements of approved production plans at minimum cost, within quality limits, and consistent with manufacturing policies and good operating practices.

2. To maintain the plant inventories for which he is responsible at optimum levels for maximum long-term profitability.

3. To manufacture all products according to written product-quality standards and specifications. When forced to deviate from standard because of limitations of materials, equipment, or personnel, the Plant Manager must obtain written permission from the Director of Manufacturing.

4. To receive and process customer orders, and assemble and ship finished goods to fill these orders, in accordance with customer-service policy.

5. To direct the local accounting, credit, and collection activities.

6. To direct the maintenance of the approved system of control reports to permit responsible individuals to exercise firm control over costs, product quality, production, and other critical factors.

7. To analyze results of plant operations and determine variances from standard. To correct the conditions causing the variances, informing the Director of Manufacturing of the action taken.

8. To prepare the capital budgets for improvement, re-equipment, and expansion of the plant and offices.

9. To administer the expenditure of funds to carry on plant operations.

10. To arrange for the procurement of raw materials, packaging materials, and operating supplies to meet local production requirements. To supervise the purchase of maintenance equipment and supplies according to policy.

11. To direct the traffic function through the Plant Controller in accordance with traffic and customer service policies.

12. To develop improved manufacturing methods, layouts, equipment, and techniques and submit recommendations to the Director of Manufacturing for their adoption. These recommendations must include the necessary justification.

13. To conduct a continuous cost-reduction program throughout the entire plant and offices.

14. To participate in negotiating labor contracts, as required, by:

    a. Advising management of contract needs.

    b. Participating in contract negotiations.

    c. Advising the Vice President for Employee Relations and the Director of Manufacturing during the course of contract negotiations.

15. To administer the labor contract in accordance with its provisions and corporate policy, using the advice and counsel of the Supervisor–Employee Relations.

16. To administer a program for safety, hygiene, and fire protection to safeguard the health and welfare of the personnel and preserve the plant facilities.

17. To maintain the plant building, equipment, and grounds in good operating condition and appearance.

18. To make shipments of overstocked finished goods to other plants as directed by the Director of Manufacturing on the recommendation or with the approval of the Supervisor–Planning and Procurement.

19. Through the printing facilities, to provide printed material, such as soap wrappers and promotional literature, to all plants as required.

20. To recruit, train, and develop the necessary personnel to staff the plant and offices for the forecast level of operations.

PLANT MANAGER

A Paper Manufacturer

OBJECTIVE: To direct the activities of the _____ Plant to produce items of specified quality, at lowest cost, in line with established production plans, customer service requirements, and profit objectives.

RESPONSIBILITIES AND AUTHORITY

1. Organization and Staffing

   a. Recommends the establishment of organizational elements, responsibility, and authority, to conduct the plant's operations effectively.

   b. Determines when operating conditions require revisions of the plant's basic organizational structure and complement; applies and follows accepted procedures to accomplish those revisions.

   c. Approves internal changes in work assignments which will not affect basic organization structure or complement.

   d. Hires, or delegates hiring of, personnel for hourly and entry salaried positions. Selects personnel to fill higher salaried vacancies.

   e. Evaluates present personnel and recommends candidates to fill existing vacancies in other plants or organizational elements.

f. Reviews manning and workload for hourly and salaried positions to achieve optimum staffing.

2. *Supervision*

a. Provides for proper training and communication throughout the plant.

b. Administers all phases of union contracts covering all jurisdictional groups within the broad scope of unlimited contract clauses, or follows procedures which outline the interpretation of specific clauses.

c. Represents management and makes decisions on grievances through the third stage. Consults staff Industrial Relations or his supervisor as he deems necessary to insure his position and to insure that his decision is in line with the joint contract provisions.

d. Approves individual wage-rate changes in accordance with union contract schedules and approves job-rate changes submitted to him and previously approved by the Labor Relations Department.

e. Recommends salary adjustments in accordance with existing salary policy.

f. Approves demotion, discharge, or other disciplinary action, referring to his supervisor only such cases as are unusual in view of community relations or union reactions.

g. Approves vacations and other absences within the limits of existing policy.

h. Maintains effective employee morale and safety programs.

3. *Policy and Procedures*

a. Establishes internal policies, procedures, and rules governing plant operations which are consistent with Division and local plant policies.

b. Enforces policies and interprets and clarifies them for his subordinates.

c. Recommends revisions of local plant, Division, or internal policies or procedures applicable to the operations and organizational elements for which he is responsible.

4. *Assets and Operations*

a. Reviews annual budget recommendations for all areas for which he is responsible, adjusts them, and submits a plant budget for approval.

b. Keeps informed of competitor activities and customer requirements.

c. Keeps informed of product improvements and developments within the carton-converting industry.

d. Plans production and allied operations to meet customer requirements, marketing trends, and Division production programs.

e. Recommends capital expenditure programs for the plant.

f. Administers plant expenditures allotted under the approved budget and any special or capital expenditure programs.

g. Approves payment from allotted funds of expenses up to $2,500 per item.

h. Assures that standards, manning, and accounts are realistic and appropriate and that variances are investigated and resolved.

i. Strives to reduce operating costs and improve efficiency through coordination of projects pertaining to plant layout, material handling, machine design and modification, and process or methods improvement.

j. Controls inventory levels consistent with market requirements and minimal financial investment.

k. Maintains desired standards of quality for all products produced in the plant. Assures that adequate quality evaluation programs are established and applied.

l. Makes decisions on operating problems referred by plant personnel in the event of breakdowns affecting production, order-loading conflicts, quality problems, and other similar matters.

m. Provides for experimental and developmental projects and evaluates results and potential.

n. Assures that maintenance and general upkeep of plant property are properly handled.

o. Provides effective housekeeping, fire prevention, insect and rodent control, safety, and other programs of benefit to both the plant and its employees.

5. *Relationships*

a. Keeps his superior informed of plant progress and significant events.

b. Communicates and cooperates with personnel of other Divisions to obtain or furnish materials; implement programs; exchange experience, ideas, and solutions to operating problems; improve communication, and the like.

c. Cooperates with staff elements by making equipment and personnel available for experimental orders, machine-trial orders, and similar experimental or developmental activities.

d. Familiarizes himself with staff services available and uses such services in solving problems and obtaining advice or information in specialized fields.

e. Protects confidential developments, specifications, materials, and other such data in contacts with competitors or others.

f. Collaborates with sales personnel to utilize production equipment effectively so as to meet marketing requirements.

g. Participates in negotiating union contracts.

h. Contributes to sound customer relationships through personal or staff visits to customer plants at the request of sales personnel.

i. Acts as the local Company representative and fosters good community relationships by maintaining membership and representation in local clubs and organizations, by participating in civic affairs, and by providing for plant tours.

WORKS MANAGER

Allegheny Ludlum Steel Corporation

BASIC FUNCTION: Responsible to the General Manager of Production for the profitable operation of the _____ Works on a continuing basis; for fulfilling customers' requirements in accordance with established schedules and accepted quality standards; for the execution of management policies through active planning, directing, coordinating, and controlling the Works' operations within the scope of the basic objectives and policies established by corporate management and within the scope of authority delegated by the General Manager of Production; for the maintenance of a sound plan of organization; for the controlling of costs; for making recommendations to the General Manager of Production on matters requiring his action; for the appraisal of performance and results at his Works; for the maintenance of existing plant, facilities, and equipment; and for the coordination of modernization, replacement, or extension of plant, facilities, and equipment.

BASIC OBJECTIVE: To administer the operations of the _____ Works in a manner which will enable it to meet the Corporation's objectives, assuring a coordination of effort that will result in optimum operating efficiency, manufacturing cost, profit, product quality, performance to schedule, forward planning and growth, product development, and industrial relations.

MAJOR DUTIES AND RESPONSIBILITIES

1. *Organization and Personnel*

   a. To develop, maintain, and administer an organization which is capable of carrying out the functions of the _____ Works.

   b. To assign definite duties, responsibilities, and authorities to immediate subordinates; to approve the position and job descriptions of immediate subordinates; and to see that all Corporation and Works policies and procedures are understood and followed within the Works.

   c. To review and appraise periodically the performance of each immediate subordinate as prescribed by Corporation policy and to take or recommend any necessary remedial action.

   d. To counsel with and recommend to the General Manager of Production regarding the employment, dismissal, or change in compensation or status of personnel under his immediate supervision.

   e. To direct the administration of all industrial relations functions, including the receiving and handling of employee grievances in accordance with established procedures and carrying out of all applicable provisions of contractual union agreements and corporate industrial relations policies; to direct salary administration; to administer and develop further Works safety and good housekeeping programs; to develop and maintain apprentice, on-the-job, and executive development training programs; and to improve employee morale by providing adequate employee services and by stimulating inter-Works and intra-Works competition through recognition of employee achievements.

   f. To review and approve newly created or recommended changes in incentive wage plans covering Works personnel.

2. *Manufacturing*

   a. To direct the Manager of Operations in his functions of production planning, scheduling, and expediting: insuring that the necessary utilities, transportation, and other services are immediately available to secure uninterrupted production; insuring that all equipment and facilities are in good operating condition; directing the actual performance of scheduled operations to see that they are accomplished in the most efficient manner consistent with quality requirements and delivery dates; and keeping the

Customer Service Department informed with respect to deviations from production schedules.

3. *Planning*

   a. To direct the planning of the Works production program in accordance with sales forecasts, customer orders, and availability of materials, equipment, and facilities.

   b. To direct the activities of the Works Engineer in planning and making recommendations for the modernization, replacement, or addition of equipment and facilities; to review and approve all changes or additions recommended; and, following corporate approval, administer the execution of construction projects in a manner satisfactory to the Vice President in Charge of Engineering.

   c. To direct the work of the Manager of Industrial Engineering in planning and making recommendations for changes in operating practices, methods, standards, equipment, and plant layout.

   d. To be a member of the product-line committees for sheets, strip, and magnetic materials so as to obtain cooperation and coordination among the Sales, Research, and Production Divisions. Committees will meet at frequent intervals to consider and take action on matters affecting orders, prices, costs, margins, investment, and return on investment.

4. *Material Control*

   a. To direct the requisitioning and procurement of needed materials, equipment, or services, including the receiving and storing of materials and equipment.

   b. To establish controls over inventory and maintain inventory levels at predetermined or otherwise authorized levels as established by corporate management.

5. *Quality Control*

   a. To direct adherence to the techniques, processes, and standards developed by the Technical Division and to develop supplemental policies, procedures, and programs as necessary to assure competitive standards of quality for the Works' products.

   b. To develop inspection techniques to insure maintenance of quality up to established standards.

   c. To administer the Works' metallurgical functions in accordance with corporate and Technical Division policies and procedures.

   d. To direct the review, investigation, and resolving of customer complaints and claims arising from inferior product quality.

    e. To see that technical counsel is made available to assist the Sales Division in developing customers' applications and quality standards and to coordinate all requested customer contacts made by Works personnel.

6. *Costs and Budgets*

    a. To analyze facility, equipment, and Department performance and cost records, locating and correcting improper or inefficient operations in order that the lowest cost consistent with established corporate objectives and policies may be realized.

    b. To analyze cost studies and justification of investment return on proposals for new facilities and equipment in order to secure reduced operating costs.

    c. To review and approve recommendations from the Industrial Engineering Department for cost reduction due to alterations in plant layout and better methods or practices.

    d. To analyze profitability of the various Works products in order to recommend Sales Division emphasis on the more profitable products; to correct unfavorable conditions affecting the less profitable or to recommend adequate substitutes.

    e. To direct the Works Controller to assist the operating departments in the further development of cost and performance records and budgetary controls.

    f. To counsel with the General Manager of Production in the preparation and submission of an annual budget for the _____ Works covering requirements for facilities and equipment additions and replacements.

7. *General*

    a. To submit a quarterly and annual report to corporate management showing in detail the progress being made in meeting all phases of Works objectives.

    b. To see that his organization is currently informed on Corporation affairs.

    c. To approve the expense accounts of his immediate subordinates.

    d. To represent the Corporation in local community organizations and affairs.

    e. To perform any additional duties as requested by the General Manager of Production.

SHOP SUPERINTENDENT

A Machinery Company

FUNCTION: To supervise, directly and through Foremen, the activities of the Manufacturing Departments engaged in the machining, assembly, and testing of the Division's products; to coordinate the various operating phases to insure the proper flow of work through the Departments; to be responsible for quality and quantity of work, maintenance of production schedules, and operating costs.

ORGANIZATIONAL RELATIONSHIPS: Reports to: Manager of Manufacturing. Supervises: General Foremen and other Foremen. The Shop Superintendent must work closely with Personnel, Production Control, Methods, and Standards, Engineering, and other Manufacturing Departments, cooperating on joint problems and making suggestions to improve the over-all efficiency and effectiveness of the Division.

SPECIFIC RESPONSIBILITIES: The Shop Superintendent shall be accountable for the following broad responsibilities, which he shall fulfill through delegation of responsibility and authority and by initiation and execution of action in keeping with the authority vested in his office and the applicable Company policies and procedures.

1. To achieve economical operating costs by effective utilization of the facilities and employees' time.

2. To keep currently informed on status of production schedules and take appropriate action to clear away any difficulties that arise.

3. To assure that the established standards of quality, accuracy, and performance are maintained, directing corrective measures when necessary. To call attention of appropriate individuals to all cases of inaccurate manufacturing information.

4. To collaborate with Methods and Standards in the development of economical manufacturing methods and the administration of the wage incentive system.

5. To administer Company personnel policies, enforce safety and health regulations, and take prompt action on employee complaints to achieve good employee morale. To represent the Department at all stages of the grievance procedure and arbitration. To maintain current status with respect to employee morale. To keep management informed on status of employee morale. To maintain discipline.

6. To maintain equipment and tools in good working condition, ma-

chinery guards operative at all times, and working areas clear for safe, efficient operation.

7. To be alert to opportunities for improvement in the operation of the Departments and plant.

8. To keep Departmental expenses within budget allowance.

9. To develop and maintain training programs to provide efficient personnel for Department requirements. To check the job performance of subordinates and advise them on their good points and shortcomings; to give counsel on growth potential.

AUTHORITY: The Shop Superintendent is vested with the following authority, to be exercised in keeping with all established Corporation and Division policies and procedures in carrying out the responsibilities of the office.

1. To initiate or approve purchase requisitions for tools and supplies required in the operations of the Departments.

2. To requisition productive employees as necessary to maintain production.

3. To penalize or discharge any employee in the Departments who is found guilty of an infraction of Company rules that calls for such a penalty.

4. To adjudicate any issues, including those of time standards, which arise within the Departments, according to the policy and practice of the incentive system.

5. To settle complaints and grievances within the limits of personnel policies and labor-agreement obligations.

6. To recommend salary, wage-rate, and personnel-status changes for subordinates.

PRODUCTION SUPERINTENDENT

A Paper Manufacturer

OBJECTIVES:

1. To print, cut and crease, finish, pack, move, store, and ship cartons of standard cost or lower, within established specifications, consistent with the customer's required level of quality, and in line with established production schedules.

2. To receive, move, and store incoming materials.

3. To furnish, as a service to the Production Departments, accurate and economical dies, properly formulated inks, and good-quality, re-usable printing plates.

RESPONSIBILITIES AND AUTHORITY

1. *Organization and Staffing*

   a. Recommends changes in production-area organization to recognize manufacturing methods changes, to achieve better control, to reduce expense, or to adjust the organization to recognize other changes.

   b. Recommends personnel within his sphere of responsibility for promotion, demotion, transfer, or other assignment to assure adequate staffing for the present and to plan for the future, either inside or outside his primary responsibility area.

   c. Interviews candidates to fill salaried positions within his area of jurisdiction, evaluates them, and recommends his selection to the Plant Manager .

   d. Recommends to the Plant Manager, and justifies, any requests for additional employees or reductions in workforce which he deems necessary for efficiency.

2. *Supervision*

   a. Exercises direct supervision over three Shift Superintendents, Die Room Foreman, and Materials Handling and Shipping Foreman. Delegates to these employees the responsibility for supervising all hourly and salaried personnel in their areas (i.e., Working Foremen, Shift Foremen, and operators).

   b. Provides for proper training and communication throughout his area of responsibility.

   c. Represents management and makes decisions in grievances. Consults Industrial Relations staff and/or his supervisor as required to insure his position and to insure that his decision properly interprets current labor relations policy and practice.

   d. Approves individual rate changes in accordance with union contract schedules and approves job-rate changes submitted to him prior to approval by the Plant Manager.

   e. Recommends salary adjustments in accordance with existing salary policy.

   f. Approves vacations and other absences within the limits of existing policy.

   g. Conducts work-performance and personnel-appraisal reviews.

h. Maintains effective morale and safety programs.

i. Recommends office equipment for his assigned area.

3. *Policy and Procedures*

   a. Enforces Division policies and interprets companywide policies at all levels under his direct chain of command and supplements these policies with plant-level releases when deemed necessary and in order.

   b. Recommends revision of Division or internal policies or procedures applicable to the operation and organizational elements for which he is responsible. Submits all recommendations to the Plant Manager for review and approval.

4. *Assets and Operations*

   a. Submits for review by the Plant Manager a program providing for major repair and overhaul of equipment, with projections for additional items of equipment of a capital nature. (Does not include primary production center items ordinarily submitted through the Plant Manager to the Central Division Planning and Management staff for approval.)

   b. Continuously reviews existing budget allowances, production standards, waste standards, and manning and performance standards to initiate and put into effect changes required to maintain a good competitive manufacturing position from the cost, quality, and service standpoints.

   c. Formulates with the Plant Accounting Section realistic and competitive budgets for cost elements, covering labor (manning); service labor (including training and teaching); salaries; overtime (for both salaried and hourly personnel) ; maintenance (including direct and indirect labor and materials); and the raw materials and supplies used in the production processes. Submits his recommendations to the Plant Manager.

   d. Analyzes current plant production processes and usage of materials, manpower, and machinery on a continuing basis to improve methods of operation and insure efficient use of present materials and new materials, equipment, and so forth, to enable the plant to manufacture present products more effectively and economically or to manufacture new products.

   e. Evaluates and recommends improvements in usage of equipment, material, and manpower after appraising current backlogs, overtime demands, service requests, performance levels, quality levels, and cost effects.

   f. Investigates and answers all customer product complaints by review of quality control records, sampling, and other in-plant methods, as well as personal observation at customer's premises. Reports findings and recommendations to the Plant Manager regarding the plant's responsibilities in the matter.

g. Exercises daily control over the utilization of machines, materials, and manpower as required. Reviews all control reports, including daily production reports, daily performance reports, weekly reports, quality reports, and the like, both to keep informed and to determine the type and application of control required. Makes recommendations to the staff areas of the plant as required to assure that such areas continue to provide useful and current information to facilitate control of operations in the plant.

h. Approves revisions of standards. Approves all new specification authorizations and authorizations for changes in current specifications.

i. Makes decisions on operating problems referred by plant personnel in the event of breakdowns affecting production, quality problems, or other similar matters.

j. Meets with salesmen and customers. When required, resolves questions relating to conversion of orders which deviate from normal conditions.

k. Reviews with all areas under his jurisdiction new methods, new products, and product styles which require experimental or trial runs to determine the probability of their acceptance. Cooperates with various staff areas in the insertion of experimental orders into the production schedules. Institutes and follows the progress and end results of the trials and takes such final action as may have been implied in the initial request.

l. Is responsible for assuring proper operating condition and maintenance of all production and auxiliary equipment within his area of jurisdiction and for maintenance of all work spaces.

m. Establishes such schedules and programs as are required to recondition or replace defective materials produced by another Division plant.

n. Maintains a knowledge of product improvement and developments within the industry and weighs possible application to the plant production facilities.

o. Assures effective housekeeping, fire prevention, insect and rodent control, safety, and other programs of benefit to both the plant and its employees.

p. Attends, either in an advisory capacity or as chairman, meetings on the following matters: fire brigade, safety, quality, grievances, union/management, service, and the like.

q. Takes active part in the plant profit-planning program.

5. *Relationships*

a. Keeps his supervisor informed of production progress and significant events. Reviews his major activities and plans with the Plant Manager.

b. Meets with representatives of customers and suppliers on matters of quality, service, or policy decisions which deviate from the normal.

c. Cooperates with and utilizes central and plant staff services in solving problems and obtaining advice or information in specialized fields.

d. Contributes to customer relationships by personal visits to customer plants as assigned.

e. Meets with general management, sales management, salesmen, and customers as required to resolve questions of quality, service, or costs relative to the conversion of raw materials to finished products in the plant.

f. As delegated by the Plant Manager, in his absence maintains contacts with local civic leaders and plant callers.

PRODUCTION SUPERINTENDENT

Diamond Crystal Salt Company

REPORTS TO: Plant Manager.

DEPARTMENTS: Power, Processing, Screening and Grading, and Packaging (Production).

TITLES OF POSITIONS SUPERVISED DIRECTLY: General Foreman.
Screening and Grading
Foreman.
Packaging Foreman.
Night Superintendents (3).

NUMBER OF EMPLOYEES SUPERVISED INDIRECTLY: 123.

BASIC FUNCTION: To coordinate and direct the operation of the plant's Power, Salt-Processing, Screening and Grading, and Packaging Departments to meet the Company's operating standards, quality requirements, and shipping schedules in the most efficient manner practicable within the limitations of the Company's rules and policies and the working agreement.

MAJOR RESPONSIBILITIES

1. Personnel Relations: The standard of performance for this responsibility is met when all Company rules and policies and the working agreement are complied with so that harmonious relations exist between management and employees in areas reporting to the Superintendent of Power and Processing. To meet this responsibility, the Production Superintendent:

  a. Establishes sensible and adequate safety rules for employees to follow and coordinates these with the maintenance program to correct unsafe conditions.

  b. Assists in developing and directing programs and procedures to create and maintain employee interest and participation toward working safely.

  c. Advises subordinates of the proper interpretation and application of Company personnel policies to maintain just treatment of employees.

  d. Advises subordinates of the proper interpretation and application of the terms and conditions of the working agreement to maintain just relations between employees and management.

  e. Assists at Company and labor relations meetings and contract negotiations.

2. Power Production: The standard of performance for this responsibility is met when all power requirements are accomplished by the efficient utilization of employees, raw materials, and equipment. To meet this responsibility, the Production Superintendent:

  a. Directs the inspection and major maintenance of the plant's boilers and turbogenerators so that they are maintained in a satisfactory condition.

  b. Provides technical assistance to the Purchasing Department on the purchase of coal. Runs boiler tests and interprets the results, so that future coal purchases can be made on a sounder basis.

  c. Reviews all power reports and operating conditions with the General Foreman to assure that all operations are as efficient as practicable; takes corrective measures to improve operations wherever possible.

3. *Salt Production*: The standard of performance for this responsibility is met when all quality standards and quantity requirements are accomplished by the efficient utilization of employees, raw materials, and equipment. To meet this responsibility, the Production Superintendent:

    a. Directs the long-range development and maintenance of the brine fields for the most effective use of properties to insure an adequate supply of quality brine for production requirements.

    b. Coordinates operations with the Maintenance and Shipping Departments so that necessary maintenance work on processing equipment may be accomplished without interfering with salt production required to meet shipping schedules.

    c. Reviews all processing reports and operating conditions with the General Foreman to assure that all operations are as efficient as practicable; takes corrective measures to improve operations wherever possible.

4. *Product Grading and Blending*: The standard of performance for this responsibility is met when the proper quantities of salt are graded, blended, and binned and when special products are prepared in accordance with established standards to meet customer needs. To meet this responsibility, the Production Superintendent:

    a. Informs the Screening and Grading Foreman of short- and long-range product requirements and assists him in the scheduling of his manpower, equipment, and chemical needs so that product shipping schedules are met.

    b. Directs the Screening and Grading Foreman when producing special grades, blends, and new products so that quality and production standards may be established to meet customer needs.

    c. Reviews production reports and operating conditions with the Screening and Grading Foreman to assure that all operations are as efficient as practicable; takes corrective measures to improve operations wherever possible.

5. *Product Packaging*: The standard of performance for this responsibility is met when the proper quantities of product are packaged in accordance with standards of packaging, weight control, and scheduling to meet customer demands and transportation rulings. To meet this responsibility, the Production Superintendent:

    a. Informs the Packaging Foreman of short- and long-range product requirements and assists him in the scheduling of his manpower, equipment, and packaging materials so that product shipping schedules are met.

    b. Provides technical assistance to the Purchasing Department on the purchase of packing and packaging materials. Cooperates with the Quality Control Superintendent on the testing and evaluation of raw materials so that future purchases can be made on a more sound basis.

c. Reviews production reports and operating conditions with the Packaging Foreman to assure that all operations are as efficient as practicable; takes corrective measures to improve operations wherever possible.

6. *Building and Equipment*: The standard of performance for this responsibility is met when equipment and buildings are maintained in a manner that provides for quality production and efficient operation within established standards for repair and maintenance and with minimum interruption of scheduled operation because of mechanical failure. To meet this responsibility, the Production Superintendent:

a. Establishes and directs programs whereby the conservation and maintenance of buildings and equipment through preventive maintenance, adequate repairs, and good housekeeping are practiced by all subordinate employees.

b. Reviews all recommendations for revising and repairing buildings and equipment and takes appropriate action when the expenditure is justifiable.

c. Establishes and directs procedures to assure that all buildings and equipment are maintained in compliance with regulations established by such outside agencies as the insurance companies and government agencies.

d. Directs the scheduling of maintenance work which affects more than one Department so that it can be accomplished with minimum interference with other maintenance schedules and shipping requirements.

7. *New Equipment Methods and Processes*: The standard of performance for this responsibility is met when new equipment, methods, materials, and process developments are recommended wherever advisable. To meet this responsibility, the Production Superintendent:

a. Reads technical publications, attends technical meetings, and meets with representatives of other companies so that knowledge can be gained about new equipment, methods, materials, and process developments which can be used to improve plant operations.

b. Initiates and supervises tests on new equipment, methods, materials, and processes and interprets their results so that their possible application to the Company's operations may be correctly evaluated.

c. Assists the Maintenance Superintendent on specifications, design, and installation of approved capital projects whenever possible.

8. *Management Development*: The standard of performance for this responsibility is met when the responsibilities of all subordinate supervisory positions are established and incumbents are generally meeting their responsibilities, and when adequate replacements are available or in training to fill foreseeable vacancies. To meet this responsibility, the Production Superintendent:

   a. Establishes position responsibilities and advises supervisors of their responsibilities so that, when supervisors work toward understood goals, an efficient organization will be maintained.

   b. Analyzes subordinate personnel and recommends potential employees for future training for possible promotion to supervisory positions.

   c. Reviews position responsibilities with incumbent Supervisors and guides them in areas where improvement is deemed necessary.

PRODUCTION SUPERINTENDENT

A Petroleum and Carbon Producer

REPORTS TO: Plant Manager.

GENERAL RESPONSIBILITY: To supervise and coordinate all functions of the Production and Maintenance Departments of the _____ Plant as directed.

DUTIES

In connection with this responsibility, the general duties are:

1. To supervise and coordinate all production activities to the end that schedules are met, product quality conforms to established specifications, and production costs are held to the lowest controllable point.

2. To confer with and assist the Foremen of the Production and Maintenance Departments in the maintenance of quality and conformity to established specifications.

3. To recommend the improvement of production methods and processes and to put such improvements into practice upon proper authorization.

4. To cooperate with the Technical Superintendent in the maintenance of quality standards, the administration of the inspection function, and the development and installation of authorized improvements in processing and product specifications.

5. To counsel and assist the Maintenance Foreman in the establishment and administration of a sound preventive maintenance program.

6. To require adherence on the part of all subordinate personnel to established specifications, policies, and procedures.

7. To delegate appropriate authority and responsibility to the Foremen of the Production and Maintenance Departments to the end that all subordinate supervisory personnel shall discharge their duties in an efficient manner.

8. To supervise compliance of Production and Maintenance personnel with Company and Division policies and instructions, legal regulations, established procedures, and provisions of the union contract.

9. To initiate preventive measures against the occurrence, or claimed occurrence, of accidents and industrial diseases; to direct health, welfare, and safety programs established under Company policy.

10. To assist the Plant Manager in estimating manpower and material requirements, production and maintenance costs, and quality and process control programs, as well as in other related phases of administering the production activities of the plant.

11. To submit to the Plant Manager any recommendations for changes in processing or handling of procedures designed to increase productivity or reduce costs.

12. To establish and maintain high standards of work output and to participate actively in the training of subordinates, so that the best practice is uniformly adopted.

13. To notify the Plant Manager immediately of any situation that will interfere with scheduled plant operations.

14. To perform special assignments as requested by the Plant Manager.

AUTHORITY

1. Trains and directs the personnel assigned to him by the Plant Manager and approves their selection.

2. Recommends employees to the Plant Manager for promotion, separation, disciplinary action, or adjustments in compensation; takes
   immediate action to resolve grievances within the limits of established policies.
3. Initiates and approves requisitions for purchases in accordance with
   established procedures for the approval of the Plant Manager.
4. In the Plant Manager's absence, when directed acts in his place.

SUPERINTENDENT–ASSEMBLY SECTION

A Machinery Company

DIRECTS: All activities of the Assembly Section.

REPORTS TO: Manufacturing Manager, on all phases of his work.

SUPERVISES DIRECTLY: Foreman–Armature Assembly.
Foreman–Motor Assembly.
Foreman–Upright Assembly and Canister
Assembly.
Foreman–Cleaning Tool Assembly.
Foreman–Polisher Motor and Floor Washer
Assembly.

DUTIES

1. Directs the work of his five Foremen in the subassembly, final assembly, and packing operations for motors, brushes, dusting tools,
   cleaners, hose, and floor washers. This covers a wide variety of
   assembly and fabricating operations. However, since the great bulk
   of the parts used in assembly, both purchased and shop-made, are
   drawn from finished stores, the Superintendent of the Assembly
   Section must maintain close coordination with the Production Control function to see that each and every part will be available as
   needed for assembly. In addition, he must coordinate the activities
   of the various Departments in his Section in order to meet his production schedules. This involves, among other things, assisting his Foremen in overcoming obstacles, such as equipment breakdowns,

shortages of parts or materials, and others requiring cooperation from staff functions like Production Control and Inspection.

2. Assists the Manufacturing Manager in administering and enforcing all management policies applicable to his Section. May be called upon to make policy recommendations, particularly in cases affecting his Section (as on smoking).

3. Guides and assists his Foremen in carrying out their responsibilities, delegating to them the full authority necessary for this purpose.

4. Utilizes fully the services, controls, reports, and recommendations provided by the various staff functions to control over-all operations and improve performance in his Section. For example:

   a. Using the production schedules and delinquency reports furnished by the Production Control function, to follow up with his Foremen on the meeting of schedules.

   b. Following up on the variance reports and recommendations of the Cost Control function to see that corrective action is taken by his Foremen.

   c. Utilizing inspection reports and recommendations as a means of checking action taken by Foremen to improve quality and reduce scrap.

5. Cooperates with Operations Control and Plant Engineering in scheduling new layouts, major installations, machine inspection, and maintenance requiring appreciable shutdowns.

6. Tours each Department in his Section at least once each day and discusses with each Foreman such matters as production against schedule, productivity, indirect labor, costs, safety, housekeeping, and discipline; commends or criticizes as indicated. Analyzes Foremen's problems as to methods, procedures, or any of the matters mentioned above; reaches decisions and recommends possible solutions and improvements. When problems involve more than one section, takes action by consulting with appropriate Superintendent to reach a satisfactory solution within the framework of Company policy. If no solution is found, decides further course of action, such as referring to Manufacturing Manager for decision.

7. Consults with Manufacturing Manager and Labor Relations Manager on important problems involving the union. Would not, for example, suspend or discharge an employee represented by the bargaining unit without such consultation.

8. Follows up on special projects, such as employee suggestions and Foremen's job method proposals, which are being tried out in his Section to make sure that action is being taken and that projects are completed on the specified dates.

9. Maintains records and makes reports as required by the Manufacturing Manager and the various staff functions, such as Operations Control and Inspection, plus any others which, in his opinion, are needed to carry out his responsibilities. Also records and reports on special projects and various budget items, such as indirect costs.

FINISHING SUPERINTENDENT

A Paper Manufacturer

FUNCTION: To be responsible to the Production Superintendent for the efficient and economical performance of equipment and manpower in the Finishing Section, operating on a three-shift basis; to participate in the development of schedules; to maintain schedules and quality, production, and cost standards. To supervise all employees involved in carrying out this function.

DETAILED DUTIES

1. Supervises three salaried Shift Foremen and approximately 175 hourly employees involved in the waxing and gluing operations of the _____ Plant.

2. Is responsible for the efficient operation of the following: ten waxers (three paraffiners, one saturator, four dippers, and two velvet waxers); one Glamakoter, six Staudes, four straight-line and one right-angle gluer; one hot-spot dewaxer, and two cellophane machines; wax storage; the blending and delivery system; and the case sealer and conveyor system.

3. Is responsible to the Production Superintendent for the most efficient operation and maintenance of all machines in the production area under his supervision. Is responsible for the quality of production; assures that all standards and specifications are adhered to properly.

4. Schedules the workload of shifts as operations require, keeping in mind production needs and minimizing operational costs whenever possible. Attempts to utilize employees in the most efficient manner when shutdowns occur, and to maintain enough production on all machines to utilize available manpower.

5. Works closely with the plant Industrial Engineer in attempting to keep waste at a minimum and to establish more efficient control of

all operations. As necessary, and through the Production Superintendent, requests methods studies to improve productivity. Advises on circumstances surrounding various operations that would affect standards within the areas under his supervision.

6. Receives and analyzes cost breakdowns of the finishing operations from the standpoints of labor, expense, and materials; takes corrective action when necessary. Assigns various cost-item controls to the Foremen. Investigates maintenance charges, life of material, quality, and other factors related to his operations.

7. Receives daily, weekly, and monthly production and efficiency reports; takes steps if necessary to correct any activities under his supervision.

8. Administers adequate quality checks in the Finishing Section to assure that quality products are processed. Determines, when necessary, whether questionable products should be held up for sorting or junking and determines the disposition of such items. Attends quality meetings weekly. Reviews complaints and takes corrective action to eliminate work of repeatedly bad quality.

9. Attends production meetings weekly with the Customer Service and Production Services employees, Production Superintendent, Plant Manager, and Industrial Relations employees. Reviews future production and service requirements and problems of either general or specific nature.

10. Works closely with the Engineering Department on scheduling maintenance, whether general, preventive, or emergency. Follows up on all maintenance charges and investigates as necessary. Recommends machine changes to reduce maintenance and improve efficiency.

11. Orders and maintains an adequate inventory of operating supplies as approved by the Production Superintendent. Establishes inventory levels, depending upon usage, and decides on suppliers.

12. Works with Technical Services in processing experimental orders and assists in evaluating the orders as to production feasibility.

13. Recommends allowances on expense items and proposes the annual budget for operation and equipment maintenance and change-over and replacement parts for the Department. Includes any contemplated renovation of equipment.

14. Establishes workloads, evaluates work performance, and is responsible for the working conditions and morale of salaried and hourly employees in the Finishing Section. Selects, trains, instructs, and counsels employees; recommends demotions and promotions; and approves rate changes. Handles disciplinary action and termination of hourly employees.

15. Insures that all employees in the Finishing Section follow established safety regulations and practices and that they use the available safety devices. Takes corrective action if safety regulations are not followed. Is responsible for insuring that working conditions and equipment follow good safety practice.

16. Gives authoritative and complete information to any employee requesting counsel. Carries out programs to instill quality- and efficiency-consciousness on the part of both shift foremen and hourly employees.

17. Informs the Production Superintendent of situations, conditions, and problems or difficulties worthy of his attention. Keeps him informed at all times of the over-all function of the Finishing Section.

18. As required, assists the Foremen in developing answers to first-stage grievances. Represents the Department in any second-stage grievances involving employees from his area.

19. Is responsible for unloading, waxing, giving Materials Control inventory figures, and blending to specifications. Equipment involved: eight storage tanks, pipes, valves, fittings, and pumps. Is responsible for issuing work-order requests.

BACKGROUND REQUIREMENTS: Must have a technical knowledge of the products processed at the _____ Plant, particularly as to the quality of such products. Must have a thorough knowledge of the raw materials that go into the converted products from a quality and economy point of view. Must have a working knowledge of all equipment, from an operating and maintenance point of view, and an over-all knowledge of the capacity of the equipment over which supervision is exercised (waxers, dewaxers, gluers, Glamakoter, etc.). Must have the administrative ability to plan and schedule the finishing operations effectively from both a short- and long-range point of view. Must know the union contract and the interpretation of clauses that would affect employees under his jurisdiction. Must know the bases of costs, standards, and efficiency as they apply to the finishing operations. Must have a working knowledge of the customers, particularly of their respective requirements in respect to quality. Must possess a thorough knowledge of the staff areas of the plant (Accounting, Production Service, Industrial Engineering, for example) and their operations.

A high school education is the minimum educational background requirement, although a college degree is desirable. Practical experience of two to four years' production work in finishing operations, with an additional three to five years as Foreman in the same area, is desirable. In addition, one to two years on the job as Superintendent is required for satisfactory proficiency.

Application of Knowledge: Judgment and analysis are required in making operating decisions on a day-to-day basis in regard to machinery changes, proposed methods of operation and manning, cost minimization, and increased efficiency. Judgment is required in determining the status and disposition of questionable products. Analysis and ingenuity are required in anticipating operating problems and fluctuating workloads. The Superintendent is expected to visualize long-range production requirements; to acquaint himself with methods and equipment that would be beneficial to the over-all operation; and to make recommendations to the Production Superintendent. Judgment and discretion are required in scheduling employees, handling disciplinary problems, working with union representatives, and generally handling all employee situations that may arise within his area.

Contacts

Internal: Has daily contacts with all Departments of the _____ Plant; occasional contacts with Central Staff Technical Departments, such as Central Industrial Engineering, Central Plant Engineering, Commercial Development, and Process Engineering; and occasional contacts with sales representatives concerning service orders being processed. Controversy in these contacts is permissible.

External: As the occasion demands, contacts are made with representatives of vending companies that supply raw materials or equipment.

Supervision: Directly supervises three salaried Shift Foremen and, through these Foremen, approximately 175 hourly employees on a three-shift basis involved in the Finishing operations of the _____ Plant.

Exercises all elements of supervision: the selection, training and counseling, promotion, demotion, discipline, and termination of employees. Establishes workloads, evaluates work performance, and initiates personnel activities resulting from these evaluations.

Is responsible for satisfactory working conditions and morale of salaried and hourly employees reporting to him. As required, assists the Foremen in developing answers to first-stage grievances and represents the Department in any higher-stage grievance in which Department or employees are concerned.

Responsibilities

1. Assumes full responsibility for the building facilities and equipment within the Finishing area, including ten waxers, six Staudes, four straight-line gluers, one international gluer, one hot-spot dewaxer, one Glamakoter, two cellophane machines, wax storage and distribution equipment, case sealer and conveyor system, and miscellaneous materials handling equipment and auxiliary equipment in the Fin-

ishing Section. Is responsible for all operations within the Section from waxing to the delivery of finished, quality products for shipment. Operates within established budgets and explains any variances that may occur. Is responsible for quality and low waste as reflected in the cost of the finishing operation. Is responsible for housekeeping and maintenance of the physical areas of operations.

2. Is responsible to the Production Superintendent for recommending improvements in methods, procedures, and processes to eliminate excess waste and costs. Works with Technical Services and Plant Engineering and Industrial Engineering in the development of new machinery and modifications to existing processes to effect material saving, improve quality, and reduce waste. Institutes and carries out machine modifications (feed mechanisms, new dries, feed wheels, for example) that create better production efficiency.

3. Reviews and checks cost reports of production, waste, and over-all production activities. Is responsible for the preparation of the weekly work schedule. Is responsible for time sheets, vacation schedules and authorizations, and absentee reports for all employees under his supervision. Checks quality control reports daily for corrective action. Is responsible for all production records and reports, proper execution of finished-goods load tickets, and other paperwork prepared in or related to his Section's operations.

WORKING CONDITIONS AND HAZARDS: Is required to be present in areas of the Finishing Section where there is moving machinery and is thereby subject to the normal conditions and hazards encountered in a converting area. Occasionally travels on Company business (once or twice per month) to _____ area, to customer premises to answer customer complaints, to manufacturers of equipment or machinery, and to technical society meetings.

SUPERINTENDENT, FABRICATING SECTION

A Machinery Company

DIRECTS: All activities of the Fabricating Section.

REPORTS TO: Manufacturing Manager on all phases of his work.

SUPERVISES DIRECTLY: Foreman–Enameling and Iron Assembly.
Foreman–Machine.

Foreman–Tubing and Plating.
Foreman–Special Products.
Foreman–Bags, Service Parts, Stick and
Commercial Cleaners.

DUTIES

1. Directs the work of his five Foremen in the fabricating and finishing of numerous metal, bakelite, and paper parts; in the subassembly operations for cleaners, dusting tools, irons, and service parts; and in the final assembly of floor polishers, special products, and stick and commercial cleaners. This covers a wide variety of machining, polishing, plating, enameling, and assembly operations and the operation of semi-automatic machines for paper bags. The parts fabricated in the Fabricating Section many times require processing in two or more Departments of the Section. Since it is desirable to maintain a minimum stock of finished parts, and since each and every part must be available in order to complete assemblies in Final Assembly operations, the Superintendent of this Section must co-ordinate the activities of his various departments in order to accomplish these objectives. This involves, among other things, assisting his Foremen in overcoming all obstacles, such as machine and tooling breakdowns, conveyor malfunctions, raw material shortages, and those requiring cooperation from other groups, such as the originating Section.

2. Assists the Manufacturing Manager in administering and enforcing all management policies applicable to his Section. May be called upon to make recommendations toward the establishment of policies, particularly in cases where his Section is affected—as, for example, a policy on smoking.

3. Guides and assists his Foremen in carrying out their responsibilities, delegating to them the full authority necessary for this purpose.

4. Utilizes fully the services, controls, reports, and recommendations provided by the various staff functions to control over-all operations and improve performance in his Section. Examples of these are:

    a. Using the production schedules and delinquency reports furnished by the Production Control function to follow up with his Foremen on the meeting of schedules.

    b. Following up the variance reports and recommendations of the Cost Control function to see that corrective action is taken by his Foremen.

    c. Utilizing inspection reports and recommendations as a means of checking Foremen on action being taken to improve quality and reduce scrap.

5. Cooperates with the Operations Control and Plant Engineering functions in the scheduling of new layouts, major installations, machine inspection, and maintenance requiring appreciable shutdown periods.

6. Tours each Department in his Section at frequent intervals, at least once each day, and discusses with each Foreman such matters as production against schedule, productivity, indirect labor, costs, safety, housekeeping, and discipline; commends or criticizes as indicated. Analyzes Foremen's problems as to methods, procedures, or any of the matters mentioned above; reaches decisions; and recommends possible solutions and improvements. When problems cut across sectional lines, takes action by consulting with appropriate Superintendent to reach a satisfactory solution within the framework of Company policy. If no solution is forthcoming, decides further course of action, such as referring to Manufacturing Manager for decision.

7. Consults with Manufacturing Manager and Labor Relations Manager on action to be taken on important problems involving the Union. Would not, for example, suspend or discharge an employee represented by the bargaining unit without such consultation.

8. Follows up on special projects (such as employee suggestions and Foremen's job method proposals) which are being tried out in his Section to make sure that action is being taken and that projects are completed on the specified dates.

9. Maintains records and makes such reports as are prescribed by the Manufacturing Manager and the various staff functions, such as Operations Control and Inspection, plus any others which, in his opinion, are needed to carry out his responsibilities. Also records and reports on special projects and on various budget items, such as indirect costs.

AREA SUPERINTENDENT

A Chemical Company

REPORTS TO: Plant Manager.

SUPERVISES: Assigned Unit Supervisors, Area Engineers, Area Foremen, and Process Engineers.

Scope: The Area Superintendent is administratively responsible to the Plant Manager for the safe and efficient performance of all facilities employees and operations personnel within his assigned Area. He directs the operation and maintenance of the process units to insure desired production rates, satisfactory product quality and yields, low costs, and the optimum utilization of manpower, raw materials, and operating materials in conformance with the budget.

Duties

1. To exercise complete functional supervision and responsibility in all matters relating to his assigned Area.

2. To direct the planning and coordination of all activities within his assigned Area, including production, maintenance, safety, and employee relations.

3. To prepare a semi-annual operating budget covering expenses and labor forces within his Area; to actively participate in a periodic review of costs with employees in his Area so as to assess performance.

4. In conjunction with the Production Coordinator, to plan operations to meet requirements. To work with the Quality Control Supervisor to maintain desired quality. To be responsible for setting and adhering to standards of quality and quantity of work. Within limitations provided by design and equipment, to strive to eliminate contamination of streams and atmosphere. In given situations, is responsible for product shipments with respect to strict adherence to requirements for container appearance, quality, and shipping schedule.

5. To be responsible for adherence to standards of appearance and for the safety of all facilities within his Area.

6. To be responsible for maintenance costs through investigation of more modern methods or utilization of new procedures and/or equipment.

7. To call on Staff Divisions as necessary for assistance in accounting, industrial relations, recruiting, safety, design of new equipment (for example) in order to maximize the efficiency, safety, and quality of the Area for which he is responsible.

8. To be responsible for seeing that training programs on skills, safety, fire prevention, and supervisory responsibilities are carried out effectively.

9. To recommend merit increases for those who report to him; to recommend disciplinary measures, leaves of absence, and other administrative measures as necessary; and to participate from time to time in labor negotiations with the various bargaining groups.

10. To keep informed of current trends and advances in the industry through outside study and contacts with professional societies in an effort to advance in management development, personnel techniques, and other administrative aspects of his job.

EXPERIENCE AND TRAINING: A college degree, preferably in chemistry, chemical engineering, or mechanical engineering, and at least five years of related industrial plant experience or equivalent practical experience.

SHIFT SUPERVISOR, PRODUCTION

A Chemical Company

REPORTS TO: Area Superintendent.

SUPERVISES: All hourly employees at work in assigned Area on his shift.

SCOPE: Is responsible during his shifts for operations in Area assigned to his jurisdiction.

DUTIES

1. Supervises hourly personnel in assigned Area to insure prompt and efficient discharge of assignments and to insure that instructions, safe practices, proper charge rates, estimated yields, and specifications are complied with in the most efficient fashion.
2. Makes minor adjustments in process operations to fulfill desired requirements for product quantity and quality.
3. Schedules and assigns workmen to tasks; confers with them about problems, personnel matters, and the quantity and quality of their work; insures that adequate tools and materials are available to them.
4. Inspects equipment to determine need for repair work and reviews repair work requisitions submitted by workmen for approval.
5. Is responsible for operation of his assigned equipment within budgeted costs.
6. Holds safety meetings and oversees training of all employees on his shifts.

7. Coordinates, with Night Superintendent, the operations of his assigned units on shifts where other units are affected.

8. Prepares operating reports specified by Area Superintendent.

EXPERIENCE AND TRAINING: Degree in chemistry or engineering and two years of experience in Process or Utilities, or ten or more years of experience as an operator on operating units. Orientation of at least one month on other units, such as Laboratory, Maintenance, or Warehouse.

Foremen

In addition to general foremen there are foremen in charge of particular operations, shift foremen, and assistant foremen.

GENERAL FOREMAN

A Proprietary Products Manufacturer

The General Foreman of the _____ Department is responsible for the production of all items at minimum cost, of specified quality, and according to production schedules. He is responsible to the Production Supervisor and directly supervises 11 foremen, 2 clerks, and 120-250 hourly workers.

RESPONSIBILITIES

1. To schedule operations in the Department to attain maximum output, specified quality, and minimum cost as stated in the plant performance reporting guide; and to adhere to these schedules on shift, daily, weekly, and monthly bases.

2. To be responsible for employee relations at the Department level, including adherence to the labor contract, seniority agreement, and so forth; the carrying out of administrative and personnel functions; and the training of both supervisory and hourly employees.

3. To supervise the maintenance of equipment for all operations in the department.

4. To maintain the quality of manufactured products.

5. To administer safety programs, including good housekeeping.

6. To recommend to the Production Supervisor items for inclusion in both the capital expenditure program and the cost reduction program; and to bring to a successful conclusion those items programed.

DUTIES

1. To supervise the scheduling of production by quarters, months, weeks, and days, according to production facilities and requested budgets, so as to permit lowest possible cost and minimum disturbance of labor.

2. To supervise the production of scheduled items to permit quality merchandise to arrive at the warehouse on time. To make changes in schedules as directed by the Production Supervisor.

3. To maintain close contact with Purchasing to assure that raw materials, packing materials, and operating supplies will be on hand to meet production schedules.

4. To maintain close contact with Quality group to assure that all materials used or produced meet quality specifications.

5. To make recommendations to the Production Supervisor for changes in methods, quality standards, standard practice instructions, cost standards, and organizational setup for the improvement of Departmental operations.

6. To supervise the training of supervisory personnel on assigned and related jobs to increase flexibility of assignments. To coach various supervisory employees in their methods of training hourly workers. To make out performance rating sheets on supervisory employees and review these with them on a regular basis.

7. To carry out plant and Department programs of safety, fire protection, and good housekeeping to safeguard the health and welfare of the employees.

8. To supervise the making-up of job assignments in accordance with the labor contract and seniority agreement. To meet with the union delegate on Department labor problems and render decisions in accordance with Step 2 of the contract. The decisions are subject to review by the Production Supervisor.

9. To review all control reports covering Departmental activities. To explain variances on daily and monthly bases. To take corrective action and report to the Production Supervisor.

10. To maintain liaison with the Industrial Engineering group on all improvements in methods and incentive rates.

11. To make up job description sheets for evaluation. To initiate requests for job analysis and rating subject to approval by the Production Supervisor.

12. To make recommendations for the improvement, replacement, or expansion of Department facilities, complete with necessary justifications, so that such changes may be included in the capital expenditure budget.

13. To review the maintenance work necessary to keep the equipment in good operating condition and recommend approval for all overtime work.

14. To make recommendations for the inclusion of items in the cost reduction program, with the assistance of Industrial Engineering, and to carry out this program.

15. To set up layouts for special deals and supervise them until actually in production.

16. To perform various duties as requested by the Production Supervisor, such as holding conference-type training sessions and escorting visitors.

GENERAL FOREMAN

An Instrument Company

REPORTS TO: Superintendent.

SUPERVISES: Foreman, Section Foremen, Assistant Foremen.

SUMMARY: Supervises, through Foremen or Section Foreman, employees engaged in the performance of fabricating, processing, foundry, or assembly operations.

DUTIES

1. Supervises any worker group which cannot be supervised effectively by one Supervisor and one Section Foreman. May be assisted by any number of Foremen, Section Foremen, and Assistant Foremen.

2. Coordinates and directs activities within his area of responsibility and maintains the quality and quantity of work produced in compliance with all applicable Company policies and procedures, including Production Control and Accounting.

3. Is responsible for the efficient and economical utilization of labor and material and the detection of opportunties for economies through the improvement of methods and the elimination of wasteful practices.

4. Collaborates with Production Control in planning work schedules within the area of his responsibility and maintains regular check on the progress of the work to insure performance in accordance with schedules.

5. Must have a thorough up-to-date knowledge of the processes for which he is responsible. Contributes technical assistance to Manufacturing Engineering in the development of efficient processing methods and procedures and in the accumulation of data. Collaborates with Product and Project Engineers in the development and design of new products, giving technical assistance on manufacturing processes and problems. Gives technical advice to subordinates in the solution of operating problems.

6. Recommends improvements and modifications in plans, organization, and facilities, including the procurement of new equipment and tool accessories. Requisitions tools, materials, and operating supplies and authorizes other indirect expenses.

7. Is responsible for forecasting labor requirements to insure an adequate labor supply in the proper classifications to meet production schedules known to him.

8. Collaborates with Supervisors of other Shop Departments to coordinate work.

9. Maintains harmony among employees within his jurisdiction and between employees and management, assisting subordinates to settle grievances and arguments and to determine proper disciplinary action.

10. Is responsible for the observance of safety regulations; recommends measures to remove unnecessary work hazards.

11. Assures that operations and personnel for which he is responsible comply with all applicable provisions of Federal and state labor laws and the terms of labor agreements.

MANUFACTURING FOREMAN

Badger Meter Manufacturing Company

REPORTS TO: Plant Superintendent.

GENERAL RESPONSIBILITIES: The Manufacturing Foreman is responsible for the performance of the workers assigned to his Department in the manufacture of parts and assemblies and in other work assignments.

SPECIFIC RESPONSIBILITIES

1. *Planning*: To plan the work of the Department so that jobs can be assigned, material requested, and production performed in accordance with production schedules.

2. *Training*: To be responsible for training all subordinate personnel in their present jobs and, where practical, for alternate jobs.

3. *Quality*: To maintain constant surveillance over trends in the quality of all work performed in the Department and take immediate corrective action when required.

4. *Expenses*: To be responsible for maintaining expenses within budget limits.

5. *Supervisory Responsibilities*: To maintain constant follow-up to assure the efficient utilization of workers and machines. To take immediate corrective action when production troubles arise. To personally assist and direct workers who have production or quality problems and be responsible for the motivation, morale, and discipline of workers assigned to his Department. To review the accuracy of time cards, move tickets, and other reports of pieces produced and work performed. To recommend personnel and rate changes to the Plant Superintendent.

6. *General*: To report to the Plant Superintendent all items that require the attention of the Production Control, Industrial Engineering, and Maintenance Departments. To actively support all management policies, programs, and procedures. To make suggestions to the Plant Superintendent on all matters pertaining to the improvement of the over-all production operation. To contact the Plant Superintendent frequently so as to report any significant current or anticipated deviations from production schedules, quality standards, or budget allowances.

DEPARTMENT FOREMAN–MANUFACTURING

Olin Mathieson Chemical Corporation

REPORTS TO: Superintendent–Manufacturing.

MAJOR FUNCTIONS: Under the general direction of the Superintendent–Manufacturing as to scope of operations, the Department Foreman–Manufacturing supervises, controls, and directs through subordinate Foremen the various manufacturing operations and production personnel employed in one or more of the following production areas: Barrel Shop, Gun Parts Shop, Broach Shop, Screw Shop, or M/14 Shops. He performs related duties as required.

RESPONSIBILITIES INCLUDED

1. Supervising and directing Foremen in the formulation of daily and/or weekly production tasks in accordance with the outlines of the master production schedule; recommending revised schedules as required by equipment down time or other interruptions in production.

2. Directing the over-all assignment of work within the production area and coordinating the activities of the Foremen and others in charge of related activities in attaining production schedules.

3. Maintaining adequate production records in order to review continually production efficiency, volume of scrap work, and quality of work being performed. Assisting in the revision of work or force schedules in order to meet increased or decreased production schedules.

4. Implementing programs of work simplification and/or cost reduction and conducting investigations into the causes of excessive scrap or rejects in order to initiate positive correction action. Reviewing and evaluating employee suggestions as submitted.

5. Working with related Manufacturing Departments in order to keep other units informed of the status of work in process and the capability to meet production schedules. Assisting in arranging to secure maintenance services for Department equipment.

6. Enforcing effective safety programs designed to provide safe operating equipment and safe working practices and to maintain hazard-free working areas. Conducting and/or attending meetings relating to safety, quality control, production scheduling, budgets, and so on.

7. Preparing and submitting for approval the proposed annual budget requirements for the assigned production area. Continually review-

ing the status of allocated funds, manpower, and facilities in order to insure optimum utilization.

8. Performing personnel functions such as recommending the selection, hiring, change in status, or termination of assigned hourly and salaried employees. Observing qualifications of employees for selection as Foremen. Assisting in administering the provisions of the labor agreement and/or corporate policies and procedures.

SUPERVISION EXERCISED: Directly, 3-4. Indirectly, 75-100.

EDUCATION REQUIRED: Graduation from high school or trade school plus additional supervisory and technical courses equivalent to two years of college or the equivalent.

PREVIOUS EXPERIENCE PREFERRED: At least seven to ten years' experience in manufacturing operations, including at least three to five years' experience in a supervisory capacity.

RELATED EXPERIENCE ACCEPTABLE: Experience in machining operations plus mechanical background, technical courses, and/or supervisory training.

———————

GENERAL FOREMAN–ASSEMBLY

A. O. Smith Corporation

PRIMARY FUNCTION: To direct and coordinate through subordinate Foremen the operations necessary to conduct subassemblies and over-all assemblies of product systems such as S. S. pumps, hand pumps, product repair units, counters, meters, meter accessories, and submersible pumps. Supplementary operations also included are pump and meter testing, degreasing and bonderizing, and spray painting.

DUTIES AND RESPONSIBILITIES

1. To organize Sections under his jurisdiction in order to meet operational requirements, and staff them with qualified Foremen. To hold Foremen responsible for their Sections' operations.

2. To assist Industrial Engineering in establishing realistic time allowances in new-product assemblies and to determine proper manpower requirements for appropriate operational assembly levels. To assume or reassign duties of absent Foremen. To spot-check various stages

of all operations under this jurisdiction in order to insure meeting the production schedule.

3. To direct through subordinate Foremen the operations specified in the general description above.

4. To perform personally the following duties:

   a. Consulting with the Manager of Manufacturing and Manufacturing Services relative to incorporating engineering changes in the product or process. Explaining official engineering changes to the Foremen if they are not aware of them.

   b. Informing the Production Scheduling Section of delays that might cause changes in the schedules.

   c. Expediting rush orders and insuring that they are shipped as "rush" on schedule.

   d. Locating bottlenecks and taking steps to correct them, such as expediting material shortages in product systems already in production.

   e. Discussing with salesmen material problems such as paint of the wrong color and other characteristics that do not meet required quality standards.

   f. Determining minimum levels of lube models and S. S. pump chassis, meters, and so on, in anticipation of future customer orders.

   g. Analyzing underwriters' procedures in order to insure that assembly operations comply with their requirements.

   h. Directing subordinate Foremen in the conducting of annual in-process inventories.

   i. Conferring with packaging vendors about the proper type of cartons for shipment of new products which will meet the carriers' codes.

5. To maintain costs within limits consistent with assembly operational requirements by comparing actual operating costs against past cost experience; initiate steps to prevent recurrence of controllable high costs. Also, periodically to vary manpower assignments in each Section dependent upon operational loads in order to insure minimum labor costs at desired operating levels.

6. To maintain product quality by spot-checking for vendor- or plant-produced defective work; to take steps to prevent its recurrence if plant-produced; and also to insure that it is charged to the proper account.

7. To improve production methods by sketching or verbally explaining improved tooling and fixtures which will facilitate assembly.

8. To notify Maintenance personnel of any breakdowns and follow up to insure repair.

9. To administer Company personnel policies as they apply to employees under his direct and indirect supervision with reference to training, vacations, merit increases, promotions, safety, and housekeeping. To retain final approval within the Department relative to the hiring of new hourly-paid employees and to hold disciplinary powers up to and including discharge.

GENERAL FOREMAN, PARTS FABRICATION

A. O. Smith Corporation

REPORTS TO: Manager of Manufacturing and Manufacturing Services.

SUPERVISES: 12 Production Foremen and 190 hourly production workers.

PRIMARY FUNCTION: Directs and coordinates the machining and fabrication of parts for positive-displacement liquid meters and gasoline service station pumps. This includes supervision over machine shop, tool crib, and welding operations in a job-shop type of operation with short production runs and frequent machine setup changes.

DUTIES AND RESPONSIBILITIES

1. Collaborates with Production Control and Manager of Manufacturing and Manufacturing Services in the development of the master production schedule. Checks daily production against schedule. Investigates and determines reasons when schedule is not met and takes corrective action.

2. Supervises the incorporation of engineering changes in blueprints and parts lists. Informs Production Foremen of engineering changes and follows up to insure that they are incorporated into the manufacturing process.

3. Cooperates with Quality Control Manager in determining cause of scrap or rework. Takes corrective action to eliminate the repetition of errors. Conducts production tests for Service Laboratory in an effort to determine whether or not specified materials are defective. Notifies Engineering of improperly specified materials, or Purchasing in cases where materials do not meet correct specifications.

4. Maintains charts on each Department and records on each Foreman showing realization of labor, scrap, and rework. Takes corrective action on any deviations from standards. Assumes full responsibility for the machining of quality products.

5. Supervises the maintenance of stores of tools and shop supplies. Notifies Maintenance Man or Tool Fabrication Foreman of breakdowns and changes to be made in Machining Department. Assists Maintenance Man on breakdowns. Insures that tooling is repaired and that new tools are requisitioned.

6. Determines manpower needs of Department in cooperation with Production Foremen and recommends adjustments in size of workforce to Manager of Manufacturing and Manufacturing Services.

7. Counsels each Foreman on any problems related to his operation. Performs duties of Foremen when they are on vacation or absent for other reasons.

8. Recommends new methods to increase production and cut costs. Analyzes and evaluates worth of methods suggestions made by subordinates and recommends feasible suggestions to Manufacturing Superintendent.

9. Position requires a knowledge of a variety of metals such as stainless steel, brass, aluminum, cast iron, cast steel, and regular steel with reference to tolerances, feeds, speeds, and the like. It also requires a knowledge of a variety of products, such as meters, eliminators, strainers, counters, flow control valves, and stop-stop valves, with the different parts used and their identifying numbers.

10. Reviews for approval merit increases recommended by Foremen, disciplinary action taken by Foremen against employees, and so forth. Administers Company personnel policies regarding the Foremen with reference to training, promotions, vacations, merit increases, and safety training.

GENERAL FOREMAN, MACHINING

New Holland Machine Company

REPORTS TO: Manager, Plant.

SUPERVISES: Foremen, Press and Shear.
Foremen, Machine Shop.
Foreman, Tooling.

Duties (Under Direction)

1. To manage the machining personnel and activities, including punching, machining, and producing production parts and castings; and developing, making, issuing, and maintaining tools, jigs, dies, gauges, and fixtures.

2. To organize and control men, machines, materials, and parts flow to produce production parts and tools at minimum cost in accordance with over-all manufacturing plans.

3. To follow up and check Shop Foremen and other personnel on the progress of work under their supervision.

4. To investigate and correct the cause of production problems such as delays, scrap, rework, and shortages.

5. To cooperate with Production Engineering and Shop Foremen in designing and developing new tooling, modifying existing tooling, and estimating cost or production rates as required.

6. To review, revise, recommend, and/or approve new layouts, methods, procedures, processes, and equipment.

7. To initiate or approve requisitions prepared by Foremen for material, supplies, or equipment as required.

8. To cooperate with tooling, standards, and industrial engineers in determining methods, installing new procedures and processes, and establishing and administering the wage incentive program.

9. To cooperate with Accounting in establishing operating budgets and counsel with Foremen as necessary to control expenditures within approved budgets.

10. To keep abreast of new developments in manufacturing, training, and Company plans and policies by attending meetings as required, reading publications, and visiting other industrial plants as directed.

Activities Supervised

1. Developing, manufacturing, assembling, modifying, repairing, sharpening, storing, issuing, and following up tools, jigs, dies, gauges, and fixtures from piece-part prints, sketches, verbal instructions, and/or tool prints and specifications.

2. Punching, shearing, roll-forming, welding, grinding, milling, turning, broaching, hand-forming, and finishing production parts and castings according to blueprints and specification sheets.

3. Cooperating in determining methods, installing new processes, and administering wage incentive programs.

SECTION FOREMAN

An Instrument Maker

REPORTS TO: Foreman, General Foreman, or Superintendent.

SUPERVISES: Assistant Foremen and assigned employees.

SUMMARY: Supervises the activities of a group of up to 40 employees. May have the assistance of one or more Assistant Foremen.

DUTIES

1. Coordinates and directs activities within his area of responsibility and maintains the quality and quantity of work produced in compliance with all applicable Company policies and procedures.

2. Is responsible for the efficient and economical utilization of labor and material and for the detection of opportunities for economies through the improvement of methods and the elimination of wasteful practices.

3. Maintains a continuous check to assure the highest standards in quality of work produced, reporting to Manufacturing Engineering or his superior any necessary changes in tooling or processing procedures. Recommends to his superior the procurement of new equipment and tool accessories and requisitions perishable tools and materials.

4. Instructs, assists, and gives technical advice to employees under his supervision when difficulties arise.

5. Collaborates with Project and Product Engineers in the development and design of a new product, giving technical assistance on manufacturing problems and processes.

6. Cooperates with the Time Study Department in the setting of standard times for operations performed under his supervision. Is responsible for performance of work in accordance with assigned schedules; maintains a regular check on progress of work to insure that schedules will be met.

7. Maintains harmonious employee relations within his area of responsibility and takes proper and judicious disciplinary measures when required. Handles first-step grievances, consulting with his immediate superior when necessary.

8. Is responsible for the observance of shop rules and safety regulations and the elimination of unnecessary work hazards.

9. Is responsible for compliance with provisions of Federal and state labor laws and the terms of union contracts insofar as they apply to the operations for which he is responsible.

FINISHING FOREMAN

A Paper Manufacturer

FUNCTION: Is responsible to the Finishing Superintendent for the efficient performance of equipment and manpower in the Finishing Section during his shift. Carries out the orders of the Superintendent within the policies and procedures established; maintains schedules and quality, production, and other standards. Supervises all personnel involved in carrying out this function.

DETAILED DUTIES

1. Is responsible to the Superintendent for the efficient operation of the equipment during his shift and for the maintenance of quality and production standards.

2. Supervises approximately 50 male and 4 female employees during the eight-hour shift.

3. Is responsible for the efficient operation of the following machines in the Finishing Section: ten waxers (three paraffiners, one saturator, four dippers, and two velvet waxers), one Glamakoter, six Staudes, four straight-line gluers, one hot-spot dewaxer, one international gluer, two cellophane machines, the case sealing and conveyor system, the wax receiving, handling, and distribution system, and auxiliary equipment within the Section.

4. Is responsible for initiating maintenance activities to assure continuous operation of machines under his jurisdiction during his shift. Advises the Superintendent of maintenance projects to be undertaken on weekend maintenance or during the day shift. Calls in Maintenance personnel during the night shift; notifies the Superintendent or Production Superintendent in the event of major breakdowns during the last two shifts if considered worthy of their attention.

5. In accordance with seniority contract clauses and the schedule prepared by the Superintendent, places employees as necessary during his shift to maintain continuous operation and to fulfill order schedules. Is responsible for deciding on utilization or dismissal of employees when shutdowns occur or other emergency circumstances upset the original schedule.

6. Makes decisions on all quality problems arising during his shift, utilizing past experience and any information available. Acquaints himself with customer likes and dislikes; confers with Quality Inspectors on his shift regarding details of problems at hand; receives and studies complaints that are received at the _____ Plant to familiarize himself with any other information available. Studies reports issued by Quality Control, attends staff meetings, and so forth. Determines when questionable products must be set aside for sorting or packed for shipment and acts accordingly.

7. Exercises all elements of supervision over the hourly employees under his jurisdiction. (This includes training and counseling individuals in their respective duties, the operations of the Department, safety rules and regulations, and the like.) At the end of a new employee's probationary period, recommends permanent hire, extended probationary time, or termination. Evaluates work performance and progress of respective employees and makes recommendations accordingly. Handles first-stage grievances occurring within his shift.

8. Handles any unusual situations that arise within the Section during the course of his shift whether relative to operations, equipment, personnel, raw materials, or other. Checks with the Foreman on the previous shift concerning unusual orders or problems present; checks with the Production Scheduler to see what is needed for service during his shift; gives specific instructions to the Gluer Operators and Wax Line Operators on machines to run, make-ready to be performed, and so on; checks as necessary to assure that instructions are being followed and gives instructions and special attention to individual employees on those orders when required. Makes routine checks every hour on the quality of cartons run on all machines and makes routine checks on loads going to the warehouse to assure that labels, fibers, load tickets, and the like are in order.

9. Assures that waste is kept at a minimum in the Finishing Section at all times during his shift and explains any excessive waste to the Superintendent.

10. Instructs and trains all new help on his shift; offers authoritative information and counsel to individual employees as necessary at all times.

11. Maintains a daily time report of all personnel on the shift.

12. Insures that all employees under his supervision follow established safety regulations and practices and that they use safety devices available. Takes corrective action if any safety regulations are broken and reports serious infractions to the Superintendent.

13. Assumes full responsibility for buildings and equipment under his jurisdiction during his shift. Keeps the Department clean and orderly. Makes out the daily performance report on waxers and gluers and maintains a log of the machines under his jurisdiction.

14. Is responsible for an assigned portion of the operating materials uitilized by the Section as to operating inventory, cost control, usage figures, maintaining of life figures, ordering and replenishment, recommending of suppliers, and so forth.

15. Is responsible for calling to the attention of the Superintendent commercial orders which are outside of specification. He must obtain approval from the Superintendent prior to running them on a commercial basis.

16. Advises the Superintendent of over-all conditions of operation during his shift, pointing out particular situations, conditions, and problems or difficulties worthy of his attention.

KNOWLEDGE

1. *Knowledge Requirements.* Must have a thorough knowledge of the finishing operations performed in the Section, including knowledge of products, equipment and operations, raw materials, costs, and personnel engaged in the operations. Must possess a working knowledge of other operations preceding those processes directly supervised. A working knowledge of production scheduling procedures and practices and familiarity with budgets, costs, and production records are required, along with a thorough knowledge of union contracts and interpretations of clauses affecting the personnel under his jurisdiction. A knowledge of customer requirements reflected in the quality of finished products and a good knowledge of operating supplies and materials utilized by the Section are essential.

2. *Sources of Knowledge.* A high-school education or its equivalent, with additional training in mechanical fields and administration, is desirable. Previous experience of approximately four years, progressing through various occupations within the Finishing Section such as Gluer or Wax Line Operator, or other pertinent previous experience also is desired. Assuming the above education and experience, an additional one-and-one-half to two years' time on the position of Finishing Foreman will generally be required to achieve normal working proficiency.

APPLICATION OF KNOWLEDGE: Judgment and analysis are required in making operating decisions on his shift in regard to allocating workloads, shifting personnel, and generally assuring continuous and economical operations at all times. Applies knowledge in making decisions on questionable products as to quality in view of customer requirements, cost factors, machine limitations, and so forth. Applies analysis and judgment in maintaining production at its most efficient point while still maintaining quality and economical operations. Analyzes situations and takes immediate action if necessary. Calls to the attention of the Superintendent those situations which he deems worthy of the latter's attention and decision. Makes decisions relative to materials assigned to him for cost control, including the recommending of suppliers, maintenance of life-usage figures, and suggestions as to normal inventory to accommodate machine requirements and minimize the costs involved.

CONTACTS

1. *Internal Contacts*: Has daily contact with all levels of personnel in all Departments of the plant. As the occasion demands, contacts are made with representatives of Central Staff Departments, usually for exchange of information. If problems arise, they are normally referred to the Superintendent for his action.

2. *External Contacts*: Has occasional contact with vendors and with representatives of other companies at technical meetings; has contacts with customers at their plants to determine quality requirements, understand their packaging problems, and discuss similar matters.

SUPERVISION: Supervises approximately 40 to 65 hourly employees engaged in waxing, gluing, Glamakoting, and other finishing operations in the plant. Exercises all elements of supervision, including the approval of employees for permanent hire; training and counseling; evaluation of work progress and work performance; and recommendations for the promotion, demotion, disciplining, and termination of such employees.

FOREMAN, ASSEMBLY

A Large Electronics Company

GENERAL DESCRIPTION OF WORK PERFORMED: Reports to General Foreman or Superintendent. Supervises senior and special apparatus technicians, production repairmen, lead operators, and assemblers in the assembly of military equipment, spare parts assemblies, and coils.

PRINCIPAL DUTIES AND RESPONSIBILITIES

1. Is responsible for training of subordinate personnel by explanation of policies and procedures; demonstration of new equipment and processes; and interpretation of drawings, prints, and instructions.

2. Controls costs through application of labor, proper maintenance of equipment, enforcement of safety rules, and good housekeeping.

3. Is responsible for the execution of work assignments as scheduled in accordance with acceptable standards of quality as required by Company and customer specifications.

4. Is responsible for dealing with grievances by oral discussion with employee or shop steward.

5. Initiates, subject to higher approval, all types of personnel actions.

FACTORS

1. *Job Knowledge*: Requires a sound knowledge of leadership principles, military specifications, assembly breakdown, standards application, organization and layout of production lines, assembly techniques, material control procedures, and training methods for unskilled operators. Must continually stay abreast of new assembly techniques, tools, and production material. Requires a high-school diploma with a minimum of three years' experience in supervision of small mechanical or electrical assembly.

2. *Mental Application*: Under general guidance from the General Foreman or the Superintendent, makes daily decisions pertaining to labor utilization and good assembly practices. As first-line management representative, projects and exemplifies corporate and Division philosophy to the working level.

3. *Responsibility for Costs*: Responsible for building scheduled quantities of quality equipment at or below standard costs.

4. *Responsibility for Contacts*: Contacts extend to representatives of all departments in the Division in order to obtain fixtures, parts, specification interpretations, and emergency rework.

5. *Responsibility for Directing Others*: Exercises direct first-line supervision. Interprets and enforces Company policy and shop rules. Is held accountable for planning, organizing, directing, and appraising the performance of assigned personnel.

FOREMAN, ASSEMBLY—SECOND SHIFT

A Machinery Company

PRIMARY FUNCTION: Directs and coordinates all activities of the Assembly Departments' second-shift operations and reports to the Superintendent of the Assembly Departments on all phases of his work.

DUTIES

1. Directs, with the assistance of a Full Supervisor and two Setup Supervisors, all work activities performed in the Assembly Departments on the second shift.

2. Checks, approves, and applies promptly all time standards issued by Industrial Engineering. Sees that these standards are applied properly. Also reports methods changes promptly.

3. Coordinates the movement of parts and material so as to maintain a smooth flow of work within his Departments and into the departments to which he supplies parts.

4. Follows closely the production schedule as set forth by the Production Control Department. This may involve advertising through the Employment Department for personnel needed for schedule increases; it may also involve reducing personnel when schedules are decreased, following the rules set forth in the "transfer, layoff, and rehiring plan" of the union contract.

5. Maintains parts produced at an acceptable quality level.

6. Approves employees' time cards, verifying such information on the cards as number of pieces produced, time spent on each operation, wage rates, and standard hours.

7. Trains and instructs personnel, with the assistance of a Full Supervisor and two Setup Supervisors, on the various operations and machines in the Departments.

8. Enlists the services of the various staff functions, such as Industrial Engineering, Plant Engineering, Tool Engineering, Inspection, Electrical Engineering, and Quality Control, to resolve mechanical and technical problems which affect the production of parts and assemblies.

9. Assists the various staff groups in special projects pertaining to the Assembly Departments by completing and following up on assignments initiated by the first shift.

10. Makes every effort to keep costs under control, using the various reports that are available (variance report from the Cost Department, scrap report from Inspection, etc.). Also improves methods wherever possible.

11. Maintains good housekeeping and safety in work habits throughout the Departments.

12. Handles first-step grievances. Answers employees' challenges on incentive rates.

13. Enforces Company rules and regulations at all times.

14. After consulting his Superintendent, initiates necessary disciplinary action for subordinates.

15. Reviews new and revised layouts, making suggestions to obtain optimum quality in layouts.

16. Maintains all records necessary to a smooth-running, well-organized, efficient department.

GENERAL: The incumbent directs the second-shift work activities of the following Assembly Departments: Armature, Motor, Upright Cleaner, Canister Cleaner, Cleaning Tool, and Polisher Motor. The major portion of his time is devoted to the two Cleaner Assembly Departments. The number of employees in each of these Departments varies from 2 to 25. The total number of employees supervised is approximately 60, the majority of whom are women.

FOREMAN, PROCESSING

A Proprietary Products Manufacturer

Is responsible to the Department Head–Processing for the production operations within the Department.

1. Assists in setting up daily departmental production schedules and in the designation of job assignments to personnel.

2. Checks operations regularly to insure that processes, schedules, and quality are maintained.

3. Supervises personnel, including process helpers, operators, and lower-grade supervision.

4. May carry on Department routine in the absence of the Department Head.

5. Makes recommendations to the Department Head concerning employee performance and review.

6. Is responsible for the cleanliness and orderliness of the Department, as well as for maintaining safe working conditions and for instilling safe working habits in employees.

FOREMAN, MACHINE DEPARTMENT

A Machinery Company

DIRECTS: All activities of the Machine Department.

REPORTS TO: Superintendent of Fabricating Section on all phases of his work.

SUPERVISES: Approximately 24 male and 6 female employees.

DUTIES

1. Directs all work in the Machine Department in accordance with specifications established by the Engineering Division. This work includes:

   a. Machining and polishing a large variety of metal and plastic parts for cleaners, irons, and dusting tools.

   b. Miscellaneous spot-welding operations.

   c. Washing parts.

   d. Balancing fans.

   e. Salvaging plastic parts.

2. Utilizes the machines, materials, services, reports, and recommendations provided by the various staff functions to control both detailed operations and over-all performance in his Department. Examples:

   a. Using the production schedules and daily status report furnished by the Production Control function to control his production and prevent delinquencies.

   b. Approving and applying promptly all time standards provided by the Industrial Engineering function and seeing to it that they are properly administered and used. Keeping abreast of all method changes in his Department, regardless of where initiated, and being fully responsible for reporting all such changes promptly to the Industrial Engineering function.

c. Utilizing Inspection reports and recommendations as a guide to improve quality and reduce scrap.

d. Using the variance reports and recommendations from the Cost Control function as a guide to corrective action necessary to keep costs in line with his budget.

e. Applying the proper occupation rates, as established by the Industrial Engineering function, to all work being performed in his Department.

f. Using process analyses provided by Inspection to determine whether the machines and processes in his Department are capable of producing parts consistent with blueprint specifications.

3. Makes every effort to overcome obstacles, such as material shortages or machine and tooling breakdowns, which may interfere with meeting schedules or maintaining quality; uses his own best judgment in these cases, going to his Superintendent only when he cannot get help, action, or results unaided. Can enlist the aid of Tool Design and Engineering, Production Control, Plant Engineering, and other Departments.

4. Trains and assists his workmen to:

a. Maintain product quality in accordance with specifications.

b. Keep scrap at the lowest practicable level.

c. Maintain high productivity, without lowering quality standards.

d. Maintain a smooth flow of work within his Department and into the Departments to which he supplies parts.

e. Control costs to meet his budget.

f. Work safely.

g. Maintain good housekeeping throughout the Department.

5. Carries out special projects in his Department. Such projects may result from employee suggestions; better method proposals by Foremen and Superintendents; suggestions from the Manufacturing Manager, Operations Control Manager, and others.

6. Cooperates with the Quality Engineer on the installation of statistical quality control techniques.

7. Answers grievances of his employees at the first step of the challenge or grievance procedure. Consults his Superintendent before replying when he judges that other Departments may be affected.

8. Assumes full responsibility for the quality of all parts leaving his Department and for the accuracy of all production counts for which the workers are paid. May delegate, but is still fully responsible.

9. Maintains such records as may be prescribed by his Superintendent, Operations Control, and others. Simple records of daily production and indirect hours are typical.

10. Keeps his Superintendent informed verbally and makes reports only upon special request by authorized individuals.

CHEMICAL PRODUCTION FOREMAN

A Proprietary Drug Company

ESSENTIAL JOB ELEMENTS: Directs and supervises the efficient, safe, and profitable operation of his shift. Advises and recommends programs and procedures to the Chemical Production Manager.

WORKING RELATIONSHIPS

1. Reports to: Chemical Production Manager.

2. Supervises: Chemical Operators, Dryer Operators.

3. Works with other Chemical Production Foremen and Chemical Engineers, and the Process Development, Quality Control, Materials Handling, Maintenance, and Industrial Engineering Departments.

AUTHORITIES AND RESPONSIBILITIES

To be responsible for the following functions and any additional responsibilities which the Chemical Production Manager may assign.

1. *Production Scheduling*: Is responsible for scheduling the starting and completion of operations and batches in such a manner so that production is not delayed and the manpower of his and the following shifts will be most efficiently utilized.

2. *Production Control*: Insures adherence to standard compound operating procedures and accepted techniques in all operations and activities. Performs simple laboratory tests on samples of in-process and waste materials to insure proper operation and equipment func-

tion. Cooperates with the Chemical Engineers in making approved changes in the standard procedures or techniques. Deviates from the standard compound operating procedures in the event of an emergency, a batch abnormality, or equipment failure which makes adherence to standards inadvisable.

3. *Personnel*: Is responsible for making all job assignments for the members of his shift. Is responsible for training and evaluating the performance of his subordinates. Reports to his Supervisor any excess or shortage of personnel and suggests changes in procedures or methods to make the most economical and safe use of personnel. Collaborates with other Chemical Production Foremen in training, performance evaluation, corrective action, and other personnel matters to insure coordination. Is responsible for communication and for interpreting and upholding Company policies.

4. *Facilities*: Exercises proper care and utilization of buildings, equipment, and services. Cooperates with the Maintenance Department in the accomplishment of maintenance activities. Reports and makes requests for routine or emergency maintenance. Makes suggestions concerning changes in facilities to his Supervisor to insure accomplishment of all elements in his job.

5. *Materials Handling*: Cooperates with the Materials Handling Department in positioning materials in the chemical plant. Requests the handling of raw materials, finished goods, and waste materials during the normal working hours of the Materials Handling Department.

6. *Processes*: Makes recommendations to his Superintendent to improve yields and reduce waste, labor, material, maintenance, handling, and other costs. Cooperates with Chemical Engineering and other Departments in the investigation of present processes, in making approved trial runs, and in experimental work.

7. *Records*: Provides required records concerning the activity of his shift, including personnel, raw-material usage, process information, finished goods produced, maintenance, and the like.

8. *Standards*: Cooperates with the Industrial Engineering Department in establishing and maintaining standards.

9. *Material Identification and Sampling*: Insures the proper identification of all raw materials, in-process materials, batches, and finished goods in the Chemical Production Department. Cooperates with the Quality Control Department in providing samples of any materials requested.

FACTORY NIGHT FOREMAN

Hersey–Sparling Meter Company

PRIMARY FUNCTION: To supervise all production and maintenance work done on the second shift.

ELEMENTS OF SUPERVISION

1. *Develop skills of employees*: Train new employees and retrain older employees to develop highest skills of each. Develop versatility in the men so that schedules can be followed within machine limitations.

2. *Maintain quality of workmanship*: Manufacture to standards established by the Engineering Department. Interpretations and exceptions are to be secured from the Inspection Department. Arrange night work for inspection of day shift. Inspect work periodically.

3. *Assign work* based on schedules established by Day-Shift Foreman.

4. *Control costs*:

   a. Direct labor to meet production standards after training period.

   b. Eliminate unnecessary indirect labor costs.

   c. See that tools and supplies are used properly and effectively.

   d. Keep scrap to a minimum.

5. *Keep necessary records*: Keep Day-Shift Foreman informed through reports.

6. *Maintain good working conditions* as far as practicable considering work to be done; have clean, orderly Department.

7. *Develop morale*: Assert leadership instead of relying on Foreman's authority, build up confidence of employees in himself and the Company. Interpret Company policy to employees. Instill interest in their jobs and pride in their work; welcome suggestions.

8. *Straighten out grievances* that occur during the second shift. Confine decisions to the scope of the Foreman's authority, reserving a decision until the next day if any question exists concerning authority or the proper decision. Consult with Departmental Day-Shift Foreman in all cases where possible before giving a decision so that the Company policy on the day shift will be the same as on the night shift. When in doubt, consult the Superintendent or the Personnel Director.

9. *Wage reclassification*: Action is to be initiated by the Day-Shift Foreman but must be approved both by the Day and by the Night

Foreman. The Night Foreman is to be responsible for establishing the degree to which the worker meets the requirements for a change in classification in such areas as supervision needed and ability to meet production rates.

10. *Supplies and equipment*: Refer to Day-Shift Foreman when supplies may be needed or machines or equipment is to be repaired.

11. *Maintenance work*: The Foreman of Building Services is to give a copy of his work schedule for the second-shift workers to both the Factory Night-Shift Foreman and the Foundry-Shift Foreman outlining the jobs he has scheduled. Workers will be responsible to the Factory Night Foreman, but when working in the Foundry they will be under the direction of the Foundry-Shift Foreman, who can reassign them to do necessary work should this develop. If a mechanical impasse is reached and technical assistance is required to decide the best way to do a job, the Foundry-Shift Foreman can ask the assistance of the Factory Night Foreman. Upon completion of the Foundry assignment, the Foundry-Shift Foreman will notify the Factory Night Foreman.

ASSISTANT FOREMAN

An Instrument Maker

Reports to: Superior Foreman or Supervisor.

Reporting to Him: Group of assigned employees.

Duties

1. Assists a Superior Foreman or Supervisor in the direction and supervision of the activities of a group of employees. Acts in accordance with general instructions of his superior, performing such supervisory functions, exercising such supervisory authority, and fulfilling such responsibilities as are delegated to him by his superior.

2. Is generally required to:

   a. Insure employees' compliance with Company policies and procedures.

b. Check the utilization of labor and materials to eliminate wasteful practices and to insure maximum efficiency and economy of operation.

c. Maintain a continuous check to assure the highest standards in quality of work produced, reporting any necessary changes in tooling and procedures to his superior.

d. Cooperate with the Time Study Department in setting time standards.

e. Maintain a regular check of performance to insure compliance with schedules.

f. Instruct and assist employees when processing difficulties arise.

3. Takes disciplinary action, consulting with superior when necessary.

3. Manufacturing Staff Services

Sᴛᴀғғ ᴘᴏsɪᴛɪᴏɴs in manufacturing—that is, those which provide special services to line management—are presented in seven categories: heads of manufacturing (or production) services; materials handling and related functions; plant engineering and maintenance; industrial engineering; quality control and reliability engineering; manufacturing engineering and research; and production planning and control.

Heads of Manufacturing Services

In certain companies, manufacturing services report to a single individual, in some cases at the vice-presidential level.

VICE PRESIDENT IN CHARGE OF PRODUCTION

CORPORATE STAFF

John Labatt Limited

Fᴜɴᴄᴛɪᴏɴ: As a staff member of management, the Vice President in Charge of Production is charged with advising the President and furnishing functional advice to the General Managers of the Operating Divisions on production, transportation, and traffic; with conducting all construction activities of the Company, including the installation of new production and research equipment; with conducting the quality control, product research, and new product research activities of the Company; and with the establishment and maintenance of technical production procedures, in which latter capacities he will act as a line member of management.

RESPONSIBILITIES AND AUTHORITY: Within the limits of his approved program and Company policies and control procedures, the Vice President in Charge of Production is responsible for and has commensurate authority to accomplish the fulfillment of the duties set forth below. He may delegate to members of his Department appropriate portions of his responsibilities, together with proportionate authority for their fulfillment, but he may not delegate or relinquish his over-all responsibility for results or any portion of his accountability.

1. *Activities*

   a. He will formulate or receive and recommend for approval policies on production research, product development, construction, and quality control of products; will administer such policies when approved; and will communicate them to the Operating Divisions.

   b. He will establish and administer quality control and technical production procedures, procedures leading to the discovery of new products which may or may not be allied with the brewing industry, and procedures leading to the improvement of existing products.

   c. He will recommend new products to be manufactured and the methods to be used to produce such new products.

   d. He will assess methods and means of transporting Company products and recommend changes in these methods and means.

   e. He will conduct all plant construction and remodeling and the installation of research and plant production equipment and machinery.

   f. He will conduct control tests to insure that products are of specified quality.

   g. He will advise and assist the Secretary in all matters pertaining to patents and copyrights of labels, packages, and new products.

   h. He will develop and recommend new production and plant operating techniques.

   i. He will recommend changes in plant design.

   j. He will review and approve or otherwise deal with the capital expenditure budgets of all Operating Divisions.

2. *Organization of His Department*: He will recommend changes in the basic structure and complement of his Department.

3. *Personnel of His Department*:

   a. Having ascertained the availability of qualified talent within the Company, he will hire personnel for or make appointments to positions other than management within the limits of his approved basic organization.

   b. He will approve all salary and wage changes for non-union personnel in Salary Class 12 or under and will recommend salary changes for personnel in Class 13 and up.

   c. He will recommend promotion, demotion, release, and retirement for personnel of his Department.

   d. He will approve vacations and personal leaves and recommend salary payments in excess of those provided by Company policy to sick employees.

   e. He will prepare necessary job and position descriptions.

   f. He will do whatever is necessary to maintain the morale of the employees of his Department at a high level.

4. *Finances of His Department*

   a. He will prepare the annual budget.

   b. He will administer funds allotted under the approved annual budget, approved extraordinary or capital expenditure programs, or any appropriations.

   c. He will approve payment of operating expenses and capital expenditures not in excess of $1,500 for any single expenditure which may not be covered by the approved budget, any approved expenditure programs, or any appropriations. Such additional expenditures are to be limited to $5,000 in any fiscal year.

   d. He will recommend extraordinary or capital expenditure programs and appropriation.

   e. He will administer fiscal procedures.

   f. He will receive for review and recommendation the items of the annual operating budgets of other Head Office Departments and Operating Divisions within his province.

RELATIONSHIPS: The Vice President in Charge of Production will observe and conduct the following relationships. He may delegate portions of the conduct of such relationships to members of his Department, but may not delegate his over-all responsibility or accountability for their proper conduct.

1. *The President*

   a. He is accountable to the President for the fulfillment of his function, responsibilities, authority, and relationships and for their proper interpretation.

    b. He will relieve the President of administrative detail as outlined in this guide or as otherwise specified by the President.

2. *Other Head Office Department Heads:* He will advise and assist other Head Office Department Heads in the fulfillment of their respective functions in matters within his province and will coordinate his activities and cooperate with them in matters of mutual concern. But, in so doing, he will not assume, nor will he be delegated, any function, responsibility, authority, or relationship belonging to any other member of management.

3. *General Managers of Operating Divisions:* He will review and assess the effectiveness of the methods and procedures of the General Managers of the Operating Divisions in the fulfillment of their functions in matters within his province, will advise and assist them therewith, and will coordinate his activities and cooperate with them in matters of mutual concern. But, in so doing, he will not assume, nor will he be delegated, any function, responsibility, authority, or relationship belonging to any other member of management.

4. *Others*

    a. In these relationships, he will establish and maintain those contacts necessary to the fulfillment of his function.

    b. The President may specify from time to time other relationships to be conducted by him.

5. *The Public:* He will maintain such relationships outside the Company as are necessary to accomplish his function, acting in such instances only as the representative of the President.

DIRECTOR OF MANUFACTURING SERVICES

CORPORATE STAFF

International Business Machines Corporation

BASIC FUNCTIONS: The Director of Manufacturing Services is responsible for providing staff guidance in matters relating to manufacturing, purchasing, and traffic; for giving advice and counsel to Corporate and

Division executives in these fields; and for providing specialized services to the Divisions in the areas of building construction and selected purchasing activities.

The Director of Manufacturing Services will:

1. Develop Corporate policies and programs in the areas of manufacturing, purchasing, traffic, and facility location and construction.

2. Review and recommend approval of the manufacturing, purchasing, and traffic aspects of Division and Subsidiary annual and long-range plans and revisions thereto.

3. Conduct staff studies both inside and outside the Corporation in manufacturing research and on the best methods of industrial engineering; manufacturing engineering; manufacturing controls; purchasing and traffic administration; and facilities planning, construction, and maintenance. Disseminate pertinent information to Division managements.

4. Assist Divisions in establishing standards of performance and systems for reporting and measuring accomplishments with regard to basic significant factors in the areas of manufacturing, purchasing, traffic, and facility construction.

5. Keep appropriate executives informed regarding long-range trends, outside developments, special study projects, and effectiveness of policies.

6. Advise Division General Managers on the professional excellence of their purchasing, traffic, and manufacturing functions.

7. Provide the following specialized services:

   a. Building and construction service which will furnish specialized knowledge about site selection, architect and contractor negotiations, and construction supervision necessary to meet Divisional facilities requirements.

   b. Negotiation of Corporate supply contracts against which the Operating Divisions may issue purchase orders when desired.

   c. Standard Company data for establishing direct and indirect labor time standards at manufacturing locations; alternative method charts for selecting "best method"; and annual audit of direct and indirect labor standards, insuring accuracy and consistency.

8. Give advice and counsel in assigned functional areas. For example:

   a. Advise Divisions of factors to be considered in preparation of their annual plans and, when requested, give advice in the preparation of these plans.

 b. Assist Divisions in the determination of new facility requirements.

 c. Provide guidance on operating and policy problems when requested by Division executives.

 d. Advise Divisions in techniques for conducting studies or projects.

MANAGER, MANUFACTURING SERVICES

A Business Forms Manufacturer

REPORTS TO: General Manufacturing Manager.

PRIMARY FUNCTION: To direct and supervise the Departments listed below or later assigned; to effectively integrate these Departments with other activities of the Company:
 Pre-Press.
 Receiving, Warehousing, and Shipping.
 Maintenance.
 Design/Mechanical Art.

SPECIAL DUTIES AND RESPONSIBILITIES

1. To know, to fully understand, and to comply with the several duties and responsibilities separately stated in "General Responsibilities of Management Positions."

2. In cooperation with the General Manufacturing Manager, to prepare labor and overhead budgets for the areas assigned.

3. To insure that Departments assigned operate within the budgets so determined.

4. To cooperate fully with the Controller in respect to Items 2 and 3 above.

5. To insure that the Service Departments assigned give prompt and efficient support to other Departments of the Company as required; to keep continuously informed of the changing nature of such requirements.

6. Constantly to study ways and means of improving services rendered,

initiating or recommending improvements according to the organizational responsibilities involved.

7. To assist the General Manufacturing Manager as a supporting line executive when such help may be requested or required.

8. To correctly administer established personnel policies; to efficiently and adequately staff all activities required to accomplish his duties; and to supervise, direct, and control the hiring, training, promotion, or separation of all personnel acquired or assigned.

9. To supervise and maintain close liaison with the Managers of the Service Departments assigned; to aid and direct them daily as may be required to accomplish effective administration by such Department Managers.

10. To carry out such special projects as may be assigned.

PRODUCTION SERVICES MANAGER

A Proprietary Drug Company

ESSENTIAL JOB ELEMENTS: Directs the activities of the various control functions of the Production Division. Insures the development and implementation of plans and programs to meet the Company's objectives in regard to inventories, product quality, warehousing, production control, quality control, inspection, and industrial engineering.

WORKING RELATIONSHIPS

1. Reports to: Vice President–Production.
2. Supervises: Production Control Manager.
   Quality Control Manager.
   Material Handling Manager.
   Industrial Engineering Manager.
3. Serves on: Product Committee.
   Safety Committee.
4. Maintains contact with all Departments and Divisions to insure coordination of objectives, plans, and programs.

AUTHORITIES AND RESPONSIBILITIES: Is responsible for the following functions and any additional responsibilities which the Vice President–Production may assign.

1. *Policies and Objectives*: Develops and recommends production policies and objectives to the Vice President–Production. Insures that his subordinates understand and adhere to approved policies.

2. *Plans and Programs*: Develops and recommends plans and programs to reduce production costs; increase capacities; improve product quality, uniformity, and marketability; and improve safety conditions.

3. *Costs*: Is responsible for the development and maintenance of the Company's standard cost program. Reviews variations with Department Managers concerned and pinpoints areas for improvement. Prepares cost estimates for proposed products. Assists the Industrial Engineering Manager and the Data Processing Manager in establishing production overhead rates and working on cost control.

4. *Methods and Work Standards*: Assists Department Managers in improving and standardizing methods, equipment, and working conditions. Suggests revisions in plant layout to improve methods and efficiency.

5. *Quality Control*: Is responsible for sampling, inspection, and analysis of all raw materials, packing materials, and finished goods, according to specifications and standard procedures. Assists in establishing quality specifications for raw materials and finished goods. Assists in the establishment of general inspection practices and procedures. Recommends, to Vice President–Production, rejection or price adjustment of materials that do not meet specifications.

6. *Specifications*: Is responsible for development of specifications for all packaging materials and supplies to insure adequate product protection and proper handling by production machinery. Assists in establishing specifications for all raw materials to insure product quality at minimum cost.

7. *Production Control*: Is responsible for establishing schedules for the purchase of raw materials and the monthly scheduling of Pharmaceutical, Chemical, and Biological Production to maintain inventories at the most economical level. Assists in scheduling finished goods in quantities to meet sales forecasts.

8. *Material Handling*: Provides for the receipt, warehousing, protection, and dispersion of all raw material and finished product inventories at _____, except bulk storage of liquid chemical raw materials. Maintains for all Departments services such as waste disposal, mail delivery, and deliveries of equipment and supplies as

required. Is responsible for packing and shipping merchandise to customers. Is responsible for inventory control of all material.

9. *Industrial Engineering*: Provides Industrial Engineering services to all areas of the Company as directed by the Vice President–Production. Assists in planning plant layout and estimating equipment, labor, and material costs for proposed or revised products. Assists in the development of account hour budgets for Departments using standard hour or standard cost systems.

10. *Budgets*: Develops budget for Production Services function. Directs preparation of and reviews budgets of Production Control, Material Handling, Quality Control, and Industrial Engineering Departments. Submits all operating budgets to the Vice President–Production for approval.

11. *Returned Merchandise*: Is responsible for the inspection, recording, sorting, and disposal of all returned merchandise.

12. *Records and Reports*: Is responsible for maintaining and protecting adequate department records. Furnishes periodic reports to the Vice President–Production concerning all phases of his work.

Materials Handling and Related Functions

The materials handling function includes shipping, receiving, warehousing, loading, unloading, stores, and traffic.

MATERIAL HANDLING MANAGER

A Proprietary Drug Company

ESSENTIAL JOB ELEMENTS: Administers the material handling activities of the Company. Warehouses all finished products and raw materials except bulk chemical liquids. Transports materials to and from various Departments and directs packing and shipping of orders. Is responsible for receiving all materials, supplies, and equipment.

WORKING RELATIONSHIPS

Reports to: Production Services Manager.

Supervises: Warehousing Group Leader.
Shipping Group Leader.
Truckdrivers.

Contacts all Divisions and Departments to provide receiving and shipping services.

AUTHORITIES AND RESPONSIBILITIES: Is responsible for the following functions as well as those outlined in standard practice job description and any additional responsibilities which the Production Services Manager may assign.

1. *Warehousing*: Is responsible for the warehousing of raw materials except bulk chemical liquids and finished products; designates their storage areas.

2. *Material Handling*: Is responsible for the loading and unloading of trucks and freight cars, supplying production units with raw materials and supplies, and the handling of finished products from production areas to storage; for loading of trucks for branch orders as requested; for performing for all Departments such services as waste disposal, mail delivery, deliveries of equipment and supplies, and out-of-town trips as required to pick up or deliver materials or personnel.

3. *Receiving*: Is responsible for receiving, inspecting for damage in shipment, and counting all materials, supplies, and equipment received by the Company. Prepares receiving reports and notifies the Department concerned.

4. *Shipping*: Directs the packing and shipping of merchandise to all customers served from the _____ office. Insures proper identification and marking of products and packages to meet various state and foreign requirements. Is responsible for packing techniques and procedures and a knowledge of shipping schedules, rates, and requirements. Cooperates with Traffic Manager in the scheduling of branch trucks and the economical delivery of merchandise.

5. *Inventories*: Is responsible for all inventories under his control. Periodically takes physical inventories to verify perpetual records. Notes irregularities and takes necessary corrective action.

6. *Budgets*: Develops budget for Material Handling function. Submits operating budget to the Production Services Manager for his approval. Adheres to budget and analyzes expenditures against budget.

7. *Facilities*: Insures that his facilities are properly protected, maintained, and utilized. Cooperates with Maintenance to see that facili-

ties are maintained at peak operating efficiency. Insures that all vehicles assigned to his Department are properly maintained.

8. *Safety*: Insures safety and health of employees by proper training, maintenance of equipment, and provision of necessary safety equipment and clothing. Knows properties of various chemicals to insure their safe storage and the safety of his employees when handling them.

9. *Quality Control*: Cooperates with the Quality Control Departments to insure proper sampling of raw materials or finished products. Obtains release before moving material to storage or to shipping.

10. *Inter-Building Messenger Service*: Is responsible for inter-building messenger service, including pick-up and delivery at post office and local suppliers.

11. *Records*: Maintains records of all transactions; assigns RM numbers, makes out receiving reports, fills out IBM cards, and keeps records of all inventoried material.

TRAFFIC SUPERVISOR

A Machinery Maker

FUNCTION: To supervise, directly and through subordinate supervisors, the activities of the Department engaged in the receiving and shipment of all materials, parts, and products in accordance with established procedures; to be responsible for obtaining the most economical transportation consistent with delivery dates and essential dependability. To arrange transportation and hotel reservations for employees.

ORGANIZATIONAL RELATIONSHIPS

1. *Reports to*: Manager of Manufacturing. *Supervises*: Shipping and receiving activities.

2. The Traffic Supervisor reports directly to the Manager of Manufacturing. His duties require close working relations with Purchasing, Inventory Control, and Production Control, cooperating on mutual problems to provide efficient and timely customer service.

SPECIFIC RESPONSIBILITIES: The Traffic Supervisor shall be accountable for the following broad responsibilities that he shall fulfill through delegation of responsibility and authority and by initiation and execution of action in keeping with the authority vested in his office and the applicable Company policies and procedures.

1. To keep fully informed with respect to developments in the transportation industry by attending meetings and conferences of transportation service organiations, reading trade bulletins, and interviewing representatives of carriers and government agencies so as to select most economical transportation.

2. To select appropriate carriers and routings on the basis of the economics and delivery schedules involved; requisition freight cars or schedule pick-ups; prepare shipments by package, crate, box skid, and/or load and brace in freight car; mark, label, and prepare bills of lading and other shipping papers; expedite in-plant delivery to shipping area to meet shipping schedules.

3. To maintain records of all shipments and trace shipments in response to inquiries. To prepare, file, and execute claims against carriers for loss, damage, or delay of shipments en route. To control and record all demurrage charges. To audit carriers' transportation charges and approve for payment or initiate action in case of discrepancies.

4. To check incoming materials, parts, subcontracting, supplies, and the like against purchase orders; record receipt of and store or arrange for delivery of incoming items to appropriate location; prepare and distribute receiving reports. To compute "chargebacks" to vendors when material is incorrectly shipped or proper allowance is not made on material sold "delivered." To investigate all the latest phases of modern materials handling procedures for improving Department facilities in order to expedite loading and unloading and reduce damage to materials.

5. To compile data and prepare reports of shipping activities as directed, including reports to Headquarters Traffic Department. To study prospective classification and rate adjustments and prepare analysis for presentation.

6. To arrange for personnel travel via rail or air and make necessary hotel reservations. To effect the transportation and movement of transferred employees and their household goods.

7. To administer Company personnel policies in the Department supervised, enforce safety and health regulations, and take prompt action on employee complaints to encourage good morale. To represent the Department at all stages of grievance procedure and arbitration. To maintain current status with respect to employee morale. To maintain discipline.

8. To check and review the job performance of subordinates, advise them of their good points and shortcomings, and counsel them about their growth potential. To train and develop men for advancement.

9. To plan and schedule work in order to use employees' time effectively and to keep Department operating expense within the budget.

AUTHORITY: The Traffic Supervisor is vested with the following authority to be exercised in keeping with all established Corporation and Division policies and procedures in carrying out the responsibilities of the office.

1. To initiate purchase requisitions for tools, supplies, and materials essential for efficient operation of the Department.

2. To hire authorized personnel; recommend salary, wage rates, or employee status changes in the Department; and penalize or discharge any employee supervised who is guilty of an infraction of Company rules which calls for such action.

3. To settle complaints or grievances in the Department within the limits of Company personnel policy and labor contract terms.

4. To select appropriate carriers.

5. To reject incoming material, parts, subcontracting, supplies, and the like that fail to meet specifications on purchase orders.

STORES SUPERVISOR

An Electronics Company

GENERAL DESCRIPTION OF WORK PERFORMED: Supervises the activities of all Storekeepers and Material Handlers in the receipt, storage, and issuance of production material within the stockrooms. Works under the general guidance of the Manager of Material Control.

PRINCIPAL DUTIES AND RESPONSIBILITIES

1. The Stores Supervisor shall be responsible for the proper storage and issuance of all material used by Manufacturing in all warehouses and shall see that proper paperwork is authorized and correctly processed.

2. Shall be responsible for maintaining the stockrooms in a neat and orderly manner; storing material to be issued on a first-in, first-out basis; and maintaining the proper staff for the workloads involved.

3. Shall be responsible for seeing that material is handled with care between issue from Stores and delivery to assembly areas, since material is unpacked at the time of issue.

4. Shall be responsible for seeing that all material received is correctly packaged for storage and initiating action with Purchasing or the Shop for correction when indicated.

5. It shall be his further r sponsibility to constantly investigate new techniques in storage and material handling methods for adaptation to our needs.

6. Handles personnel problems and appraises performance of assigned Storekeepers and Material Handlers.

FACTORS

1. *Job Knowledge*: Requires an extensive knowledge of receiving, packaging, storage, and planned use of material for which he is responsible. He must continually investigate, through study of technical journals and other media, material handling and storage methods as they relate to potential use at the _____ Division. Requires a high-school diploma in addition to three to five years' experience in the supervision of material issuance and storage.

2. *Mental Application*: With limited guidance and basing his judgment primarily on past practice, determines most practical location and method of storing material as related to its potential use. Requires continual re-evaluation of storage facilities in order to meet changing stock requirements.

3. *Responsibility for Costs*: Poor decisions pertaining to improper storage and issuance will result in costly stock losses and obsolescence.

4. *Responsibility for Contacts*: Demonstrates above-average tact and diplomacy during frequent contacts with plant management pertaining to condition, location, and quantity of material under his control.

5. *Responsibility for Directing Others*: Supervises from 15 to 25 Storekeepers and Material Handlers in the storage and warehousing facilities. Initiates, subject to higher approval, all types of personnel actions.

GENERAL FOREMAN–RECEIVING, MATERIALS HANDLING, AND WAREHOUSING

A. O. Smith Corporation

REPORTS TO: Manager of Manufacturing and Manufacturing Services.

SUPERVISES: Foreman—Receiving and Raw Materials Storage.
Foreman—Finished Goods and Parts Storage.
Foreman—Materials Handling and Transportation.
Mechanic and Driver.
Operators—Fork-Lift Truck (4).
Fillers—Parts Orders (2).
Clerk—Returned Defective Materials.
Clerks—Receiving (2).
Stock Clerks (22).

PRIMARY FUNCTION: Develops Division receiving, materials handling, storage, and warehousing policies. Exercises general supervision over subordinate Foremen in their supervision over operations required to insure availability of (1) productive materials for Manufacturing Departments; (2) certain non-productive materials and supplies for Manufacturing, Maintenance, and Plant Service Departments; and (3) finished goods inventories (parts and complete product systems) to meet shipping requirements. Operations include: receiving, productive materials storage, raw materials storage, returned materials storage, PSD parts storage, finished goods (in-plant) storage, materials handling and transportation, and finished goods (out-of-plant) warehousing. End objective is to maintain minimum inventories consistent with customer demands and production capabilities.

DUTIES AND RESPONSIBILITIES

1. Defines and develops organizational structure and functional responsibilities of Sections under his supervision. Staffs Sections with qualified personnel. Delegates authority without relinquishing accountability. Holds subordinate Foremen responsible for meeting their functional responsibilities.

2. Develops and recommends to Manager of Manufacturing and Manufacturing Services the establishment of receiving, materials handling, storage, and warehousing policies and procedures.

3. Provides direction to subordinate Foremen in their supervision of respective activities, including:

a. *Receiving and Materials Storage*: Receiving productive and certain non-productive materials (e.g., purchased parts, sheet and plate steel, bar stock and pipe, resins, paints, lubricants, welding supplies, etc.); checking against bills of lading; systematically storing such materials until they are requisitioned by Manufacturing, Shipping, Maintenance, or Plant Service Departments.

b. *Purchase Requisitioning*: Processing requisitions for raw materials and certain non-productive materials, job (production) orders, and requisitions for production processing by vendors outside of plant; handling petty cash and charge purchases for over-the-counter sales in plant.

c. *Returned Materials Processing*: Arranging with Purchasing and Shipping Departments for return to vendors of defective materials rejected by Manufacturing Departments; delivering to Manufacturing Departments materials returned by customers for repair or substitution.

d. *Finished Goods Storage and Warehousing*: Storing PSD parts, other parts, subassemblies, and complete product systems in plant storage (3,000 square feet) and two local leased warehousing facilities (5,000 square feet and 18,000 square feet).

e. *Materials Handling and Local Transportation*

(1) Loading and unloading trucks, freight cars, and conveyors, either manually or by fork-lift trucks; transporting materials to and from Departments and work stations within plant and warehouses, using hand trucks, tote boxes, fork trucks, and so forth.

(2) Operating and performing preventive maintenance on automotive vehicles used to transport materials, equipment, supplies, and men from one location to another, outside plant and within 150-mile radius of plant; coordination, dispatching, and moving of automotive vehicles.

f. *Scrap Segregation*: Segregating metallurgically dissimilar metals which can be separated visually in preparation for scrap sales by Purchasing and Cost Accounting Departments.

g. *Physical Inventory*: Conducting annual physical inventory of "free bin" items.

4. Exercises direct supervision over the General Stores Department (main stockroom), consisting of over 20,000 items of productive materials, purchased parts, and certain non-productive materials.

a. Makes daily work assignments based on Section's operational requirements, which are specified in materials requisitions received by the Section. Periodically follows up to insure that Section's operations are fulfilling the productive materials requirements of the Manufacturing Departments.

5. Controls product quality to the extent of directing subordinate Foremen to insure that received materials comply with material and/or part numbers specified in purchase orders, and that materials, parts, and finished goods are so handled, stored, and transported as to prevent product damage or malfunction.

6. Develops and installs methods improvements pertaining to Departments under his jurisdiction, including:

   a. Standardization of parts numbers for inventory control and co-ordination of Stores function with cycle control system.

   b. Collaboration with Product Engineering and Purchasing Departments on purchased parts standardization (e.g., obsoleting extra sizes and types of fasteners).

   c. Development of special methods for storing heavy rotors (to support weight and stress), blades (vertically, rather than horizontally, to prevent warping), and critical components (inserting bearings in sealed containers or incorporating bearings in sub-assembly housings, to prevent damage from dust).

   d. Development of record-keeping forms for internal Department use.

   e. Rearrangement of storage and warehousing facilities for more efficient use of space.

   f. Revision of routing, scheduling, maintenance, and dispatching of power-lift and automotive trucks to provide centralized in-plant and local-area transportation service.

7. Contacts Purchasing Department regarding status of purchased materials specifications to insure a current supply of productive materials which will meet specifications.

8. Represents Manager–Service Planning on matters pertaining to purchasing, traffic, inventory control, product repair, shipping, and warehousing in monthly meetings of Product Service Division Parts Committee, which coordinates _____ Division finished goods and parts inventory status in PSD branches and forecasts such requirements for both Divisions.

9. Is a member of Product Performance Committee, which evaluates and improves product performance through planning and coordination of new engineering, procurement, production control, and plant service methods.

10. Administers personnel policies which affect Departments and personnel under his supervision; trains subordinates and augments training provided by subordinate Supervisors; consolidates and

approves vacation scheduling; has final authority in hiring non-supervisory employees; interviews and recommends selection in hiring supervisory personnel; has final authority on salary adjustments for non-supervisory employees; recommends salary adjustments for supervisory personnel; takes additional disciplinary action, including determination of discharge for a subordinate.

FOREMAN–MATERIAL HANDLING

A Petroleum and Carbon Producer

REPORTS TO: Assistant Production Superintendent.

GENERAL RESPONSIBILITY: To manage the activities of the Material Handling Department in an economical and efficient manner; to accomplish, through the disposition of his workforce and the use of equipment assigned to his Department, the unloading of all incoming raw materials and supplies, to direct either processing or storage; to accomplish any required, subsequent intra-plant movement of these raw materials and supplies from storage to processing locations; to transport stock, as requested, to various storage locations; to load all outgoing shipments of bulk or scrap; and, in addition to these general services, to maintain the plant grounds, roadways, and paved areas in good condition; and to perform various other miscellaneous jobs that may be assigned to his Department.

DUTIES

1. Directs the activities of his Department in accordance with established methods and practices, planning the disposition of his workforce and the use of assigned equipment in an economical and efficient manner, so as to accomplish the movement of all materials at the lowest possible cost.

2. Performs all requested and authorized services in Material Handling to all Operating Departments in the plant.

3. Maintains close contact with the local representative of the railway company and with the Processing Department Foremen, so that incoming materials may be delivered to the Department, or Departments, in accordance with processing needs.

4. Estimates manpower and equipment requirements and advises the Assistant Production Superintendent in advance of his needs for each.

5. Notifies the Assistant Production Superintendent and the affected Department Foreman immediately of inability to meet schedules.

6. Requests maintenance service, whenever such service is required, so as to maintain the equipment assigned to his Department in satisfactory operating condition.

7. Cooperates with the personnel assigned to the Quality Control function, and with the administration of the Process and Product Control and Technical Departments, to assure that necessary samples are taken of incoming materials and that the quality of incoming materials does not deteriorate in the process of unloading and transfer.

8. Supplies all Production Departments with additional service as required on weekends, holidays, and other periods not included in a normal work schedule.

9. Makes accurate reports in accordance with established procedure.

AUTHORITY

1. Approves the selection of personnel assigned to him; directs and trains them.

2. Recommends employees for promotion, disciplinary action, and separation; takes immediate action to resolve grievances within the limits of established policies.

3. Initiates purchase requisitions in accordance with established procedure, subject to the approval of the Plant Manager.

FOREMAN–MATERIALS HANDLING AND TRANSPORTATION

A. O. Smith Corporation

REPORTS TO: General Foreman–Receiving, Materials Handling, and Warehousing.

SUPERVISES: 3 Mechanics–Drivers and 4 Operators of Fork-Lift Trucks.

PRIMARY FUNCTION: To supervise those centralized plant service operations required to insure efficient and orderly handling and flow of materials among Storage and Manufacturing Departments on plant premises. To supervise transportation of materials, parts, and finished goods to and from vendors and warehousing facilities. Operations include materials handling and in-plant transportation; coordination and movement of materials by automotive equipment between plant and vendors, and between plant and outside warehouses; and minor automotive maintenance.

DUTIES AND RESPONSIBILITIES

1. Assigns men to work stations, routes, and/or equipment according to their vocational specialties and the Section's operational requirements as specified by materials requisitions and instructions received in the Section. Modifies work assignments per receiving, manufacturing, maintenance, storage, and shipping requirements. Periodically follows up to insure that Materials Handling and Transportation Sections and Garage are fulfilling these assignments.

2. Supervises the following operations within Sections under his jurisdiction:

   a. Loading and unloading trucks and freight cars for the Shipping and Receiving Departments; loading and unloading conveyors either manually or by use of power-operated fork-lift trucks; transporting materials to and from Departments and work stations, using tote boxes, hand trucks, fork-lift trucks, and so on, within confines of plant premises (including various plant Storage Sections).

   b. Coordinating, scheduling, and dispatching of automotive vehicles to transport raw materials, purchased parts equipment, in-process and finished goods and parts, and supplies from one location to another, to and from plant premises, and within 150-mile radius of _____. Performing preventive maintenance on automotive vehicles (Company-owned and/or leased pick-up trucks and cars).

   c. Weighing, packaging, and dispatching of parcel-post orders.

   d. Performing receiving function at two local-area warehousing facilities.

3. Controls product quality to the extent that all materials are handled and transported so as to prevent product damage or future malfunction.

4. Makes minor methods improvements, such as development of new materials handling and transportation techniques and schedules, to improve services to other Departments.

5. Administers personnel policies as they affect employees under his supervision (i.e., training, safety and housekeeping, rate adjustments, vacations, discipline, hiring and firing, etc.).

FOREMAN–SHIPPING, RECEIVING, AND STOCK DEPARTMENTS

An Electronics Company

GENERAL FUNCTIONS: To supervise Shipping, Receiving, and Stock Departments; plan and schedule work for the Departments; make recommendations pertaining to personnel and functions of Departments; train members of Departments. Is responsible for proper stocking, shipping, and receiving of all materials purchased or manufactured in the _____ Plant.

SPECIFIC DUTIES OF JOB

1. To supervise employees (approximately 23) of the Shipping, Receiving, and Stock Departments.
2. To plan, schedule, and assign work for Departments.
3. To be responsible for administration, conduct, quality, and quantity of work in Departments.
4. To recommend pay increases, promotions, transfers, and dismissals for members of Departments.
5. To interview applicants for jobs in Departments.
6. To train members of Departments in functions and duties of their jobs.
7. To institute and/or recommend changes in operations performed by the Departments.
8. To be responsible for the receipt, storage, and distribution of raw material, parts, and finished goods.
9. To be responsible for the packaging and shipment of finished products according to Company procedures; to eliminate bottlenecks, and to maintain quality standards.
10. To be responsible for the accurate count of all parts in the most economical manner.

11. To maintain all trucks, bins, and other equipment in good condition and report to the Supervisor of Production Planning any suggestions for improvement.

12. To expedite critical parts or finished goods in order to maintain an even production flow.

13. To review methods of material storing and handling and any changes in shipping procedures in order to reduce costs.

14. To maintain a Kardex system on all raw parts, coordinating with Cost Department on special items.

15. To be responsible for materials handling between Receiving, Raw Material Inspection, Stock, and all Production Departments.

16. To maintain an up-to-date file of labels for all _____ offices and be responsible for all packaging material.

17. To advise and assist the Supervisor of Production Planning in formulating proposals for new policies and improvements and changes in procedures, package design and specifications, processes, tools, equipment, and other items that would lead to cost reduction.

18. To investigate high costs of operation in Departments and take corrective measures.

19. To encourage suggestions for improvement in shipping, stock, and receiving processes and give full credit to employees when earned.

20. To conduct regular Department inspections to insure cleanliness and safety. To arrange for proper maintenance, operation, and orderliness of buildings, machinery, equipment, facilities, and material in process within the area of his jurisdiction.

21. To control the use of material, supplies, and tools to reduce operating expense within his Departments.

22. To fulfill the requirements of standard practice instructions or personnel manual with respect to records, requisitions, report forms, and authorizations which apply to his Departments or to the plant.

23. To prepare, as required, reports on progress, shipments, work on specific jobs, attendance, discipline, and general Department problems.

24. To attend meetings to give and receive information on improvement or utilization of material, tools, personnel, and methods.

25. To cooperate with the Service Departments in helping to solve internal Department problems and the problems of other Departments.

26. To maintain standard safety procedures and participate in plant inspection tours and report on results.

27. To coordinate work carefully among the Order, Cost, Production and Inspection Departments.

28. To investigate thoroughly each recommendation for monetary expenditures and base all requests upon factual evidence.

29. As requested by superiors, to perform allied duties, fill in on other jobs, perform higher classification functions such as promotional training, and perform any work done in like or lower job classifications.

FOREMAN–STOCK AND SHIPPING GROUP

The Carborundum Company

I. GENERAL RESPONSIBILITY: To be responsible for receiving all materials used in the plant; routing them to proper location; storing and issuing all stock and stores items; transporting materials within the plant; coordinating the transportation of materials and personnel between Coated Abrasives Division and other parts of the Company; taking cycle and general physical inventories; handling all shipping, housekeeping, and yard operations; handling and disposing of salvage and scrap materials; maintaining stock area in an orderly manner; keeping records; approving requisitions and issuing reports on stock and shipping operations, employee relations, and labor contract administration; consulting with Operation Department Heads on methods of supply and with Traffic Manager and Bonded Abrasives and Electro-Minerals Divisions' Shipping Department Heads on shipping and traffic coordination and routing. Also consults with government inspectors.

II. ORGANIZATIONAL RELATIONSHIPS

A. *Line:* Is responsible to: Manager, Production Control Department. Supervises: Assistant Foreman–Raw Stores, Receiving and Housekeeping Unit; Assistant Foreman–Shipping and Finished Stock Unit.

B. *Staff:* Advises and receives advice from: Division, Branch, and Department Heads and their subordinates; Traffic Manager; Bonded Abrasives and Electro-Minerals Divisions' Shipping Department Heads and their subordinates.

III. Specific Duties

KIND OF ACTIVITY	SCOPE	TYPE OF ACTION

A. Line or Operational

1. Receiving and storage: Materials, returned merchandise, issuing records.	Stock and Shipping Group.	Supervises the receiving of all materials used in the plant; the checking-in, reporting of receipt, routing to storage areas, handling, and disposal of returned merchandise; and the storing and issuing of raw materials and supplies.
2. Housekeeping and yard operations: Cleaning, scrap disposal, boiler coal.	Stock and Shipping Group.	Supervises and coordinates the cleaning of offices, plant, and yard, including snow removal, removal of scrap from plant, incinerator operation, disposal of ash and other material, unloading of coal, and supplying coal to boiler house. Negotiates with Purchasing and outside vendors on supplies and services purchased.
3. Finished stock and shipping operations: Storing, issuing, packaging, shipping.	Stock and Shipping Group.	Supervises the storing and issuing of finished stock, packaging of broken lots, packing and marking of export shipments, consolidation of district shipments, assembling and release of customer shipments, routing changes, loading of shipments on rail cars and trucks, preparation of labels and bills of lading, and reports in connection with shipping operations. Coordinates handling of government shipments with Sales Branch

III. Specific Duties (cont'd)

KIND OF ACTIVITY	SCOPE	TYPE OF ACTION
A. *Line or Operational* (cont'd)		
		and government inspector for release, marking, samples, and necessary certificates.
4. Physical inventories: Planning, coordinating.	Stock and Shipping Group.	Supervises the taking of cycle and general physical inventories as required, including planning of personnel and equipment and changes in procedures required; coordinates physical inventories with Inventory Record groups, Finance Branch, and Operating Department Heads.
5. Requisitions approved: Issuing, approval records.	Stock and Shipping Group.	Supervises the issuing and approval of material requisitions for replenishment of operating and packaging supplies obtained from Bonded Abrasives Division Stores; supervises the maintenance records in Receiving Office, stock areas, and Shipping Office as required.
6. Transportation: Intra-plant, inter-plant.	Stock and Shipping Group.	Supervises the transportation of materials from storage areas to operating departments and from operating departments to storage areas and shipping room; transportation of materials, papers, and personnel between Coated Abrasives Division and other parts of the Company; and other general transportation as required.
7. Personnel relations: Size of workforce,	Stock and Shipping Group.	Recommends additions to and reductions of workforce in Group; administers labor contract, including assisting in

III. SPECIFIC DUTIES (cont'd)

KIND OF ACTIVITY	SCOPE	TYPE OF ACTION

A. Line or Operational
   (cont'd)

contract administration, morale.		Step *B* of grievance procedure; administers employee progress review pertaining to salaried personnel; maintains good employee morale; interviews new employees; terminates unsatisfactory probationary employees.
8. Programs, policies and procedures.	Stock and Shipping Group.	Implements approved policies, programs, and procedures in the Group, assists in studies leading to improvements in stock and shipping operations, prepares special reports for Department Head and Manager of Manufacturing.

B. Staff or Functional

1. Shipping and stock operations.	Manufacturing Branch.	Consults with Operating Heads and their subordinates regarding coordination of operations and improved procedures and supplying methods. Is an active member of inter-division task force on shipping practices. Coordinates with other divisions and Central Traffic Department on consolidated shipments through branch warehouses. Recommends and assigns over-the-road carriers for incoming and outgoing materials. Interviews representatives of outside carriers. Places tracers on shipments.
2. Transportation.	Manufacturing Branch.	Consults with Company Traffic Manager and Bonded Abrasives and Electro-Minerals Di-

III. SPECIFIC DUTIES (cont'd)

KIND OF ACTIVITY SCOPE   TYPE OF ACTION

B. *Staff or Functional*
(cont'd)

visions' Shipping Department Heads and their subordinates regarding traffic and shipping problems and combined shipments.

WAREHOUSE FOREMAN

A Petroleum and Carbon Producer

REPORTS TO: General Foreman.

GENERAL: The Warehouse Foreman works under the general supervision of the General Foreman, supervising the workers in the warehouse and yard so as to properly handle products for shipment or warehousing.

DUTIES

1. Must be able to utilize (a) good training and safety techniques for the development and protection of workers, (b) sound job relations methods for the handling of employees' problems, and (c) sound methods for the development of good job methods to increase quantities of quality production.

2. Properly interprets and administers Company policies and procedures.

3. Gathers, computes, records, and compiles required data, records, and information with respect to inventories, shipments, bills of lading, time cards, and the like.

4. Supervises the proper handling of products and supplies in the warehouse, such as bags, car strappings, chip board, tags, and staples, with respect to inventories, shipments, and the like.

5. May fulfill duties of the General Foreman during his absence.

6. Must see that all work areas are kept safe, neat, and clean.

7. Handles production and maintenance procedures as directed. Schedules; plant changes; maintenance of adequate supplies, parts, and material; purchasing; and the like are the responsibility of the Plant Superintendent, but portions of these may be delegated to the Warehouse Foreman, who will perform these management functions in accordance with the Division policy.

8. Is responsible for related or lesser duties as required.

FOREMAN–FINISHED GOODS AND PARTS STORAGE

A. O. Smith Corporation

REPORTS TO: General Foreman–Receiving, Materials Handling, and Warehousing.

SUPERVISES: 10 stock clerks and 2 fillers of parts orders.

PRIMARY FUNCTION: Supervises operations required to insure availability of finished goods (complete product systems in the Division's line of equipment for metering and handling liquids) and parts to meet Shipping Division requirements. Operations include in-plant storage (3,000 square feet) and finished goods outside warehousing (two local area facilities of 5,000 and 18,000 square feet).

DUTIES AND RESPONSIBILITIES

1. Assigns men to work stations according to their vocational specialties and the Section's operational requirements as specified in materials requisitions received by the Section. Modifies work assignments per sub- and final assembly schedules and changing requirements of Shipping Department. Periodically follows up to insure that Storage and Warehousing Sections are fulfilling needs of Final Assembly and/or Shipping Departments. (*Note*: Most shipments are drawn from finished goods inventories, rather than from production lines. In this respect the finished goods storage and warehousing functions might be termed an "industrial" products mail order house.)

2. Supervises the following activities within the Sections under his jurisdiction:

   a. Receiving finished goods and parts in Storage Section from Manufacturing Departments.

   b. Storing items in bins, on shelves, or on pallets and/or floor in convenient locations to allow easy removal when needed. Includes marking or tagging parts and models as required for identification purposes.

   c. Filling parcel-post orders for small, lightweight parts; pulling larger, heavy parts from storage location preparatory to transmittal to Shipping Department and/or return to Final Assembly Department.

   d. Maintaining inventory control records and processing requisitions for ordering additional quantities of parts and sub- and final assemblies as indicated by Finished Goods Section's minimum inventory requirements records.

   e. Coordinating with in-plant Transportation Section the delivery to Shipping and/or Final Assembly.

3. Controls product quality to the extent of insuring that all materials received by Section comply (i.e., by count, weight, and verification) with parts and/or part numbers specified in purchase orders, and that finished goods are stored so as to prevent product damage and future malfunction. Maintains tagging system to insure proper stock rotation on FIFO basis (e.g., to prevent a three-year-old "rotten" O-ring from being shipped out after normal "shelf life" and later returned by customer within warranty period).

4. Makes minor methods improvements (e.g., rearrangement of finished goods storage facilities) for more efficient use of space.

5. Administers personnel policies as they affect employees under his supervision (i.e., training, safety and housekeeping, rate adjustments, vacations, discipline, hiring and firing).

Plant Engineering and Maintenance

Plant engineer, maintenance manager, general foreman, assistant foreman, and unit foreman are some of the jobs in this classification.

PLANT ENGINEER

The Morgan Engineering Company

BASIC FUNCTION: To be responsible to the Vice President of Manufacturing for maintenance of the physical plant, equipment, and machines; for moving and rearrangement of equipment and facilities; for establishing and maintaining a preventive maintenance program; for plant construction and services and the supervision of actual construction, including outside contractors; for maintenance of plant blueprints; for economical operation of the heating plant and other utilities; for maintenance of adequate supplies; for providing standby equipment where required; for utilizing and keeping Division management fully advised of current developments in the materials, equipment, and techniques normally required in plant maintenance and engineering; for the Company's cost reduction program; for methods and standard practices which include operating methods, material handling methods, plant layout, machine and equipment procurement and replacement.

BASIC OBJECTIVE: To administer the Plant and Industrial Engineering functions in a manner which will result in well-maintained buildings, equipment, and plant operating facilities; improved operating and material handling methods; and reduced costs.

MAJOR DUTIES AND RESPONSIBILITIES

1. *Organization and Personnel*

   a. To maintain and administer an organization which is adequate for the performance of the Plant and Industrial Engineering operations.

   b. To insure that the duties and responsibilities of subordinates are clearly defined and fixed and to approve position descriptions of immediate subordinates.

   c. To recommend to the Vice President of Manufacturing major changes in the form and size of the Plant and Industrial Engineering Department required to meet changing conditions.

   d. To see that the personnel in the Plant and Industrial Engineering Department are fully and currently informed of all the pertinent Company policies and that such policies are followed in the Department.

   e. To direct the Company's personnel policies within the Department.

f. To recommend to the Vice President of Manufacturing the employment, promotion, dismissal, or change in compensation of personnel under his immediate supervision.

g. To approve the employment, promotion, dismissal, or change in compensation of personnel reporting directly to his immediate subordinates.

h. To periodically review and appraise the qualifications of Department personnel as prescribed by the Industrial Relations policies.

i. To receive and process employee grievances originating within the Plant Engineering Department as directed by the Company contract with the union, and to adhere to all other Company/union contract agreements.

j. To consult with the Industrial Relations Division with respect to orientation and training of personnel within the Plant Engineering Department and the apprentice training program.

k. To consult with the Industrial Relations Division with respect to the development and operation of the Company safety program within the Plant Engineering Department.

2. *Physical Plant Maintenance*

a. To maintain buildings and grounds in good physical condition.

b. To maintain blueprints and tracings covering buildings and grounds and including location of sewers and power, water, steam, and air lines.

c. To establish and maintain a program of plant and equipment maintenance on a continuing basis for the repair, replacement, and expansion of Company machinery, equipment, and facilities.

3. *Machines and Equipment*

a. To maintain all equipment and machines in good working condition.

b. To establish and maintain a preventive maintenance program so that all equipment is thoroughly inspected and tested periodically.

c. To move and rearrange equipment as recommended by the Industrial Engineering Department and approved by the Vice President of Manufacturing.

4. *Construction*

a. To direct and assist in the preparation of drawings and specifications required to construct, repair, or demolish new or existing building facilities.

b. To supervise the construction, repair, or demolition of new or existing building facilities.

    c. To develop proposals for outside contracting work or services for bids, except in cases of emergency repairs.

5. *Utilities*: To see that plant-generated or purchased utilities are obtained at the lowest possible costs and that supply lines servicing said utilities are properly maintained and tested.

6. *Supplies*: To see that adequate supplies of maintenance materials are carried in stock and that proper accounting is made of the supplies used, in conformance with controls established by the Finance Division.

7. *Standby Equipment*: To recommend and install standby equipment as approved by the Vice President of Manufacturing.

8. *Unskilled Labor*: To direct the supervision of unskilled labor services in an effective manner, handling odd-job assignments as required.

9. *Budgets*

    a. To prepare the annual budget for the Plant and Industrial Engineering Department, covering expenditures for the sections therein, and submit it to the Vice President of Manufacturing.

    b. To operate the Plant and Industrial Engineering Department within the approved budget.

    c. To review and approve the annual budgets covering operating expenses and capital expenses of the individual sections reporting to him.

    d. To review periodically, with the Section Heads reporting to him, their actual operating performance in relation to approved budgets.

    e. To assist various Company Divisions and Departments in the preparation of their annual budgets for capital expenditures, re-arrangement of equipment, machine repairs, and semi-expendable and expendable tools.

    f. To prepare, in conjunction with the General Manufacturing Superintendent, the annual capital budget and to submit it to the Vice President of Manufacturing for approval.

10. *Cost Reduction Program*

    a. To coordinate all cost reduction items involving technological improvements and methods changes, equipment replacement, general improvements, and suggestions originating in all Divisions.

    b. To estimate cost reduction resulting from capital investment.

    c. To prepare cost comparison reports.

    d. To maintain cost reduction records.

    e. To maintain a post-audit of cost reduction items.

11. Operating Methods: To establish and recommend to shop supervision the most effective methods for performing manufacturing operations.

12. Material Handling Methods

  a. To recommend and select material handling equipment.

  b. To make material handling analysis.

  c. To establish material handling techniques and flow.

13. Plant Layout

  a. To coordinate and establish floor area utilization.

  b. To provide adequate internal and external factory transportation arteries.

  c. To provide for future expansion and growth.

  d. To provide safety and fire protection and comply with city and state factory codes and laws.

14. Machine and Equipment Procurement and Replacement

  a. To make replacement analyses of machinery and equipment, utilizing information and records from various Company Divisions and Departments; to consider data such as space costs, depreciation, service life, purchase date, down time, and maintenance and service costs.

  b. To recommend the replacement of equipment or the procurement of new equipment to lower operating costs, increase output, improve quality, or offer greater versatility when such action will result in an adequate return for the required investment.

  c. To make post-audit follow-up.

15. Basic Data

  a. To make methods improvements and corrections in conjunction with Processing Group.

  b. To establish equipment capacities.

16. General

  a. To assist the Processing Group and Sales Division in estimating labor hours for subcontract work and unusual new jobs.

  b. To approve requisitions within the Plant Engineering Department for equipment, supplies, services, or any other expenditures as authorized in the Purchase Requisition Procedure and to recommend, to the Vice President of Manufacturing, amounts in excess of authorized limits.

  c. To consult with the interested Division Vice Presidents with respect to physical changes in areas.

d. To perform any additional duties as requested by the Vice President of Manufacturing.

PLANT ENGINEER

A Petroleum and Carbon Producer

REPORTS TO: Plant Manager.

RESPONSIBILITY: To recommend and engineer new structures and equipment, and improvements or alterations to existing structures and equipment, according to procedures established by the Chief Engineer and with his approval. Undertake projects connected therewith as assigned by the Plant Manager.

DUTIES

1. Upon request of Plant Department Heads, to engineer structures, equipment, tools, fixtures, and other devices to produce new products or improve the method of producing old products.

2. To request services of the Chief Engineer and his staff to handle major engineering projects.

3. To direct the design of minor building additions, new equipment layouts, or equipment rearrangements on a plant scale; to coordinate all construction with the Plant Department Heads affected; and to advise the Plant Manager and/or Chief Engineer of alterations or changes required to maintain structural efficiency.

4. To furnish drafting and engineering services as required.

5. To confer with and assist the Production Superintendent in establishing an adequate maintenance repair program.

6. To safeguard Plant Engineering facilities and insure compliance with Company and Division policy and instructions by all personnel under his direction.

7. To originate appropriation requests covering the purchase of equipment or facilities as authorized by the Chief Engineer.

8. To perform such other engineering duties as may be assigned to him by the Chief Engineer.

AUTHORITY

1. To administer the Plant Engineering Department and engage, train, and direct the personnel allotted to it.
2. To review and approve requisitions for plant purchase involving construction or the acquisition of equipment.
3. To initiate requisitions for the purchase of supplies, materials, or equipment required by the Plant Engineering Department in accordance with established procedures.

PLANT ENGINEER

A Machinery Company

REPORTS TO: Works Manager, on all phases of his work.

SUPERVISES DIRECTLY: Foreman–Building Services.
Foreman–General Labor.
Foreman–Mechanical and Hydraulic Departments.
Foreman–Electrical Department.
Fire Chief (Full Supervisor).
Maintenance Engineers (2).

DUTIES

1. Directs, through the individuals listed above, the over-all Plant Engineering functions for all plants in _____. This includes:

    a. Engineering and executing planned maintenance repairs, installations, rearrangements, and replacements and making all emergency repairs.

    b. Generating or procuring and distributing power, steam, and other utilities.

    c. Administering and supervising the craft groups toward the safe and efficient operation of the plant.

    d. Providing adequate fire protection in accordance with fire insurance requirements.

    e. Providing production supervision with a technical consulting service on mechanical and electrical problems.

    f. Administering other service facilities such as sanitation.

    g. Maintaining adherence to local, state, and Federal laws and codes

governing plant operations, buildings, stream pollution abate-
ment, and interference with radio and television broadcasting.

h. Extending the preventive maintenance program by accelerating
machine and equipment inspection.

i. Establishing and maintaining adequate records of machine locations, services required, and maintenance and repair costs for each
major item of plant equipment and property.

j. Establishing and maintaining adequate records and providing
periodic reports on maintenance cost in order to control this
expense.

2. Directs his Foremen in securing outside bids from contractors, and
directs the coordination and inspection of contracted work, in accordance with the over-all Plant Engineering schedule.

3. Coordinates the efforts of his Foremen in accordance with the schedules established by the Operations Control function.

4. Cooperates with shop and office supervision in the timing of repairs,
in order to minimize confusion and down time.

5. Directs the control of all liquid waste and its proper treatment to
prevent stream pollution.

6. Directs the development of lubrication charts for more adequate
control and sets specifications for lubricants, coolants, and so on.

7. Cooperates with the Operations Control function on the scheduling
of inspection and planned installations and maintenance requiring
appreciable shutdown periods during the regular work shift.

8. Directs the checking of estimates of materials and hours by the
various craft groups on installations and repairs.

9. Directs the checking of requisitions and work orders prepared by his
Foremen for large special material and equipment items.

10. Advises and assists his Foremen on design and engineering problems.

11. Is responsible for maintaining inventories of materials, supplies, and
repair parts at suitable levels and in accordance with such over-all
policy as may be established by management on total dollar value.

12. Directs the handling of the current workload of planned maintenance and the balancing of hours against the number of employees
in the various craft groups.

13. Follows up on the variance reports and recommendations of the
Cost Control function to see that corrective action is taken by his
Foremen.

14. Assists the Works Manager in administering and enforcing all management policies applicable to his Section. May be called upon to
make recommendations toward the establishment of policies, particu-

larly in cases where his Section is affected—as, for example, a policy on smoking.

15. Guides and assists his Foremen in carrying out their responsibilities, delegating to them the full authority necessary for this purpose.

16. Consults with Works Manager and Labor Relations Manager on action to be taken on important problems involving the union. Would not, for example, suspend or discharge an employee represented by the bargaining unit without such consultation.

17. Follows up on special projects, such as employee suggestions and job method proposals of Foremen, which are being tried out in his Section to make sure that action is being taken and that projects are completed on the specified date.

18. Maintains records and makes such reports as are prescribed by the Works Manager, Operations Control, and the like, plus any others needed to carry out his responsibilities. Preventive maintenance records and machine and equipment prints are typical records; monthly reports or charts showing repair costs by types or classes of machines are examples of reports.

MAINTENANCE SUPERVISOR

An Office Machine Company

POSITION DESCRIPTION

A. *General Objective of Position*: To be responsible to Manager, Central Division, for the design, improvement, and maintenance of equipment and facilities commensurate with good engineering practices and low cost.

B. *Responsibilities and Authority*

1. Personnel and organization

   a. Initiates the selection, termination, promotion, classification changes, and compensation of all non-exempt Department personnel according to Company policy and union contracts.

   b. Recommends the selection, termination, promotion, and compensation of exempt personnel.

   c. Recommends all job descriptions for Departments in this Division.

   d. Develops and directs programs designed to maximize the utilization of the talents of all Department personnel.

    e. Recommends the changes required in organizational structure to increase the efficiency of the Department.

    f. Total employees supervised: 23.

    g. Directly supervises: Maintenance Dispatcher.
                          Electricians (5).
                          Oilers (2).
                          Firemen (3).
                          Plumbers (3).
                          Carpenters (2).
                          Welder.
                          General Maintenance Men (5).
                          Painter.

2. Operational

    a. Compiles, recommends, administers, and operates within the approved budget.

    b. Directs work of Electrical Department and General Maintenance Department to meet work schedules.

    c. Initiates and follows up on cost saving projects.

    d. Checks Department performance by comparison with records of past performance.

    e. Promotes cooperation and team spirit among employees under his supervision.

    f. Promotes safety and good housekeeping practices.

    g. Makes all necessary records to keep superior informed.

    h. Executes all approved policies.

    i. Is a member of the management committee that meets with unions to handle problems and grievances.

    j. Directs and assists in developing training programs and training material.

    k. Recommends the purchase of new machines, equipment, and materials. Recommends changes in process as necessary.

    l. Checks on the use of materials and supplies and takes steps to control waste.

    m. Recommends layout of utilities for the plant.

    n. Performs all other duties as assigned by superior.

C. *Relationships*

1. Within the company

    a. Consults with Supervisors of most Departments concerning the maintenance of equipment and facilities.

  b. Is a member of Factory Management Council.

 2. Outside the company

  a. Maintains, through the Purchasing Department, contact with outside vendors of material, equipment, and supplies for all the plant.

  b. Maintains contact with public utilities.

  c. Acts in the best interest of the Company to further good public and community relationships.

D. *Results Expected*

 1. To maintain or reduce maintenance cost.

 2. To meet work schedule by assuring adequate personnel performing according to production requirements commensurate with economical cost.

 3. To maintain good employee relations.

 4. To develop subordinates to maximum effectiveness.

 5. To keep all equipment in best possible operating condition.

 6. To insure clean and safe working conditions throughout the plant.

 7. To meet construction, equipment installation, and major repair schedules, maintaining a high degree of quality, good engineering products, and at the lowest possible cost.

E. *Measures of Performance*

 1. Review of costs on work orders and budget figures.

 2. Number of lost-time hours of production equipment.

 3. Review of grievance records and quality and quantity of work.

 4. Number of subordinates performing effectively and ready for promotion.

 5. Number of breakdowns of equipment.

 6. Inspection of plant. Review of frequency of accidents involving time loss.

 7. Meeting of specifications, estimates, and scheduled dates.

F. *Comments*:

The effectiveness of the Maintenance Division can be improved by a well-planned method of scheduling work to be done and by cooperation of all other Departments concerned. Obtaining material from the outside more speedily will result in a more efficient maintenance operation. Advance notice of a reasonable time limit should be given to the Maintenance Division in order that jobs may be planned correctly and carried out completely.

POSITION SPECIFICATIONS

A. Education and Training

  1. College graduate with engineering degree or its equivalent.

  2. Special courses in conference leadership and human relations.

B. Experience

  1. Three years in engineering.

  2. One year in supervision.

C. Other Personal Qualifications

  1. Minimum age: 25 years.

  2. Should be classed as "Engineer-in-training" with the state as a step toward obtaining professional engineer's license.

  3. Must be able to analyze both human and mechanical problems and organize individual as well as group approach for finding and applying solutions.

  4. Must be able to organize material for group discussion.

  5. Must have patience and self-control.

  6. Must be a good salesman.

  7. Must be able to see relationship of cost and profit.

  8. Must be able to adapt to change.

  9. Must be able to delegate work responsibilities commensurate with authority.

  10. Must be enthusiastic and aggressive.

MANAGER–MAINTENANCE

Allegheny Ludlum Steel Corporation

BASIC FUNCTION: Is responsible to the Works Manager for maintaining all productive equipment, buildings, and yards; for performing all construction work his Department can handle; for generating steam and electricity and for distributing utilities; for administering a preventive maintenance program; for seeing that electrical work is carried out; for maintaining and operating machine shop facilities; and for administering the erection and relocation of machinery.

BASIC OBJECTIVE: To see that the men, material, and equipment constituting the Maintenance Department are directed and supervised in such a manner that the Production Departments can maintain production at economical cost in accordance with planned schedules and quality standards.

MAJOR DUTIES AND RESPONSIBILITIES

1. *Organization and Personnel*

   a. To develop, maintain, and administer an organization qualified to erect, relocate, or maintain all productive facilities in a safe and efficient working condition; to perform such construction work as his Department is qualified to do with its normal complement of men; to generate steam and electricity and to distribute all steam, electricity, water, compressed gases, and sewage; to carry out an effective preventive maintenance program.

   b. To see that all employees are kept fully and currently informed on all applicable Corporation, Works, and Department policies, and to see that these policies are followed.

   c. To insure that the duties, authorities, and responsibilities of subordinates are clearly defined and fixed and to approve the position and job descriptions of immediate subordinates.

   d. To review and appraise periodically the performance of each immediate subordinate as prescribed by Corporation policy and to take or recommend remedial action.

   e. To confer with the Works Manager and recommend to him the employment, dismissal, or change in compensation or status of personnel under his supervision.

   f. To receive and handle employee grievances in accordance with established procedures; to carry out all applicable provisions of labor contracts and the policies of the Industrial Relations Department.

   g. To cooperate with the Industrial Relations Department in the development and administration of a successful safety program.

2. *Maintenance and Construction*

   a. To maintain all operating equipment in the Works in satisfactory condition; to schedule needed repair work so as to interfere least with production, in order that Production Departments may meet production control schedules based on promises to customers.

   b. To be responsible for the quality of his Department's work to assure that producing equipment will turn out end products up to the specifications and tolerances set by the Quality Control Department.

c. To develop and administer, with the cooperation of the various Production Departments, an effective preventive maintenance program designed to eliminate down time of equipment

d. To perform such construction work as his Department is qualified to do with its normal complement of men; to consult with the General Engineering Division, Works Engineering, Industrial Engineering, and the various Production Departments regarding desirable modifications of existing equipment and facilities and the installation of new equipment and facilities.

3. *Utilities, Transportation, and Other Services*

a. To be responsible for the efficient operation of the steam plant, gas-generating plant, air compressors, and their related distribution facilities and the other facilities necessary to the distribution and usage of electric power and water.

b. To be responsible for the efficient maintenance of intra-Works Transportation facilities, including a diesel locomotive, yard crane, lift trucks, jitneys, multipurpose trucks, and overhead traveling cranes.

c. To provide janitorial services.

d. To operate a machine shop.

4. *Costs*

a. To analyze the performance and cost records of his Department, locating and promptly correcting improper or inefficient operations in order that lowest costs consistent with established schedules and quality standards may be realized.

b. To analyze cost studies of proposals for new facilities and equipment in his Department designed to secure reduced operating costs; to make recommendations thereon to the Works Manager.

c. To maintain adequate records, controls, and statistics necessary to permit thorough and regular review of his Department's operating costs; to meet regularly with his immediate subordinate to review and analyze these costs.

d. To prepare an annual budget anticipating the needs of the Maintenance Department.

5. *General*

a. To determine standards of performance for projects undertaken by the Maintenance Department and to inspect the results of such work to insure conformity to these standards.

b. To be responsible for requisitions originating within his Department for equipment, supplies, or services.

c. To plan for, provide an adequate supply of, and insure control over spare parts and other maintenance supplies.

d. To approve invoices for payment of items connected with repair and construction projects.

e. To be responsible for the prompt and accurate preparation of all reports required from his Department.

f. To make maximum use of reports, controls, and statistics as made available by the Works Controller's Department in order to determine those areas requiring the most attention for improved performance.

g. To plan and make recommendations to the Works Manager concerning changes in the organization, personnel, equipment, and facilities requirements of his Department.

h. To meet periodically with his immediate subordinates for the purpose of reviewing operating policies, plans, performance, and problems.

i. To perform any additional services requested by the Works Manager.

SUPERINTENDENT OF PLANT AND TOOL MAINTENANCE

A Tubing and Forged Products Company

PURPOSE OF THE POSITION: The Superintendent of Plant and Tool Maintenance shall be responsible to the Vice President of Manufacturing for over-all plant maintenance, including tool procurement (other than original tooling); repair and maintenance of all tools; engineering modifications of existing tools and machines; procurement, modification, and maintenance of plant facilities; maintenance of all plant equipment. He shall be responsible for participating in the over-all planning of plant activities as a member of the staff of the Vice President of Manufacturing.

ORGANIZATIONAL RELATIONSHIPS

Reports to: Vice President of Manufacturing.

Supervises directly: Foreman—Machining Section.
Foreman—Electrical Section.
Foreman—Plant Maintenance Section.
Chief Guard—Plant Security Section.
Engineer—Building and Grounds Section.

MAJOR DUTIES AND RESPONSIBILITIES

1. *Execution of the Following Activities*

   a. Recommending improvements in existing tools, machines, methods, and processes to the Superintendent of Manufacturing Engineering.

   b. Providing plant facilities; repairing and maintaining machinery, equipment, tools, and plant facilities to prolong plant and equipment life, to minimize replacement expense, and to facilitate manufacturing activities.

   c. Administering a preventive maintenance program to assure continuous operation of production facilities, buildings, and equipment.

   d. Procuring machines, tools, and equipment for processing new products or for major revisions of existing products or processes, as requested and specified by the Manufacturing and Product Engineering Departments and as approved by the Vice President of Manufacturing.

   e. Moving, rearranging, and installing equipment, machinery, and utility services in accordance with specifications.

   f. Maintaining a janitorial and general housekeeping activity in accordance with established procedures.

   g. Maintaining a continuous supply of all utility services, including electricity, heat, process steam, gas, water, and air for the plant and offices.

   h. Receiving all purchased machinery, machined parts, equipment, tools, dies, and purchased plant-repair services; inspecting equipment received for projects initiated by the Manufacturing Department.

   i. Analyzing workloads and scheduling the fabrication of machines, tools, equipment, and plant facilities in accordance with priorities established by the Vice President of Manufacturing.

   j. Advising operating personnel as to the condition and state of repair of plant machinery, tools, and equipment; recommending corrective action as necessary.

   k. Making approved changes and improvements in existing tools, machinery, methods, and processes; notifying the Manufacturing Engineering Department for recording purposes.

   l. Reviewing Product and Manufacturing Engineering Department specifications and recommending practical modifications thereto.

   m. Maintaining good labor relations consistent with plant procedures and the provisions of the labor agreement.

    n. Directing and maintaining fire protection and plant security programs, including training the fire brigade and plant-protection personnel.

    o. Reviewing performance of all plant and tool maintenance and security personnel and recommending changes in status, including wage and salary changes, to the Vice President of Manufacturing.

2. *Organizational Planning*

    a. Participating in the over-all planning of the plant organization as requested by the Vice President of Manufacturing.

    b. Reviewing Plant Maintenance Division organization, policy, procedure, and standards on a continuing basis and recommending changes to the Vice President of Manufacturing.

3. *Coordination of Plant and Tool Maintenance and Security Activities*

    a. Internal. Coordinating the activities of all Plant and Tool Maintenance Division personnel through application of procedures for planning, training, communication, and control.

    b. External. Keeping the Vice President of Manufacturing, Plant Division Heads, and functionaries of departments other than Manufacturing informed of related activities so that over-all coordination is facilitated.

4. *Control of Plant and Tool Maintenance Activities*

    a. Comparing Plant and Tool Maintenance Division operating results and employee performance with established standards, budgets, and procedures.

    b. Instituting action necessary to assure compliance with Manufacturing Department policy, procedure, and standards.

GENERAL FOREMAN, MECHANICAL MAINTENANCE

A Large Steel Company

PRIMARY FUNCTION: To direct and coordinate the assigned mechanical maintenance services for Hot Mill, Cold Mill, and Galvanizing Departments.

DUTIES AND RESPONSIBILITIES

1. Gives general direction, through three subordinate Foremen, to all
   activities involved in the inspection, maintenance, adjustment, repair,
   and minor installations of mechanical equipment and piping in the
   following assigned mechanical maintenance areas.

   a. *Hot Mill*: Soaking pits, rolling mills, run-out tables, coilers, shears,
      levelers, roll grinders, cranes, pumps, piping, and auxiliary me-
      chanical equipment. A 65-man mechanical maintenance crew is
      assigned to the Hot Mill.

   b. *Cold Mill:* Rolling mills, pickling, cleaning, slitting, and shearing
      lines, annealing furnaces, cranes, tractors, roll grinders, sorting
      room equipment, pumps, piping, and auxiliary mechanical equip-
      ment in the Cold Mill Subdivision, west of _____ Street, the hot
      strip shear line, Slitter Department, Cold Mill, Physical Test-
      ing Labs, and H. N. X. Gas House. A 70- to 75-man mechanical
      maintenance crew is assigned to the Cold Mill.

   c. *Galvanizing and 56" Mills*: Rolling mills, galvanizing, pickling,
      shearing and asbestos-coat lines, annealing furnaces, cranes,
      tractors, roll grinders, and auxiliary mechanical equipment in the
      Galvanizing Department and Cold Mill Subdivisions east of
      _____ Street. A 50- to 55-man mechanical maintenance crew is
      assigned to these mills.

2. With the assistance of a subordinate Leader, supervises two mechanical parts store rooms and a staff of 10 mechanical chasers and storekeepers to prepare requisitions, store, and follow up on deliveries
   from central machine shop and outside sources. Supervises the development of spares lists and the requisitioning and storage of spare
   parts and components. Assists Purchasing Department to develop
   new sources by examining and testing equipment and mechanical
   supplies.

3. Supervises a Mechanical Engineer and two Draftsmen to redesign
   components of mechanical equipment for simplified maintenance or
   more effective operation, to investigate causes of mechanical failures,
   and to design jigs and fixtures for use in repairing and adjusting
   equipment.

4. Supervises three Inspectors responsible for preventive-maintenance
   inspection of cranes, hydraulics, and bearings throughout the assigned area.

5. Prepares requisitions for additional permanent help when required;
   interviews all applicants referred by Personnel Department and
   recommends acceptance or rejection. Allocates available manpower
   to meet emergency needs of the groups under his supervision.

6. Follows up to insure that new men are adequately trained and

reviews the employee performance reports prepared by Foremen. Gives initial approval to wage-rate changes, promotions, demotions, and requests for leaves of absence. Counsels Foremen in the solution of difficult complaints and disciplinary cases or handles such cases himself, consulting with his superior if important questions of policy are involved.

7. Investigates complaints about the quality of work or service received from his organization. Makes random checks on the condition of equipment for which his organization is responsible to insure that preventive maintenance and repairs are being carried out and to anticipate the need for repair, replacement, or overhaul of existing equipment.

8. Keeps informed on new designs and developments in mobile, material-handling, and other types of auxiliary mechanical equipment and materials by reading trade literature, visiting other plants, and so forth. Makes recommendations to Department Heads for improvements based on this information. Collaborates closely with Engineering Department and Mechanical Maintenance staff personnel to plan and install new equipment or major modifications. May assist Engineering Department by acting as Field Engineer to inspect outside contractors' work on new installations and to supervise starting-up procedures.

9. Keeps subordinate Foremen informed about Company plans and programs affecting their activities and interprets or explains Company policies.

10. Follows up to insure that safety meetings are held and adequate safety training is being provided in the assigned area.

RELATIONSHIPS

1. Reports to the Superintendent, Mechanical Maintenance Department.

2. Collaborates with the Superintendents and Foremen of Hot Mill, Cold Mill, and Galvanizing Departments to provide assigned mechanical maintenance services in these Departments.

3. Collaborates with the General Foreman and Foremen of the Hot Mill and Cold Mill Electrical Maintenance functions to carry out joint repair, overhaul, or installation projects.

4. Collaborates with Foremen of Central Maintenance functions and outside contractors who may be responsible for major construction, alteration, and overhaul projects in the assigned area.

5. Collaborates with Engineering and Purchasing Departments in planning and overseeing new construction of major overhaul projects.

MAINTENANCE FOREMAN

A Paper Company

FUNCTION: Is responsible to the Master Mechanic for the movement, proper installation, repair, and general maintenance of all machinery and equipment and the construction and repair (excluding electrical work) of buildings; lays out and plans maintenance work under the general direction of the Master Mechanic; orders materials needed to complete projects; supervises maintenance crews in accomplishing repairs, installations, and/or construction.

DUTIES

1. Receives work orders and general or specific instructions, sketches, or blueprints for jobs to be done. In cases of minor maintenance repair work, makes out work orders himself. Determines priorities on jobs for which such priorities have not been indicated. Studies projects in conjunction with the Master Mechanic, Plant Engineer, or Production Supervisors concerned to determine the most efficient and most economical methods of approach.

2. Is responsible to the Master Mechanic for maintenance of all machinery and equipment, construction and maintenance of buildings, and installation of machinery. Such work involves disassembling, finding causes of mechanical difficulties, initiating and carrying out corrective measures, and reassembling machinery. (Normally is not responsible for maintenance work being accomplished in Converting Section. On assigned weekends, however, is responsible for all maintenance work throughout the plant.)

3. Assists Master Mechanic in determining work schedules for maintenance crews. Reviews assignments of individual maintenance men to jobs by the working Foreman. Specifies individual workmen to be assigned on the more complex maintenance assignments. Shifts men as the situation demands, particularly when assigned maintenance crews need additional help on any project.

4. Supervises transport of all types of equipment from one area of the mill to another, determining the tools and equipment necessary to accomplish the projects and paying particular attention to the safety of the employees handling the work. Such changes in location of machinery are generally of a heavy-duty nature.

5. Issues instructions to the Machine Shop when repair work calls for machining, construction, or alteration of spare parts in a given piece

of equipment. If work is of a general nature and detailed instructions are not necessary, supplies the necessary information to have the particular job accomplished; otherwise has the machinists, welders, and so on proceed to the project area, take measurements, and gather the detailed information needed.

6. Is responsible for maintaining a sufficient supply of spare parts and materials necessary to handle repair projects of a recurring nature. Makes recommendations on the substitution of various parts and units when such substitutions will improve plant operations.

7. Checks Machine Shop operations and assists the employees as requested.

8. Works with the Master Mechanic, Production Superintendents, and the Plant Engineer in scheduling shutdowns to avoid unnecessary stockage of production when major projects are involved.

9. Advises and assists in estimating the cost of major projects, particularly by estimating labor time involved.

10. Supervises individual workmen to accomplish assigned maintenance projects of correct quality at the proper time and at economical cost.

11. Trains and directs the activity of individual workmen to assure an effective, efficient maintenance operation. Gives personal attention to any problems presented by new, unusual jobs and at all times attempts to give complete and authoritative information to individual workmen under his supervision.

12. Assumes responsibilities for all Company property, equipment, tools, and materials used in maintenance operations. Assures that all equipment and tools are kept in repair and efficient operating condition at all times.

13. Evaluates the work of men under his jurisdiction, watches their progress, and makes recommendations on promotions, disciplinary action, and the like.

14. Handles first-stage grievances (in conjunction with Master Mechanic or alone) or other personnel problems promptly and with good judgment and in accordance with established procedures and contract clauses. Reports any serious problems to the Master Mechanic.

15. Assures that adequate safety regulations are installed and followed and that safety devices are supplied and used by maintenance crew. Takes steps to correct infractions of safety regulations and, if necessary, reports them to proper authorities.

16. Receives calls, on a 24-hour basis, in cases of breakdown. Obtains information on the nature of the breakdown and contacts necessary millwrights to handle the repair work required. Contacts Master Mechanic and/or Plant Engineer concerning major breakdowns.

17. Generally, is required to handle any mechanical maintenance work or construction in progress in the areas of the plant under his jurisdiction. Keeps the Master Mechanic and/or Plant Engineer informed of any conditions or situations which he deems worthy of their attention or decision.

18. Prepares purchase requisitions for materials, spare parts, valves, doctor blades, and so on, necessary to complete maintenance work. Forwards requisitions to Plant Engineer for further processing. Refers to various parts catalogues as necessary, to order and describe parts required.

19. Administers first-aid treatment to maintenance crew members if they incur minor injuries. Refers serious injuries to plant Industrial Nurse and takes any other measures necessary when major accidents occur. Prepares accident report on all injuries to employees under his jurisdiction.

KNOWLEDGE

A. *Knowledge Requirements.* A thorough knowledge of all machinery and equipment in all areas of the _____ Plant, including operational problems and maintenance work that might be encountered, is required to carry out properly the duties and responsibilities of this position. A thorough knowledge of shop and building trades, including tools and equipment necessary to accomplish jobs in these trades, also is required. A working knowledge of the building and structural portions of the plant is necessary to accomplish repair, altering, remodeling, or new construction work assigned, as is a knowledge of blueprint reading. A knowledge of supervisory practices is required to maintain the morale and effectiveness of the workforce under the jurisdiction of the Maintenance Foreman.

B. *Sources of Knowledge.* A high-school education, with additional vocational training in mechanical millwrighting, is desirable. Practical experience may substitute for such training; a minimum of four to five years of such practical experience is necessary. A minimum of five to six years' previous experience as a journeyman millwright is probably the best preparatory experience. Assuming the experience and formal education listed above, approximately two years' additional time is required for the average employee to achieve normal proficiency in the performance of the job duties.

Application of Knowledge: Judgment and analytical ability are required to determine repairs necessary in all maintenance situations and to set up priorities for the various projects undertaken. Judgment is required in placing crew members to best utilize individual capabilities and to accomplish all maintenance work to be done with a minimum amount of curtailment in production. Knowledge of equipment and machinery and the accepted maintenance practices is required when directing the disassembly, inspection, replacement of parts or machinery, and reassembly of various pieces of equipment to restore them to acceptable performance. Discretion and judgment are required in handling personnel problems. The Maintenance Foreman must utilize judgment in determining repair action to be taken in emergency situations.

CONTACTS

1. *Internal*: Has frequent contact with supervisors of all plant production sections; occasional contact with personnel from Central Plant Engineering, primarily for exchanging information and taking action concerning movement, installation, repair, and/or general maintenance of plant machinery and equipment. Contact can on occasion be controversial.

2. *External*: Has occasional contact with representatives of machinery-and-parts suppliers.

SUPERVISION: Is responsible to the Master Mechanic for supervising maintenance crews throughout the entire plant. Supervises six hourly working Foremen and approximately 112 hourly employees in the various trades (millwrights, tinsmiths, pipefitters, welders, oilers, construction crew, painters, etc.). Assigns work to various hourly working Foremen, reviews work, maintains order and discipline, sits in on first-stage grievances with Master Mechanic (or may handle them in his absence), instructs and advises personnel, and generally supervises employees in accordance with union contract provisions.

RESPONSIBILITIES

1. *For Assets and Operations*: Is responsible to Master Mechanic for the proper movement, installation, repair, and maintenance of machinery, and equipment throughout the plant. Major questions on projects can be referred to his supervisor, the Project Engineer, or the Plant Engineer. Is responsible for proper use and maintenance of tools, equipment, spare parts, and so on, necessary to perform maintenance functions. Is responsible for assuring that safe working practices are followed. Is generally responsible for assuring that all machinery and equipment are in good operating condition.

2. *For Policy and Methods*: Recommends and suggests changes in methods and procedures of handling maintenance work to the Master Mechanic. Schedules men for assigned week end work, plans work-order jobs, and may establish methods in handling emergency situations. Works under general supervision of the Master Mechanic.

3. *For Records and Reports:* Originates and/or processes work orders; prepares purchase requisitions for parts needed in maintenance work; schedules week end maintenance crews; prepares cost estimates on jobs as assigned; checks and approves daily time cards of employees working on work orders; prepares Foremen's accident reports as necessary. Must follow specifications and blueprints closely in all work.

WORKING CONDITIONS AND HAZARDS: Works in all areas of the mill as necessary. May work under pressure, when repairing breakdowns, to keep work stoppage at a minimum. Is required to work in and around moving machinery. Is subject to 24-hour call. Not normally required to travel on Company business.

FOREMAN, MECHANICAL MAINTENANCE

A Large Steel Company

PRIMARY FUNCTION: Supervises the activities involved in maintaining, repairing, adjusting, and making minor installations of all mechanical equipment in the Cold Mill subdivisions located in the Main Plant and Slitter Department (electrolytic lines and tin pots excepted), the hot strip shear line, the Cold Mill, Physical Testing Labs, and the H.N.X. gas house.

DUTIES AND RESPONSIBILITIES

1. With an Assistant Foreman and five Shift Leaders, supervises approximately 63 millwrights, welders, repairmen, oilers, and helpers to provide mechanical maintenance services throughout assigned areas on a continuous basis.

   a. Repairs, adjusts, lubricates, makes minor installations, or rearranges equipment on rolling mills; pickling, cleaning, slitting, and shearing lines; annealing furnaces; cranes; tractors; roll grinders; sorting-room equipment; and a wide variety of auxiliary equipment.

   b. Provides for emergency repairs on a round-the-clock basis and schedules preventive maintenance and overhaul jobs for periodic (usually weekly) shutdown shifts.

2. With an Assistant Foreman, supervises a pipefitting crew of seven men to install, repair, dismantle, and assemble piping for water, steam, gas, air, and oil used in production processes (mills, annealing furnaces, lubrication, hydraulics, burning operations, etc.). Maintains and repairs pumps, heating equipment, washroom, and laboratory fixtures in the assigned area.

3. Determines maintenance and repair needs by inspection of equipment and by requests received from Production Foremen. Lines up daily sequence of jobs to be started or completed and assigns tasks to Assistant Foreman or Shift Leaders. Prepares shift working schedules and sets up oiling and other preventive maintenance schedules.

4. Makes temporary loans of additional employees from Central Maintenance groups or labor gangs to meet emergency needs and recommends increases or decreases in the regular workforce.

5. Insures that new men are given adequate training by Assistant Foremen or Group Leaders. Recommends wage-rate changes, promotions, demotions, leaves of absence; grants days off. Answers inquiries or complaints and takes action on cases requiring disciplinary measures —after consultation with the General Foreman if the matter is difficult or unusual.

6. Makes frequent observations to insure that standards of workmanship are maintained and makes final inspection of all difficult or complex repair and maintenance jobs in the assigned area.

7. Prepares requisitions for maintenance materials and replacement parts for equipment and has the requisition approved by the Department Superintendent. Requisitions stock items, tools, and supplies from the Stores Department, indicating proper account or work order to be charged in each case.

8. Assists the General Foreman and the Cold Mill Superintendent in planning and estimating the cost of major maintenance jobs. Strives to keep maintenance and repair costs within normal limits. Checks daily manpower reports to insure correct recording of hours worked and distributions of labor costs.

9. Holds safety meetings with employees and gives instructions in safe methods of work.

RELATIONSHIPS

1. Reports to the General Foreman of Rolling Mills Mechanical Maintenance.

2. Works closely with the Superintendent, Subdivision Foremen, and Turn Foremen of the Cold Mill Department and the Foreman of the hot strip shear line to provide routine and emergency repair and

maintenance services intended to keep the equipment of the Department in good working order at all times. Collaborates with Cold Mill Electrical Maintenance Foremen for the same purpose.

3. Works with Foremen of trade functions in the Central Maintenance organization and with outside contractors who may be responsible for carrying out major construction, overhaul, or alteration projects in the Department.

4. Cooperates with the Engineering Department in the design or modification of equipment to meet the needs of the Department. Cooperates with the Suggestion Committee to investigate, evaluate, and put into effect desirable changes suggested by employees.

ASSISTANT FOREMAN OF MECHANICAL MAINTENANCE

A Large Steel Company

PRIMARY FUNCTION: Assists the Foreman, Blast Furnace and Coke Plant Mechanical Maintenance Department, in supervising the maintenance and repair of Coke Plant mechanical equipment.

DUTIES AND RESPONSIBILITIES

1. Under general direction of the Foreman, plans, directs, and works with a crew of five millwrights, pipefitters, and oilers in repairing, adjusting, and lubricating all mechanical equipment in the Coke and By-Products Plants.

2. Assigns tasks to workmen and makes temporary loans of additional help when needed. Insures that new men are given adequate training.

3. Obtains stock materials and supplies from Stores Department.

4. Makes final inspections and decisions as to acceptability of jobs of moderate complexity.

5. Answers simple inquiries or complaints of employees.

6. Insures that jobs are carried out in a safe manner, inspects tools and equipment, and instructs employees in safe working methods.

RELATIONSHIPS

1. Reports to the Foreman, Blast Furnace and Coke Plant Mechanical Maintenance Department.

2. Collaborates with the Assistant Superintendent and Turn Foremen, Coke Plant, and the Foreman, By-Products Plant, to insure that equipment is in good operating condition at all times. Collaborates with the Blast Furnace Electrical Foreman for the same purpose.

3. Collaborates with the Assistant Foreman, Blast Furnace Mechanical Maintenance, to insure that emergency repair service is made available for coke ovens and the By-Product Plant, on afternoon, night, and weekend shifts, by the Blast Furnace shift repair crews.

UNIT FOREMAN–BUILDING AND MAINTENANCE

An Electronics Company

GENERAL DESCRIPTION OF WORK PERFORMED: Is responsible for establishing job priority and providing facility maintenance of electricity, plumbing, air conditioning, carpentry, and parking lots, in addition to organizing and conducting a comprehensive program of preventive maintenance for all in-plant machinery.

Reports directly to the Plant Maintenance Manager.

PRINCIPAL DUTIES AND RESPONSIBILITIES

1. Supervises, plans, and organizes the performance of all maintenance and requests the purchase of materials necessary to complete all maintenance programs.

2. Establishes and conducts a comprehensive preventive maintenance program for all in-plant machinery.

3. Plans and integrates maintenance so as to cause the least interference with other Department work schedules.

4. Advises the Plant Maintenance Manager of the need for contract

maintenance when any particular project is beyond the capabilities of his workforce.

5. Initiates, subject to higher approval, all types of personnel action.

FACTORS

1. *Job Knowledge*: Must have sound knowledge of building maintenance trades, city and state codes, preventive maintenance programs, job scheduling, material requirements, and purchase procedures, as well as effective leadership principles.

   Must be a high-school graduate with a minimum of three years' experience in supervision in the building and maintenance trades.

2. *Mental Application*: Under the general guidance of the Plant Maintenance Manager, makes decisions pertaining to job scheduling, material purchases, new plant layout, and securing contract maintenance.

3. *Responsibility for Costs:* Is directly responsible for performing all maintenance on a given project while remaining within budget limitations. Poor decisions relating to preventive maintenance on in-plant machinery directly increase costs through substantial damage to capital equipment.

4. *Responsibility for Contacts*: Exercises considerable tact and diplomacy in contacts with personnel of other Departments in order to minimize interference and prevent delay of manufacturing schedules during maintenance or remodeling.

5. *Responsibility for Directing Others*: Exercises direct first-line supervision over a medium-size organizational unit consisting of a crew of 10 to 20 men. Is held accountable for planning, organizing, directing, and appraising the performance of assigned personnel. Initiates, subject to higher approval, all types of personnel action.

Industrial Engineering

Industrial engineering jobs described in this section include those of the chief industrial engineer, manager of industrial engineering, and the heads of various departmental sections.

CHIEF INDUSTRIAL ENGINEER

The Morgan Engineering Company

BASIC FUNCTION: To be responsible to the Plant Engineer for the Company's cost reduction program; for methods and standard practices which include operating methods, material handling methods, plant layout, machine and equipment procurement and replacement, tool design, and service of special tools; for direct labor estimating on subcontract work and unusual new jobs.

SPECIFIC DUTIES

1. To see that personnel in the Industrial Engineering Section are kept fully and currently informed of all pertinent Company policies and that such policies are followed in the Industrial Engineering Section.

2. To supervise the Section in such a manner that all subordinates perform their functions most efficiently.

3. To supervise and coordinate the Company's cost reduction program and to supervise and coordinate the Manufacturing Division's experimental program.

4. With Design Engineering and Manufacturing, to coordinate changes in design or methods as they affect manufacturing operations.

5. To establish and maintain standards of production on all manufacturing operations through the use of recognized techniques.

6. *Cost Reduction Program*

   a. To coordinate all cost reduction items involving technological improvements and methods changes, equipment replacement, general improvements, and suggestions originating in all Divisions.

   b. To estimate cost reduction resulting from capital investment.

   c. To prepare cost comparison reports on funds not capitalized.

   d. To prepare cost reduction reports.

   e. To maintain a post-audit of cost reduction items as requested.

7. *Operating Methods*: To establish and recommend to Shop supervision the most effective methods for performing manufacturing operations.

8. *Material Handling Methods*

   a. To recommend and select material handling equipment.

   b. To make material handling analyses.

   c. To establish material handling techniques and flow.

9. *Plant Layout*

   a. To coordinate and establish floor area utilization as follows:

   (1) Determination of production centers.

   (2) Location and coordination of Departments.

   (3) Arrangement of service centers.

   b. To provide adequate internal and external factory transportation arteries.

   c. To provide for future expansion and growth.

   d. To coordinate methods of applying power and service facilities to equipment.

   e. To consider, and incorporate in Company policies, safety and fire protection regulations and city and state factory codes and laws.

   f. To recommend and assist in establishing proper lighting, heating, and ventilation facilities.

   g. To determine total area required for each operation with regard to:

   (1) Storage of material.

   (2) Material handling at the operation.

   (3) Auxiliary tools, benches, and equipment.

   (4) Ease and safety of task assignment by operator.

   (5) Convenience of making repairs and maintenance to machinery and equipment.

10. *Machine and Equipment Procurement and Replacement*

    a. To make replacement analyses of machinery and equipment, utilizing information and records from various Company Divisions and Departments; to consider data such as space costs, depreciation, service life, purchase date, down time, service and maintenance costs, and so on.

    b. To recommend the replacement or procurement of new equipment to lower operating costs, increase output, improve quality, or offer greater versatility when such action will result in an adequate return for the required investment.

    c. To initiate requisitions and work orders for purchase and installation of all items in the approved capital budget.

    d. To dispose of all worn-out or obsolete machinery and equipment as approved by the Plant Superintendent and Plant Engineer.

11. *Tool Design and Service Methods and Standard Practice*

    a. To expedite special tool service of tools, jigs, dies, and fixtures.

    b. To design special tools, jigs, dies, and fixtures.

    c. To coordinate tool inventory control.

    d. To estimate special tool cost for inquiries and new jobs.

12. *Process Planning for Subcontract and Unusual New Jobs*

    a. To determine operations required.

    b. To establish sequence of operation, equipment to be used, and direct labor hours required.

    c. To determine tool requirements and assist in special tool development.

    d. To suggest to Engineering design changes involving Processing.

    e. To supply cost estimating with estimated direct labor hours on proposals.

13. *Basic Data Processing*

    a. To make methods improvements and corrections in conjunction with Processing group.

    b. To establish equipment capacities.

    c. To develop basic data and establish formulas for calculating standards.

14. *Capital Budgets*: To confer with and assist the various Company Divisions and Departments in the preparation of their annual budgets for capital expenditures, rearrangement of equipment, and machine repairs and tools; to compile such information in a form suitable for use by the Plant Engineer.

15. To provide technical service to Production Departments and Plant Engineering.

INTERMITTENT DUTIES

1. To insure that the duties and responsibilities of subordinates are clearly defined and fixed, and to approve position and job descriptions of immediate subordinates.

2. To recommend to the Plant Engineer major changes in the form and size of the Industrial Engineering Section that are required to meet changed conditions.

3. To recommend to the Plant Engineer the employment, promotion, dismissal, or change in compensation of his immediate subordinates and of the personnel reporting directly to these subordinates.

4. To review and appraise the qualifications of each subordinate periodically as prescribed by the Industrial Relations policies.

5. To confer with the Industrial Relations Division with respect to the development and operation of the Company safety program.

6. To approve requisitions within the Industrial Engineering Section for equipment, supplies, services, or any other expenditures as authorized in the Purchase Requisition Procedure and to recommend to the Plant Engineer amounts in excess of authorized limits.

7. To perform any additional duties requested by the Plant Engineer.

INDUSTRIAL ENGINEERING MANAGER

A Machinery Company

REPORTS TO: Operations Control Manager, on all phases of his work.

SUPERVISES: Section Head–Product Estimating, Methods, and Job Evaluation.
Section Head–Plant Layout, Material Handling, Tool and Die Estimating.
Section Head–Direct Labor Standards.
Industrial Engineers, assigned to projects outside the scope of the above Sections, who report directly to the Industrial Engineering Manager.

DUTIES: Directs the above parties and conducts own activities in performance of the following:

1. Making manufacturing-cost estimates for new or revised products. These estimates cover costs of labor, burden, material, tooling, equipment, facilities, rearrangement, and material handling. Includes determining make vs. buy, operation requirements, routing sequence, and direct labor standard hours.

2. Making manufacturing-cost analyses for proposed changes in design, revised methods of manufacture, new materials, and so on. These proposals may originate within the Industrial Engineering staff, may be requested by other Departments and Divisions, or may be the result of formal programs such as the Job Methods Program, Production–Automation Committee activities, Material and Cost Control Campaign, and the like.

3. Making quotations on piece and tool costs for commercial sale of aluminum and zinc die castings.

4. Preparing and maintaining estimated and actual production routing schedules specifying bills of material, material descriptions, specification numbers, and usage; describing operations required, operation numbers, sequence assignment, standard hours for incentive payment, occupational rate coding, and departmental assignment.

5. Preparing new or revised plant layouts specifying the location of equipment and obtaining and furnishing costs involved.

6. Studying, recommending, specifying, and designing material-handling requirements (conveyors, trucks, trays, pans, chutes, etc.).

7. Conducting studies for requirements and costs of facilities (building, land, and equipment) arising from added production demands, new or added models or products, and short- or long-range expansion planning.

8. Scheduling, coordinating, following up, and closing out trial runs of proposed new materials (raw material approval program).

9. Maintaining tabulated decks for purpose of determining machine loadings and added equipment requirements resulting from schedule adjustments.

10. Developing specifications for packaging aluminum and zinc die castings for commercial sale, export shipments from _____ Plant, interplant and intraplant shipment of products manufactured at _____ and _____ Plants, and materials purchased for _____ Plant manufacturing operations. Packaging requirements for _____ Plant finished goods for domestic sale are specified by the Engineering Division.

11. Conducting studies on feasibility and economics of make vs. buy. Auditing practices in effect for changes in economics.

12. Controlling movement and maintaining records of location for all items of plant equipment.

13. Estimating Company cost of constructing tools, dies, and fixtures for comparison with outside quotes.

14. Preparing occupational descriptions and determining proposed occupational rates by job evaluation. Submitting evaluations to Manager of Labor Relations for approval and negotiation with union. Maintaining and updating occupational descriptions and rates.

15. Initiating, developing, and administering direct and indirect work standards for incentive payment and/or work measurement purposes wherever advisable, practical, and economically desirable. Calculating performance for indirect work measurement programs and incentive earnings for indirect bonus systems. Auditing incentive

standards for needed revisions. Conducting studies (work sampling, etc.) for appraisal of productive efficiency in areas not covered by incentive or work measurement programs.

16. Manufacturing Division coordinating of new-model introductions. This covers the Manufacturing Engineering analysis of product designs; planning, programing, and scheduling of tooling, equipment, and facility changes; parts and material procurement; follow-up, expediting, coordinating, and reporting of progress toward target objectives.

17. Conducting special studies and analyses for Industrial Engineering and management decision making, using scientific and mathematical approaches such as probability theory, scientific sampling, linear programing, queueing theory, scientific inventory control, and economic lot size.

18. Cooperating closely with Chief Tool Engineer toward the end that new or altered tooling is designed and equipment procured to yield the planned economical operation.

19. Calling upon the services of Process Development as needed for aid on troublesome manufacturing processes. May also request its services for mechanization or automation of manufacturing processes.

20. Cooperating with Labor Relations Manager in handling labor relations problems, challenges, and grievances arising from Industrial Engineering activities. Offering recommendations to superiors for improvements in labor relations, union contract provisions, supplementary agreements, and the like.

21. Requesting services of the Factory Training Manager to conduct training programs for Industrial Engineering and other factory management personnel to aid Industrial Engineering objectives and programs.

22. Meeting with line and staff Superintendents to help solve Industrial Engineering problems and, as required, to insure success of Industrial Engineering objectives and programs.

23. Cooperating closely with Product Design on new models to achieve minimum cost consistent with design objectives.

24. Keeping informed on the most up-to-date Industrial Engineering techniques and for initiating _____ use whenever applicable and appropriate. May recommend use of consultants to initiate programs or to guide or supplement staff in carrying them out.

25. Maintaining follow-up on Production Division records stored outside the Company.

MANAGER–INDUSTRIAL ENGINEERING

Allegheny Ludlum Steel Corporation

BASIC FUNCTION: To be responsible to the Works Manager for the administration of the Industrial Engineering functions at these Works in accordance with established corporate policies and with the recommendations of the Director of Industrial Engineering of the Production Division; for the development, establishment, and maintenance of labor standards; for development and participation in the negotiation of incentive wage rates; for participation in the settlement or arbitration of grievances in connection with incentive wage rates; for conducting studies of methods and methods improvement; for plant and equipment layout, studies, and recommendations thereon to Works management and the Works Engineer; for conducting studies of material flow and material handling and making recommendations thereon to Works management; for cost reduction and cost analysis; for the development, analysis, recommendations, and primary approval of equipment justification and appropriation requests as assigned by the Works Manager; for establishing and maintaining workforce controls; for developing and maintaining job descriptions and classifications for non-exempt production and maintenance jobs; and for participation as necessary in negotiating grievances pertaining to job classification and evaluation.

BASIC OBJECTIVE: To administer the Industrial Engineering Department in a manner which will assist in meeting the Corporation's objectives of labor and production costs, operating efficiencies, and plant improvement.

MAJOR DUTIES AND RESPONSIBILITIES

1. *Organization and Personnel*
   a. To maintain and administer an organization which is adequate for the performance of the Industrial Engineering Department's functions.
   b. To assign definite duties and responsibilities to immediate subordinates and to approve position descriptions of immediate subordinates.
   c. To recommend to the Works Manager changes in the organizational structure of his Department required to meet changing conditions.
   d. To see that personnel in the Industrial Engineering Department

are kept fully and currently informed of all pertinent Corporation policies and that such policies are followed in the Department.

e. To recommend to the Works Manager the employment, promotion, dismissal, or change in compensation of personnel under his immediate supervision.

f. To review and appraise periodically the qualifications of each subordinate as prescribed by the employee relations policies.

2. *Labor Standards*

a. To develop, install, and maintain incentive labor standards for production and maintenance personnel through the use of recognized techniques.

b. To maintain complete records of all time studies, production data, calculations, and other material used to develop or change incentive labor standards.

c. To review or check incentive labor standards at the request of the Manager of Operations or the Industrial Relations Department.

d. To review periodically all incentive labor standards for any changes in equipment, processes, quality standards, and the like which might make necessary a revision in the standards; and to recommend revisions whenever they appear desirable.

e. To participate in the negotiation of wage incentive standards with the local union within basic negotiating policies and procedures set up by the Industrial Relations Department.

3. *Methods*

a. To initiate, or to undertake at the request of the Works Manager, the Manager of Operations, or the General Superintendent of any Operating Department, methods studies concerning the phases of Works operation listed below:

(1) Job and workplace simplification.

(2) Works and equipment layout.

(3) Material-handling techniques.

(4) Flow of material.

(5) Utilization and efficiency of services and equipment.

b. To conduct methods-engineering studies of production processes concurrent with or preliminary to the investigating, designing, and recommending of instrumentation and electronic control systems by the Works Engineering Department.

c. To determine necessary methods improvements and to request of Works management that they be installed to assure that incentive labor standards are based on efficient operating practices.

d. To cooperate with the Manager of Quality Control in setting up new processes or changed processes which may require joint effort in setting up work cycles, crew size, and so forth.

4. *Equipment*

   a. To assist Department management, as requested, in determining optimum machine operating speeds, operating procedures, and crew size.

   b. To recommend to Works management and the Works Engineer replacement or changes in methods of operating equipment which is obsolete, costly to operate, or unsuited to its product or use.

   c. To develop and calculate annual savings realizable through proposed equipment modernization or replacement when requested by Works management.

   d. To prepare appropriation requests for new equipment and facilities when instructed by the Works Manager, and to give primary approval thereto.

   e. To work closely with the Engineering Department and the General Engineering Division in developing equipment and facilities justification.

5. *Costs*

   a. To conduct studies of assigned problems relating to any phases of Works operation as requested by the Works Manager.

   b. To coordinate with all other interested departments all cost reduction work involving technological improvements, methods changes, equipment replacement, and general improvement.

   c. To assist Department management, as requested, in special cost surveys.

   d. As requested, to prepare for the Works Manager and the Engineering Department necessary operating, cost, and efficiency studies relating to the selection of auxiliary equipment.

6. *Job Classification*

   a. To establish and maintain production and maintenance job descriptions and classifications for all workers covered by the labor contract.

   b. To maintain complete records of all job classification forms, rates, calculations, or other information used in establishing or changing job classifications or job descriptions.

   c. To review periodically all job descriptions for changes in job content and, at any time, to review descriptions of job classifications at the request of the Industrial Relations Department or the Manager of Operations.

   d. To provide technical assistance in the Industrial Relations Department in preparing for negotiations with the local Union concerning job classifications and to participate in such negotiations as required.

   e. To serve on the Works Salary Committee for non-exempt employees.

7. *General*

   a. To establish and maintain adequate workforce controls.

   b. To write and publish an annual report concerning the activities of the Industrial Engineering Department and showing annual savings resulting from the installation of incentive labor standards, methods improvement, or any other tasks performed by the Department.

   c. To confer with and assist the Industrial Relations Department, as called upon, in processing and investigating employee grievances relating to wage incentives.

   d. To execute Corporation and Production Division policies and procedures with respect to systems and procedures under the general guidance and with the advice of the Director of Industrial Engineering of the Production Division.

   e. To hold periodic meetings with his staff to discuss and review operating policies, plans, assignments, performance, and problems.

   f. To approve the expense accounts of personnel under his immediate supervision.

   g. To perform any additional services requested by the Works Manager.

SUPERVISOR–METHODS AND STANDARDS

A Machinery Manufacturer

FUNCTION: To supervise Department activities concerned with development of methods, evaluation of employee utilization, and preparation of shop routings for current production. To be responsible for effective economical methods. To administer the incentive system to provide accurate time values in accordance with Company policy, labor contract obligations, and Department operating costs.

ORGANIZATIONAL RELATIONSHIPS

1. *Reports to*: Manager of Manufacturing.

2. *Supervises*: Routings, Standards, plus clerical personnel.

3. The Supervisor of Methods and Standards works closely with the supervision and employees of Departments engaged in incentive work to obtain cooperation in the administration of the incentive system. He must cooperate with Manufacturing and Engineering on problems involving materials, methods, and processing to achieve economical manufacturing costs.

SPECIFIC RESPONSIBILITIES: The Supervisor of Methods and Standards shall be accountable for the following broad responsibilities that he shall fulfill through delegation of responsibility and authority and by initiation and execution of action in keeping with the authority vested in his office and the applicable Company policies and procedures.

1. To administer the hourly wage incentive system in accordance with the Company's established policy, practice, and procedure; to be responsible for all hourly wages in excess of base rates paid to employees engaged in incentive work.

2. To check accuracy of engineering specifications and drawings before preparing shop routings. To analyze drawings of new or changed product designs and determine most economical methods on the basis of ordering quantities and available equipment. To prepare master routings specifying operations, sequence, and special tooling.

3. To make copies of shop routings for current production requirements on request for production control.

4. To calculate comparative cost estimates for new or changed products. To prepare analyses of the actual cost of manufacturing components, subassemblies, and complete products and conduct studies to determine more economical methods. To recommend new or changed methods, tooling, or design changes to reduce costs.

5. To break down operations into appropriate elements and make detailed time studies. To compile standard data of elemental time in charts, curves, tabulations, and the like to provide time allowances for manufacturing operations. To make check studies to insure accuracy of data and appropriate application. To revise data to reflect changes in methods, machinery, tooling, and so forth.

6. To analyze manufacturing drawings and calculate the time allowances for the operations to be performed. To investigate and reconcile complaints concerning time allowances. To furnish guidance to supervisors on incentive problems. To participate in all stages of grievance procedure and arbitration involving established time allowance.

7. To train, instruct, and assign work to employees. Within the Department to administer Company personnel policies, enforce safety and health regulations, and take prompt action on employee complaints to achieve good employee morale. To check job performance and advise employees on their good points and shortcomings; to give counsel on growth potential.

8. To plan and schedule work to make most effective use of employee time. To keep Department operating costs within budget allowance.

AUTHORITY: The Supervisor of Methods and Standards is vested with the following responsibilities and authority to be exercised in keeping with all established Corporation and Division policies and procedures.

1. To establish and maintain incentive standards and issue allowances in accordance with Company policies and labor contracts.

2. To determine methods and procedures to be used in manufacturing operations within limits of established practices.

3. To adjudicate wage incentive complaints between the Shop Committee and Standards Supervisors, Superintendents, and Foremen.

4. To initiate purchase requisitions for materials and equipment essential to the effective operation of the Department.

5. To hire authorized employees and recommend salary rate or status changes in the Department. To penalize or discharge any employee in the Department who is guilty of an infraction of Company rules which calls for such a penalty.

6. To establish special rates, applicable to employees deprived of incentive opportunity, for the convenience of the Company.

MANAGER, INDUSTRIAL ENGINEERING DEPARTMENT

American Bosch Arma Corporation

GENERAL RESPONSIBILITIES: Under the direction of the Division Manager, is responsible for planning, developing, maintaining, and administering a continuous program to reduce cost and improve operating efficiency throughout the Division, within the framework of Division policies, to improve the competitive position of the Division.

SPECIFIC RESPONSIBILITIES

1. To establish, maintain, and implement Division Industrial Engineering policies and practices to permit smooth functioning of the department in carrying forward the basic objectives of improved efficiency and reduced cost for Division operations.

2. To assist the Division Manager, through participation on his staff, by making recommendations concerning over-all Division policy and planning and by providing advice and direction on matters concerning Industrial Engineering activities.

3. To conduct specific studies to insure full utilization of Division plant and facilities, improve flow of paperwork and materials, conserve material and labor, and improve control of operations; to analyze results, make recommendations for improvement, and provide services in the implementation of approved changes.

4. To direct a continuous work simplification program within the Division to improve processes and reduce costs.

5. To direct an active cost improvement program; to serve as chairman of the Cost Improvement Committee; and to provide assistance in the analysis, development, and installation of resulting proposals.

6. To plan, in conjunction with other Departments, for continuously improving Division organization to meet changing business needs, and to implement this planning by directing the following activities:

   a. Develop, publish, review, and revise organization charts and functional organization descriptions and assist in their implementation as required.

   b. Prepare clearly defined interdepartmental standard practice instructions and maintain these instructions through periodic review and revision.

   c. Assist in establishing and implementing job descriptions.

   d. Design, review, and revise as necessary all forms used in the conduct of Division business.

7. To direct the review, appraisal, and summary of Division needs for space, facilities, and equipment for support of customer proposals and internal programs; to coordinate the preparation of forecasts of such needs as required; and to review all authorization requests prior to Division Manager approval to insure compatibility with forecasts and current needs.

8. To plan and recommend, as required, additional space best suited to the needs of the Division; to direct the allocation of all plant space in accordance with requirements, the planning of all plant layouts, the scheduling of all approved rearrangements in conjunction with the Plant Engineer, and the reporting of space allocations

to the Controller quarterly as a basis for distribution of indirect expense.

9. To direct the analysis of material-handling requirements and the design and/or development of improved or special material-handling equipment as required.

10. To direct the analysis of control information other than financial controls for the Division and to assist in the formulation of controls and control reports for over-all Division operations; to review and publish planned performance and highlight departures from predicted performance and to recommend corrective action and action necessary to revert to plan.

11. To direct activities to establish, install, and maintain fair labor standards for the Division as a basis for performance estimates and as a measure for actual performance; to assist in the application of labor standards to determine plant facilities, personnel, shoploads, schedules, and forecasts; to review performance against labor standards, analyze deviations, report trends, and recommend corrective action and/or adjust standards as required.

12. To serve as chairman of the Housekeeping Committee, conduct periodic surveys of the Division premises, and report findings to the Division Manager and to all Departments covering cleanliness, safety, fire prevention, and conformance to layout in the areas surveyed.

13. To advise and assist all departments as required in the establishment and maintenance of Department practices.

14. To handle special assignments from the Division Manager as required.

15. To introduce new and revised Industrial Engineering techniques into Department operations to improve continuously the services available to the Division.

16. To staff the Department, establish Department procedures, and supervise and authorize subordinates' activities as specified by Corporation and Division policies, standard practice instructions, and *Common Responsibilities for Personnel in a Supervisory Capacity.*

RELATIONSHIPS WITH OTHER GROUPS

1. Is directly responsible to the Division Manager for the above responsibilities and duties.

2. Is responsible functionally to the Corporate Vice President of Operations for maintaining Division Industrial Engineering activities within the framework of, and consistent with, corporate policies.

3. Works with all Departments in the conduct of Industrial Engineering studies and implementation of findings in work simplification

programs, in the analysis of CIP's, in the development of organization charts and functional descriptions, in the preparation and review of SPI's, in the allocation of space, in the utilization of space and facilities, in the planning of plant layout, in the planning of material-handling equipment, in the improvement of housekeeping, and in the reporting and analysis of control information.

4. Works with the Plant Engineer in establishing costs and schedules for moves and rearrangements, assisting in the accomplishment of moves and rearrangements as required.

5. Works with the Industrial Security Department in the incorporation, in plant layouts, of adequate security measures and fire protection for all buildings, sites, and building areas.

6. Works with the Employee Relations Department in the incorporation of adequate safety measures in all plant layouts, in the analysis of employee suggestions, in the resolution of problems arising from the application of labor standards, in the provision of supporting data for job descriptions, in the implementation of employee relations policies and controls via standard practice instructions, and in the promotion of a better understanding among employees of cost improvement, standards, and other Department activities.

7. Works with the Controller's Department in the application of standards to cost estimates, in the review and summarization of space and facilities to support proposals or forecasts, in the developing and maintaining of factory operating control reports, in the detailed analysis of CIP's, in the quarterly report of space allocations, and in the implementation of financial policies and controls via standard practice instructions.

8. Works with the Product Quality Department in the implementation of quality control policies and controls via standard practice instructions.

9. Works with the Plant Engineering, Production Control, Traffic, and Product Quality Departments in the establishment and application of indirect labor standards.

10. Works with the Production Control Department in the application of standards to shoploading and scheduling.

11. Works with the Tool and Processing Department in the improvement of tools, methods, and processes and in the application of standards to operations.

12. Serves as chairman of the Cost Improvement Committee.

13. Serves as chairman of the Housekeeping Committee.

14. Participates, through a representative, in the work of the Suggestion Committee.

15. Contacts the staff of the Corporate Vice President of Operations, as instructed, in the procurement of additional plant space and in the establishment of labor standards and standard practice instructions.

16. Contacts cognizant Department of Defense representatives, through appropriate channels, in the establishment and maintenance of a conservation program.

17. Maintains contact with other companies and organizations for the exchange and evaluation of the latest developments in the field of industrial engineering.

AUTHORITY: Has full authority necessary to carry out the responsibilities described herein, including the authority to:

1. Hire, change salaries or classifications, transfer, and discharge subordinates subject to supplementary approvals as required by Division policy and practices, and as specified in the standard practice instructions.

2. Approve authorization requests; plant rearrangements; petty-cash expenditures; purchase of books, pamphlets, and subscriptions; entertainment expenses and expenditures for special activities such as attendance at technical meetings; employee training and tuition expenses as specified in standard practice instructions.

3. Approve travel expenses for subordinates and prospective employees within the limits specified in the standard practice instructions.

HEAD–PROCEDURES AND OPERATING CONTROLS SECTION
INDUSTRIAL ENGINEERING DEPARTMENT

American Bosch Arma Corporation

ORGANIZATIONAL RELATIONSHIPS

Responsible to: Manager–Industrial Engineering Department.

Responsible for: Procedures and Operating Controls Section.

OCCUPATIONAL SUMMARY

1. Plan, coordinate, and direct the development of management controls, the maintenance of standardized Departmental organizations, and the institution of adequate controls to insure optimum Division performance at minimum cost.

2. Establish the approaches to be taken in the measurement of Departmental operations and generate the operating cost standards against which Departmental performance can be monitored.

RESPONSIBILITIES

1. Review recommendations of subordinates pertaining to proposed organizational changes in addition to staffing, equipment, and/or procedures changes in order to assure improved Departmental performance at minimum cost; may confer with various levels of Division management for the purpose of resolving problems and obtaining concurrence regarding anticipated changes.

2. Be responsible for providing analyses of Division business systems, preparation of standard practice instructions, and development of new and/or revised forms; and for the generation of recommendations for appropriate business equipment designed to provide optimum methods for Division business operations at minimum cost.

3. Direct the analyses of current and future operating programs and evaluate the resulting recommendations regarding changes in the assignment of functions and revisions to organizational structures for completeness, adequacy, and compliance to Division and corporate policy.

4. Plan, coordinate, direct and review the efforts of subordinate personnel engaged in the following activities:

   a. Analysis of current and future operating programs for the purpose of developing recommendations regarding changes in management controls, organization structure, adequacy of administrative practices, and suitability of Departmental layout and equipment for optimum Departmental operation.

   b. Planning and implementation of a Division operating controls program to report Departmental and Division performance against operating cost standards.

   c. Measurement of Departmental operating costs, including the direction of personnel from other Departments who may be assigned to participate in such study, to establish standards for Departmental operating costs, and to establish reporting techniques by which performance may be monitored on a continuing basis.

   d. Analysis of factors contributing to Departmental workload and expenditures and establishment of statistical basis for flexibility in Departmental standards to reflect variations in demand for Departmental activity as level and nature of Division activities change.

e. Review of performance versus Departmental operating cost standards; analysis of significant deviations; recommendations for corrective action to Departmental management and/or adjustment of standards as required; revision of standards when functions, equipment, or procedures change.

f. Development, recommendation, and assistance to Divisional management personnel in the installation of new and/or revised management controls for planning, forecasting, and monitoring Division and Department staffing and expenditures.

g. Periodic review of all existing Division reports, appraisal of their effectiveness, and recommendations on changes in the reporting structure and/or report formats to provide adequate management information at minimum cost.

h. Planning, preparation, and publication of an organization manual for the Division, including organizational charts and functional organizational descriptions and their maintenance on a current basis.

i. Coordination of the analysis and maintenance of organizational plans and the submission of recommendations for adequate inventory and depth of management personnel.

j. Review of proposed organizational changes for need, consistency with good organizational practice, cost, and conformance to Division and Corporate policy; initiation of action for Division and Corporate approval for any necessary deviations from established organizational policy. Editing of all organization change announcements for timeliness and conformance to organizational policy.

k. Study of Division business operations to simplify them and/or provide better and more timely controls at less cost. Preparation, issuance, and maintenance of interdepartmental standard practice instructions. Preparation and approval for use of new and/or revised forms.

l. Periodic review of Division operations to assure adequacy of and conformance to existing standard practice instructions and organizational and functional charts. Initiation or recommendation of corrective action as required.

CONTACTS

1. Maintain constant and numerous contacts with all levels of management in the normal performance of job duties which may include such controversial and delicate matters as contemplated organizational changes.

2. Initiate and maintain contacts with other companies and outside sources of information to keep abreast of the latest developments and advances in the "state of the art."

AUTHORITY

1. Effectively recommend changes in structure of management controls and establish and maintain departmental operating control standards and organizational changes in accordance with executive management planning.
2. Approve selection of subordinate personnel of rank lower than immediate subordinates; recommend selection of personnel for immediately subordinate positions; recommend approval of changes and use authority to effectively recommend hiring, firing, and disciplinary action.
3. Use authority to request and receive information relative to his activity from all personnel in the Company.

QUALIFICATIONS

1. Bachelor's degree in industrial engineering, liberal arts, economics, or business administration, or the equivalent as evidenced by the successful completion of extensive studies at an accredited college or university.
2. Eight years' diversified experience in industrial engineering with emphasis in the areas of standards, procedures, organization development work, work measurement, systems analysis, plant layout, cost control, statistical analysis, and the application of forecasting techniques. Five years of this experience should be in a supervisory capacity dealing with executive management.

HEAD–STANDARDS AND COST IMPROVEMENT SECTION
INDUSTRIAL ENGINEERING DEPARTMENT

American Bosch Arma Corporation

ORGANIZATIONAL RELATIONSHIPS

Responsible to: Manager, Industrial Engineering Department.
Responsible for: Standards and Cost Improvement Section.

OCCUPATIONAL SUMMARY

1. To plan, supervise, and coordinate the work of the Standards and Cost Improvement Section personnel in establishing, developing, and evaluating labor standards.

2. To develop and maintain a program designed to analyze and evaluate Departmental operating performance throughout the Division, including the highlighting of problem areas.

3. To maintain a sound cost improvement program for the investigation, evaluation, and installation of cost improvement proposals.

RESPONSIBILITIES

1. Analyzes labor operations with a view to establishing fair labor standards and secures understanding and acceptance of standards by affected supervision.

2. Studies Departmental operations to establish standards of operating efficiency; secures understanding and acceptance of established standards by affected management.

3. Analyzes departures from standard in both labor operations and Departmental operations to discover problem areas; recommends methods of improving performance and assists in installation.

4. Stimulates interest in cost improvement, assists in establishing Departmental quotas, and acts as chairman of Cost Improvement Committee, which examines feasibility and value of proposals.

5. Assists in the application of labor and Departmental standards to estimating and cost control.

6. Periodically reviews Division reports for need, proper content, distribution, and effectiveness as instruments for managerial control.

CONTACTS: Contacts all Department Heads and executive management in the performance of job duties.

AUTHORITY

1. Establishes and approves labor standards to improve the productive efficiency of facilities and personnel; establishes and approves operating control reports to aid management.

2. Approves selection of subordinate personnel of rank lower than immediate subordinates; recommends selection of personnel for immediately subordinate positions; makes or approves changes to superior. Has authority to effectively recommend hiring, firing, and disciplinary action.

3. Has the authority to request information relative to his activity from all personnel in the Company.

QUALIFICATIONS

1. Bachelor's degree in industrial engineering or equivalent in applicable experience or self-education.

2. Six years of diversified experience in time and motion study, statistical control, and forecasting techniques in manufacturing. Three years of this experience should be in a supervisory capacity.

HEAD–FACILITIES PLANNING SECTION
INDUSTRIAL ENGINEERING DEPARTMENT

American Bosch Arma Corporation

ORGANIZATIONAL RELATIONSHIPS

Responsible to: Manager, Industrial Engineering Department.
Responsible for: Facilities Planning Section.

OCCUPATIONAL SUMMARY: Plan, coordinate, and direct the planning and development of detailed layouts for the installation and rearrangement of new or existing equipment and facilities; be responsible for the design, development, and/or selection of standard material handling equipment; review, analyze, and affirm justification for space and equipment requirements; work with other Departments to obtain facilities and/or dispose of surplus equipment.

RESPONSIBILITIES

1. Review recommendations of subordinates pertaining to the allocation and planning of plant and office layout; review space analysis studies; review Arma estimate requests to determine equipment and space requirements, including abnormal rearrangement and leasehold improvement costs for new or proposed contracts; determine type, amount, and value of equipment to be acquired. May confer with various levels of Division management for the purpose of resolving problems and obtaining concurrence regarding anticipated changes.

2. Be responsible for analysis of, and recommendations for, current and future operating programs to provide adequate facilities for the manufacture of Division products in the most efficient and economical manner.

3. Plan, coordinate, direct, and review the efforts of subordinate personnel engaged in the following activities:

   a. Supervision of the equipment program, determining the need for equipment and machinery to produce Arma Division products.

   b. Analysis of Arma estimate requests and submission of facilities cost data to the Contracts Department and/or Controller's Department.

   c. Review of surplus and/or inactive equipment records to determine availability of needed equipment.

   d. Maintenance of active, inactive, and surplus equipment and machinery records; proposals for the disposition of such equipment as it becomes obsolete.

4. Establish and maintain a master schedule of facilities activities, including estimate requests, facility applications, equipment improvement program, master facilities plan, cost studies, screenings, authorization request reviews, and expenditure forecasts.

5. Review and analyze all authorization requests for rearrangements, equipment, and surplus equipment.

6. Supervise the preparation of facilities applications, expenditure forecasts, and housekeeping reports.

7. Review, evaluate, and summarize Division space requirements for support of customer proposals and internal programs. Supervise the layout of available space and insure most effective use of space. Allocate available plant space in accordance with operating requirements and inform Controller of such allocation.

8. Establish and maintain a master schedule of all Division plant layout activities. Check layouts for conformance to layout standards; Division policy; and safety, fire, and building code regulations. Collaborate with management to effect layout changes and describe future benefits of the change to the Company and employees.

9. Analyze material handling requirements; design, develop, and/or select improved handling equipment as required.

CONTACTS

1. Maintain numerous contacts with all levels of management in the normal performance of job duties.

2. Initiate and maintain contact with equipment and machinery manufacturers and government personnel.

AUTHORITY

1. Establish and recommend new and revised plant layouts to improve the efficiency of facilities and personnel.
2. Design and develop improved handling equipment as required.
3. Approve selection of subordinate personnel of rank lower than immediate subordinates; recommend selection of personnel for immediately subordinate positions; make or approve changes to superior. Effectively recommend hiring, firing, and disciplinary action.
4. Request information relative to his activity from all personnel in the Company and obtain information from outside sources.

QUALIFICATIONS

1. Bachelor's degree in industrial engineering, civil engineering, or mechanical engineering, or equivalent in applicable experience or self-education.
2. Eight years of diversified experience in plant layout, methods, and/ or construction work in the manufacturing industry. Two years in a supervisory capacity dealing with executive and manufacturing management.

Quality Control and Reliability Engineering

The changes in emphasis and methods which have been brought about in recent years in the field of quality management are reflected by the diversity of position titles and responsibilities found in this function.

MANAGER OF QUALITY CONTROL

An Aircraft Company

BASIC FUNCTION: To coordinate the activities of the Quality Control Department in accordance with Company standards and contract requirements.

REPORTS TO: Vice President and Manager of _____ Division.

RESPONSIBILITIES

1. *The Manager of Quality Control is directly responsible for:*

    a. Establishing and implementing a system for inspecting and auditing the quality of products or services produced, to assure that all supplies or services offered for customer acceptance and delivery conform to the requirements of the applicable contract and associated documents.

    b. Assessing the quality of the manufactured product; establishing and implementing a corrective action system, in conjunction with other responsible Departments, which will correct defects in the production processes of engineering, procurement, and manufacturing and provide acceptable product quality at optimum economy.

    c. Monitoring and assessing product reliability, recommending product reliability improvements, and coordinating the reliability functions of all Departments.

2. *To fulfill these responsibilities, the Manager supervises the duties of each Section of the Quality Control Department.*

    a. Inspection. The function of the Inspection Section encompasses quality control, process control, and factory inspection and includes the following activities:

    (1) Determining inspection requirements and establishing methods of inspection for all items in the end product, whether manufactured by the Company or procured from vendors or subcontractors.

    (2) Inspecting the product from experimental to production phases during all stages of manufacture from procurement to final acceptance, in order to insure that the end product meets all the requirements of the contract and Company policy.

    (3) Reviewing vendors' and subcontractors' quality control, reliability, capability, and performance. Evaluating vendors' conformance to established criteria, to aid in the selection of vendors.

    (4) Controlling metallurgical and chemical processes in order to assure that processed parts will meet contract requirements.

    (5) Establishing and applying inspection procedures to insure that maintenance and calibration of all equipment used to inspect the product are adequately controlled to insure the continuing ability of such equipment to perform its designated function.

b. Reliability. Functions include reliability and quality audit, quality testing, and fiscal control, as effected by the following duties:

(1) Collecting and analyzing data from process analysis, production inspection, testing, and actual performance. Reporting the results and taking necessary steps for initiating corrections to the production processes.

(2) Coordinating the reliability functions of all Departments.

(3) Assessing product reliability by means of production testing; environmental testing; and statistical analysis of engineering, manufacturing, and field data. Assuring that necessary corrective action is taken, consistent with contract requirements and the state of technological development.

c. Project control. Responsibilities are:

(1) Interpreting contracts, specifications, and engineering drawings, particularly as they affect the quality and reliability of the product.

(2) Preparing for each product a general quality control plan from which detailed plans and procedures can be devised.

(3) Maintaining continuous project surveillance to detect real or potential problems affecting product quality and reliability and project cost and schedule.

(4) Promptly resolving Department problems affecting the project.

(5) Implementing temporary special Department action when necessary to break project bottlenecks or resolve urgent problems.

(6) Coordinating with other appropriate Departments when necessary to resolve problems affecting product quality and reliability and project cost and schedule.

(7) Providing Department representatives on project task teams.

(8) Interpreting Company and Departmental policies as they may apply to project quality and reliability problems.

(9) Maintaining Departmental project control to assure that the delivered product is of the highest quality and greatest reliability consistent with requirements, project costs, and delivery schedule.

3. The Manager of Quality Control is also responsible for supervising the Value Control Coordinator in the following capacities:

a. Working as a member of the Company's Value Control group on interdepartmental and Company value control problems.

    b. Assisting the Manager of Quality Control in implementing and sustaining value control techniques within the Department.

    c. Assisting the Chief Value Control Coordinator in value control training on Company and Department levels.

    d. Investigating and making recommendations in areas of poor value control on Company and Departmental levels.

QUALITY CONTROL SUPERVISOR

A Machinery Maker

FUNCTION: To plan, direct, and coordinate activities to assure maintenance of optimum quality in manufactured products at the Division. To supervise, directly and through subordinate supervisors, all aspects of the activities of the Quality Control Department concerned with: studying, developing, installing, and maintaining quality control methods and procedures; fostering positive employee attitudes with respect to quality workmanship; inspecting manufactured products; processing quality complaints and instituting action to eliminate their recurrence; and measuring and reporting results of efforts to achieve an effective defect prevention program. To be responsible for maintaining optimum quality standards consistent with economical costs, quality and quantity of work of personnel supervised, and Department operating costs.

ORGANIZATIONAL RELATIONSHIP

1. *Reports to:* Manager of Manufacturing.

2. *Supervises:* Chief Inspector.

3. The Quality Control Supervisor works closely with employees and supervisors to assure understanding of the importance of quality to the success of the Company and to obtain cooperation on preventive measures.

SPECIFIC RESPONSIBILITIES: The Quality Control Supervisor shall be accountable for the following broad responsibilities that he shall fulfill through delegation of responsibility and authority and by initiation and execution of action in keeping with the authority vested in his office and the applicable Company policies and procedures.

1. To establish and maintain adequate quality control and inspection techniques, procedures, and coverage, such as inspection of incoming material, work in process, and finished products to assure that the established standards of quality, accuracy, workmanship, and performance are maintained. To develop special methods or procedures when necessary.

2. To investigate all quality complaints and, with Engineering, see that corrective measures are applied to prevent similar occurrences in the future. To investigate major items found to be defective and determine whether to salvage or scrap. In cases of salvage, to issue instructions on the type of repair work to be performed.

3. To compile records and initiate and maintain a continuous study of all defective and spoiled work, including scrap and rework expense, and recommend any improved methods, procedures, or other changes that will result in improved quality consistent with economical cost to the Company.

4. To stimulate and maintain employee interest in quality control. To utilize various media, such as articles in the house organ, display of scrapped parts, posters, and supervisory participation, to appeal to employees' pride in producing a quality product.

5. To establish quality controls for critical parts, be alert to any conditions which might lead to off-standard products, and recommend necessary changes.

6. To initiate and carry out equipment and process studies where it appears that design specifications are making it difficult to produce an acceptable product at satisfactory cost.

7. To maintain a current knowledge of developments in the field of inspection and testing of materials and products by attending meetings and conferences conducted by industry and service organizations, reviewing trade literature and bulletins, interviewing inspection equipment manufacturers' representatives, and so forth, in order to recommend innovations to improve the quality, economy, and effectiveness of the Company's operations.

8. To develop and maintain effective two-way communication internally and with other concerned Departments and/or Sections of the Company to assure adequate dissemination of information concerning plans, new developments, and inspection programs.

9. To train, instruct, and assign work to employees. To administer Company personnel policies, enforce safety and health regulations, and take prompt action on employee complaints so as to achieve good employee morale within the Department. To represent the Department at all stages of the grievance procedure and arbitration. To maintain current level of employee morale and keep management

informed. To review performance of employees and advise them on good points and shortcomings.

10. To plan and schedule work and make effective use of employees' time. To keep Department operating expenses within budget allowance.

AUTHORITY: The Quality Control Supervisor is vested with the following authority to be exercised in keeping with all established Company policies and procedures in carrying out the responsibilities of the office.

1. To recommend design, tooling, and methods changes to improve quality and reduce costs.

2. To establish various quality standards as required.

3. To reject any material, parts, or products that fail to meet established quality standards.

4. To initiate purchase requisitions for inspection, equipment, and supplies.

5. To penalize or discharge any employee in the Department who has been found guilty of an infraction of Company rules calling for such penalty.

6. To employ authorized personnel and recommend upgrading, downgrading, and wage and salary rate changes for Department employees.

7. To settle complaints and grievances in the Department within the limits of established policy and labor agreement obligations.

MANAGER–RELIABILITY AND QUALITY CONTROL

An Instrument Maker

REPORTS TO: Manager, Air Armament Division.

REPORTING TO HIM: Reliability and Quality Control Superintendent.
Reliability and Quality Assurance Superintendent.
Inspection Superintendent.
Test Equipment Design and Construction Supervisor.
Test Engineering Department Head.
Test Superintendent.

SUMMARY: Directs, through key supervisory personnel, employees engaged in performing test equipment engineering, design, and construction; inspection and testing of products, equipment, and incoming materials; and investigating, developing, and conducting reliability and quality control programs.

DUTIES

1. Develops, for approval, reliability and quality control organization; policies; work systems and procedures; and budget forecasts of manpower, facilities, and expenses.

2. Confers with management, customer, subcontractor, and vendor representatives in planning, scheduling, coordinating, and directing reliability and quality control programs in conformance with customer requirements, engineering specifications, and production schedules.

3. Directs, through key supervisory personnel, employees engaged in:

    a. Engineering, designing, and developing special test equipment and product test tooling programs.

    b. Generating estimates of the quality control portion of quotation estimates.

    c. Reviewing and approving engineering test specifications.

    d. Studying, evaluating, and developing test methods, techniques, and procedures.

    e. Planning and scheduling the manufacture or procurement of test equipment.

    f. Calibrating and maintaining test equipment; operating and maintaining measurement standards for the control of all instruments used in quality control and manufacturing.

    g. Performing prototype tests of new products to eliminate production problems, functional and environmental tests, special sampling tests, and so forth, in conformance with product drawings and specifications, military specifications, and standard practice instructions.

    h. Inspecting parts, materials, tools, equipment, and products; reviewing and approving inspection fixtures and gauges designed by Manufacturing Engineering.

    i. Developing, establishing, maintaining, and controlling an effective quality assurance program to facilitate detection, correction, and prevention of defects in materials, parts, assemblies, and products; evaluating and monitoring vendor and subcontractor quality performance.

    j. Establishing and maintaining reliability programs and procedures to insure that devices perform their intended functions within specified time limits under environmental conditions. Specific responsibilities include providing mathematical models, component reliability indices, and reliability standard practice instructions for design and acceptance procedures; scheduling design review audits and analyses; establishing vendor reliability ratings, devising environmental studies for parts and components; performing probability analyses of failure.

k. Preparing, maintaining, and distributing quality control Standard Practice Instructions.

l. Reviewing all Air Armament capital requests for test equipment and maintaining accountability for customer property and capital equipment.

4. Trains, motivates, develops, and counsels personnel under his direction to improve job performance and insure effective and economical operations.

5. Maintains harmonious employee relations and assists subordinates in the handling of grievances; participates in contract negotiations and changes as they affect activities under his direction.

6. Appraises employee performance and gives intermediate approval on recommendations for personnel procurements, salary increases, promotions, demotions, and dismissals in accordance with work requirements and within authorized limits.

SUPERVISOR, PROCESS QUALITY CONTROL

The Carborundum Company

I. GENERAL RESPONSIBILITY: To be responsible for supervising the quality control activities of the Manufacturing Branch to meet established specifications at economic manufacturing and inspection costs; for planning and supervising process and final inspection to minimize production of off-grade product, scrap, and waste; for using established statistical inspection, control, and sampling plans provided by Technical Branch; for collecting data appropriate to process control and reporting product quality; for relating costs of defect prevention, inspection, rework, and product failure to operator quality training and process levels specified to meet customer requirements or company standards; for carrying out gauge control and maintenance program; for conducting process capability studies;

and for training inspectors. May be assigned to supervise manufacturing operations as directed.

II. ORGANIZATIONAL RELATIONSHIPS

    A. *Line:* Responsible to: Manager, Manufacturing Services. Supervises: Process Quality Control Engineer.

    B. *Staff:* Receives advice related to process control from: Quality Control Department Manager, Technical Branch; Branch Managers; CAD Managers and Superintendents; Foremen, Manufacturing Branch. Provides advice on process control to: Inspectors, Foremen, Superintendents, Managers of Manufacturing Branch and Technical Branch, Department Managers.

III. SPECIFIC DUTIES

KIND OF ACTIVITY	SCOPE	TYPE OF ACTION
A. *Line or Operational*		
1. Inspection.	Coated Abrasives Division.	Plans, implements, and supervises in-process and final product inspection. Adjusts the amount and kind of measurement and examination within specification to match product value and need. Supervises re-inspection of rejected material by production operators or inspectors. Supervises inspection of trial or experimental material during special process studies carried out jointly with Quality Control Department–Technical Branch.
2. Quality standards.	Coated Abrasives Division.	Keeps inspection manuals containing test and inspection specifications current and accessible to inspectors. Provides and maintains suitable inspection standards such as product samples, photographs, and descriptions. Obtains replacements as necessary and protects them from damage or deterioration.

III. SPECIFIC DUTIES (cont'd)

KIND OF ACTIVITY	SCOPE	TYPE OF ACTION
A. *Line or Operational* (cont'd)		
3. Specifications.	Coated Abrasives Division.	Brings to attention of Quality Control Department the need for improvements in test and inspection specifications based on in-process experience. Identifies need for control specification and manufacturing method revision from operating experience and process capability studies.
4. Process control.	Coated Abrasives Division.	Sets up and uses statistical quality control charts and methods to minimize manufacture of defective product. Advises foremen and operators when product or process is outside of control or specification limits. Checks on corrective action taken and product quality resulting therefrom. Uses knowledge to prevent defects in future. Detects, from process control records and analysis, substandard quality due to raw materials. Identifies attributes of raw material specifications needing expansion. Prepares information and samples for discussion with vendor.
5. Reports of quality levels and costs.	Coated Abrasives Division.	Reports, routinely and effectively, product and process quality levels in each Manufacturing Department from inspection and process control data. Appraises actual versus specified quality level and relates to costs. Analyzes data for trends, shifts in plant

III. SPECIFIC DUTIES (cont'd)

KIND OF ACTIVITY	SCOPE	TYPE OF ACTION

A. *Line or Operational*
   (cont'd)

		quality, or unintentional changes. Reviews material use versus allowances, scrap, and rework. Relates prevention, appraisal, correction, and failure costs to inspection, process control, audit procedures, and training.
6. Gauging and gauge control.	Coated Abrasives Division.	Identifies gauging requirements from specifications. Selects appropriate gauging methods. Requisitions all gauging and instruments for Manufacturing Branch. Reviews preferred types with Quality Control Department–Technical Branch before ordering. Carries out gauge control program on timely basis. Schedules gauges and measuring instruments for calibration by Technical Branch or Maintenance Department as appropriate. Orders replacements or maintenance on deficient gauges. Audits use of gauges in plant.
7. Process capability.	Coated Abrasives Division.	Conducts statistical process capability studies to establish ability of equipment and operators to maintain product or process uniformity at specified levels. From such studies, identifies assignable and correctable causes that disrupt production and product quality. Develops information for maintenance.
8. Training.	Coated	Trains operators and inspectors

III. Specific Duties (cont'd)

KIND OF ACTIVITY	SCOPE	TYPE OF ACTION
A. *Line or Operational* (cont'd)		
	Abrasives Division.	in specific inspection jobs. Explains quality standards and interpretation of specifications. Audits inspection training. Qualifies inspectors. Notifies Personnel Department of qualified and incapable inspectors.
9. Administration.	Coated Abrasives Division.	Supervises record keeping, data analysis, and reporting.
10. Supervision of manufacturing operations.	Coated Abrasives Division.	May be assigned to supervise manufacturing operations as directed.
B. *Staff or Functional*		
1. Advisory.	Coated Abrasives Division.	Advises Division personnel on process control. Works with Quality Control Department to evaluate alternative inspection, process, or other quality control methods in the Manufacturing Branch.

MANAGER–QUALITY CONTROL

Allegheny Ludlum Steel Corporation

BASIC FUNCTION: To be responsible to the Works Manager, Dunkirk, for the administration of quality control functions at the Dunkirk Works in accordance with established Corporation policies and with recommendations of the Vice President and Technical Director, and the Chief Metallurgist and the Chief Chemist of the Technical Division, including metallurgical analysis and control, chemical control, physical inspection, and assigned customer contacts regarding complaints and claims arising from inferior quality.

BASIC OBJECTIVE: To administer the development and operation of quality control at the Dunkirk Works in a manner which will assist in meeting the Corporation's objectives of product quality and which will provide for the development and maintenance of an able and progressive organization.

MAJOR DUTIES AND RESPONSIBILITIES

1. *Organization and Personnel*
   a. To select, train, maintain, and administer an organization which is adequate for the performance of the Quality Control Department's functions.
   b. To assign definite duties and responsibilities to immediate subordinates and to approve position descriptions of immediate subordinates.
   c. To recommend to the Works Manager changes in the organizational structure of his Department required to meet changing conditions.
   d. To see that personnel in the Quality Control Department are kept fully and currently informed of all pertinent Company policies and that such policies are followed in the Department.
   e. To recommend to the Works Manager the employment, promotion, dismissal, or change in compensation of personnel under his immediate supervision.
   f. To review and appraise periodically the qualifications of each subordinate as prescribed by the employee relations policies.

2. *Quality Control*
   a. To coordinate the functions of the Quality Control Department to assure optimum quality at lowest cost.
   b. To direct the metallurgical analysis and control of the Works' products at each stage of production.
   c. To direct the chemical analysis and control of the Works' products at each stage of production.
   d. To direct the physical inspection of all materials in process, establishing gauges, sizes, and tolerances and paying particular attention to surface conditions and the analysis of physical test

results; to make prompt and accurate decisions on the disposition of off-test material, determining whether it can be reclaimed by further processing, can be re-applied on another order, or must be scrapped.

e. To direct the maintenance of a complete file of product specifications and quality requirements for all products made at these Works.

f. To maintain files on individual customers' special requirements or deviations from the Corporation's established levels of quality.

g. To establish and maintain a set of process specifications to serve as production instructions for all processes concerning metallurgical or chemical phases of the manufacturing cycle.

h. To contact customers, as requested by the Works Manager, regarding complaints and claims arising from inferior quality.

3. *Costs*

a. To cooperate, as requested, with the Industrial Engineering Department, advising it on the setting of labor standards for operations involving processes controlled by the Quality Control Department.

b. To direct the Quality Control Department in efforts to improve the quality of products, eliminate processes and operations through changes in manufacturing procedures, and reduce costs of existing processes wherever possible.

c. To analyze results and to make every effort to increase yield and reduce scrap.

d. To assist, as requested, any Operating or Staff Department on cost problems involving metallurgical or chemical processes.

4. *General*

a. To contact customers, as requested by the Works Manager, on technical problems involving the use of the Works' products in the customers' plants.

b. To assure that the Quality Control Department keeps abreast of the latest technological advances in its field and to recommend to the Works Manager up-to-date procedures for use at the Dunkirk Works.

c. To coordinate the efforts of the Quality Control Department to provide maximum service to the Operating Departments at the least cost and to enable them to maintain the schedules set by the Production Control Departments.

d. To execute Technical Division policies and procedures with respect to related metallurgical and chemical functions under the general guidance and with the advice of the Vice President, the Chief Metallurgist, and the Chief Chemist of the Technical Division.

e. To maintain good labor relations with all Department employees; to carry out all applicable labor agreement provisions (both U.S.W. production and maintenance and salary organizations) and all policies set by the Industrial Relations Department.

f. To encourage safe operating practices and conditions.

g. To be responsible for requisitions originating within his Department for equipment, supplies, or services.

h. To hold periodic meetings with subordinate supervisors to discuss and review operating policies, plans, performance, and problems.

i. To perform any additional duties as requested by the Works Manager.

ASSISTANT DIRECTOR, QUALITY CONTROL AND INSPECTION

An Electronics Company

GENERAL FUNCTIONS: To supervise Quality Control and Inspection Division operation in assigned plants; plan and schedule work for immediate staff; make recommendations pertaining to personnel and functions of Division; train supervisory members of Division. Be responsible for insuring that proper quality control and inspection techniques are instituted and maintained in each plant. Institute process controls and insure that customer specifications and engineering designs are specified in a manufacturable and achievable manner.

SPECIFIC DUTIES

1. Supervises Quality Control and Inspection Division in assigned plants.
2. Plans, schedules, and assigns work to members of staff.
3. Is responsible for administration, conduct, quality, and quantity of work in Division.

4. Recommends pay increases, promotions, transfers, and dismissals for members of Division.

5. Interviews applicants for jobs in Division.

6. Trains Division supervisory members in their functions and duties.

7. Institutes and/or recommends changes and procedures in operations performed by the Division.

8. Encourages and assists in professional development of his staff members, and encourages their participation in scientific societies.

9. Advises and assists the Director of Engineering and Quality Control in formulating proposals for policies, improvements, and changes in procedure, product design and specifications, processes, tools, equipment, and items that would lead to cost reduction.

10. Encourages suggestions for improvements in quality control and inspection equipment and processes.

11. Arranges for proper maintenance, operation, and orderliness of machinery, equipment, facilities, and material in process within the area of his jurisdiction.

12. Reduces manufacturing cost; controls the use of material, supplies, tools, and jigs, and the cost of labor and operating expense within the Division.

13. Fulfills the requirements of standard practice instructions or industrial relations manual with respect to records, requisitions, report forms, and authorizations which apply to the Division.

14. Prepares, as required, reports on progress, production, work on specific jobs, attendance, discipline, and general Division problems.

15. Attends meetings to give and receive information on improvement in utilization of material, personnel, and methods.

16. Uses and cooperates with the Service Departments to help solve Division problems and the problems of other Departments.

17. Maintains Company quality standards on outgoing products through the Supervisor of Quality Control and Inspection in each plant.

18. Acts as an arbiter in those instances where the Plant Manager and the Supervisor of Quality Control and Inspection do not agree as to the proper disposition of material, either in the form of finished product or as material in process.

19. Employs and appoints the Supervisor of Quality Control and Inspection in each plant with the cooperation of the Plant Manager.

20. Maintains a consulting service for the plants and engineering staff on factory experiment procedures, plant experiment procedures, and evaluation of quality control procedures.

21. Acts as customer's representative in the plant, in order to assure the

Corporation that the customer's product will arrive in acceptable and satisfactory condition.

22. Maintains a system for evaluation and investigation of complaints and product difficulties.

23. Assists the Purchasing Department in obtaining satisfactory vendor relations and vendor compliance with specifications.

24. Advises management on procedures which may help to improve operation of the Plant or of the Company business.

25. Assists management in making decisions as to the advisability of product manufacture.

26. Plans, or supervises the planning of, statistical experiments as a service to Engineering and Design Departments on production and product difficulties; analyzes or supervises the analysis of the results of such experiments.

27. Supervises or conducts investigations of process capabilities. Continually reviews specifications in order to bring them in line with customer requirements. Reviews shop capability, so as to reduce costs where necessary.

28. Maintains vendor relations and vendor rating program. Trains vendors when required.

29. Reviews customer and military specifications and prepares estimates, or assists in preparation of estimates, for performance of special test programs.

30. Keeps abreast of current developments in the statistical quality control field.

31. Conducts in-plant training programs in order to further the use of statistical quality control in the plants.

GENERAL SUPERVISOR, INSPECTION RESEARCH

International Harvester Company

GENERAL STATEMENT OF DUTIES AND MANAGERIAL RESPONSIBILITIES: As the managerial head of Inspection Research activities, is held directly responsible for initiating, developing, and conducting surveys and studies and collecting of data for procedures, manuals, bulletins, and other media for circulating information; for quality control of manufactured parts; and for performing related duties as required.

He directs, disciplines, and instructs employees and assigns work to those under his supervision; and initiates the firing, promotion, discharge, layoff, transfer, and rates of pay of such employees, with the aid of service departments.

He is responsible for carrying out Company policies; formulates rules necessary to the efficient performance of the activities under his supervision; and acts on employees' personal problems as presented.

TYPICAL DUTIES

1. To plan and direct the development of sampling methods and procedures for controlling and maintaining product quality.

2. To plan, lay out, and direct the establishment of training courses and assist Works management in training Works personnel in the application of statistical and physical control techniques of inspection programs.

3. To collaborate with the Manufacturing Standards Section in establishing standards for controlling product quality.

4. To analyze statistical control charts, graphs, reports, and related matter and direct the establishment of comparable reports, circulating results to Research and Works management in obtaining uniform methods of control in product processing.

5. To follow Works application of approved methods and procedures of quality control, recommending revisions or refinements designed to effect greater efficiency in controlling standards of quality of all products.

6. To plan and supervise the design, construction, and application of measuring devices, testing equipment, instruments, and gauges for use in inspection and quality control of Company products.

7. To keep abreast of improvements in quality control methods through the media of periodicals and technical journals, exchanging ideas in visits to other industries and universities, participating in activities of technical societies, and recommending application of valuable ideas obtained to present operations.

8. To advise higher management of progress and results attained in quality control activities.

CHIEF INSPECTOR

Controls Company of America

PRIMARY FUNCTION AND RESPONSIBILITY: To devise, develop, and direct the programs necessary to insure the maintenance of quality in accordance with specifications.

RELATIONSHIPS

1. *Line.* Reports to: Plant Manager. Supervises: Inspection Supervisors, Inspectors, Clerk–Stenographer.

2. *Staff.* Advises and assists Shop Foremen on quality matters and cooperates with Quality Control, Engineering, and Production Departments in achieving primary job function.

3. *Outside.* Contacts customers and suppliers with regard to quality. Participates in Quality Control Association as a representative of management.

TYPICAL DUTIES AND RESPONSIBILITIES

1. To formulate, institute, and insure compliance with established inspection policies concerning product quality.

2. To develop and see to the establishment of effective and economical programs insuring departmental, plant, and individual quality performance in relation to engineering specifications.

3. To direct the efforts of inspection personnel, including:

   a. Establishment of standards of performance, methods, and procedures.

   b. Assignment of work and establishment of a network of inspection designed to provide adequate coverage.

4. To institute proper controls to insure that scrap and rework costs are held to a minimum.

5. To establish acceptable levels of quality for purchased parts or material and insure their conformance to standards set. In addition, to establish an effective plant and inspection gauge control program.

6. To cooperate with Purchasing in maintaining vendor ratings. May purchase inspection items with approval of Plant Manager.

7. To serve as a member of the Plant Operating Committee.

8. To analyze rejections and refer to Engineering questions relating to design or variations from specifications.

GENERAL: Effective performance in this assignment requires knowledge in the areas of operations, methods, procedures, specifications, and standards, as well as statistical quality control procedures and application of results of effective operations. Errors of judgment, omission, or commission can result in financial loss to the Company.

CHIEF INSPECTOR (PRODUCT)

A Petroleum and Carbon Producer

REPORTS TO: Technical Superintendent.

RESPONSIBILITIES: To administer inspection and quality control functions as they relate to in-process and finished products.

DUTIES: In connection with these responsibilities, the general duties are:

1. To sample and test in-process and finished products in accordance with established procedures and to report the results to the Technical Superintendent.

2. To approve or reject the products inspected according to established procedures, specifications, and instructions.

3. To provide the Technical Superintendent with accurate data on all pieces inspected.

4. To cooperate with the Department Foremen to provide inspection service at all hours necessary to avoid the occurrence of production delays.

5. To maintain, in an accurate and usable condition, the inspection tools and equipment assigned to his Department for use in the examination of in-process and finished products.

6. To evaluate and review the effectiveness of procedures established for the inspection of in-process and finished products; to develop and recommend to the Technical Superintendent necessary improvements in inspection methods and procedures.

7. To train and direct all personnel assigned to the work of inspecting in-process and finished products and to foster high standards of work output and employee health, safety, and welfare.

8. To promote harmonious employee relations by insuring compliance with the Union contract and Company regulations.

AUTHORITY

1. To train and direct all personnel assigned to the inspection of in-process and finished products.

2. To accept or reject, with the approval of the Technical Superintendent, all products inspected.

3. To review and approve the work of employees assigned to the inspection of in-process and finished products, and to arrange for reinspection when necessary.

4. To initiate, in accordance with established procedure, requisitions for the purchase of equipment, materials, and supplies required for the inspection of in-process and finished products.

CHIEF INSPECTOR

The Morgan Engineering Company

BASIC FUNCTION: To be responsible to the Vice President of Manufacturing for quality control, including inspection of materials or equipment at vendors' plants as required; for receiving inspection; for in-process inspection; for final inspection; for the establishment of quality standards in conjunction with the Engineering Division and for maintenance of these standards.

BASIC OBJECTIVE: To direct the functions of the Inspection Department to insure that raw materials, purchased parts, in-process material, finished parts, and completed production units conform to established quality standards.

MAJOR DUTIES AND RESPONSIBILITIES

1. Organization and Personnel

   a. To maintain and direct an organization which is adequate to insure production conformance to quality standards.

   b. To insure that the duties and responsibilities of Inspection Department personnel are clearly defined and fixed, and to approve position descriptions for all such personnel.

   c. To recommend to the Vice President of Manufacturing major changes in the form and size of the Inspection Department to meet changed conditions.

d. To see that personnel in the Inspection Department are kept fully and currently informed of all pertinent Company policies and that such policies are followed in the organization.

e. To direct the Company's personnel policies within the Inspection Department.

f. To recommend to the Vice President of Manufacturing the employment, promotion, dismissal, or change in compensation of Inspection Department personnel.

g. To review and appraise the qualifications of each Inspection Department employee periodically as prescribed by Industrial Relations policies.

h. To receive and process employee grievances originating within the Inspection Department as directed by the Company contract with the Union and to adhere to all other Company–Union contractual agreements.

2. *Vendor Inspection*

a. To inspect or to direct the inspection of materials at vendors' plants as may be required.

b. To recommend to the Vice President of Manufacturing inspection of materials or equipment at vendors' plants when such inspection is deemed advisable.

3. *Receiving Inspection*: To establish the necessary controls and to direct the inspection of incoming materials and equipment; to see that established procedures are followed for rejecting or classifying received materials.

4. *In-Process Inspection*

a. To predetermine and establish control points for the sequence, types, and frequency of in-process inspection.

b. To advise and confer with the Processing Section in establishing the inspection operations to be entered on factory work order cards.

c. To see that Production Foremen are advised when operators do not conform to quality standards, in order that corrective action may be taken; to advise and confer with either the General Manufacturing Superintendent or the Vice President of Manufacturing on quality conformance.

d. To consult the Engineering Division to insure that adequate tolerances and other specifications necessary are properly maintained for quality control.

    e. To conform with established procedures in coordination with the Production Planning Department in releasing and expediting parts between operations when inspection is required.

5. *Final Inspection*

    a. To establish, jointly with the Engineering Division, final inspection checklists and to see that completed units are inspected adequately to conform with such checklists.

    b. To give final approval to all completed units before they are released for shipment.

    c. To notify the Engineering, Sales, and Manufacturing Divisions of adverse quality deviations on finished products and obtain the approval of the Sales Division before releasing completed units for shipment without correction of such quality deviations.

6. *Quality*

    a. To establish and maintain, in conjunction with the Engineering Division, standards of quality relating to all purchased material and equipment.

    b. To see that the Manufacturing Division adheres to established standards in all processing operations.

7. *Budgets*

    a. To prepare an annual budget for the Inspection Department covering anticipated expenditures for the department therein and submit to the Vice President of Manufacturing.

    b. To operate the Inspection Department within the approved budget.

    c. To periodically review with Inspection Department personnel operating performance in relation to approved budgets.

8. *General*

    a. To confer periodically with the Field Service Manager to see that developments in the field affecting quality are fully and currently made known to the Chief Inspector.

    b. To consult the Vice President of Manufacturing as required to insure proper maintenance and adherence to quality standards.

    c. To hold periodic meetings with Inspection Department personnel to review operating policies, plans, performance, and problems.

    d. To perform any other duties requested by the Vice President of Manufacturing.

INSPECTION SUPERINTENDENT

An Instrument Maker

REPORTS TO: Reliability and Quality Control Manager.

REPORTING TO HIM: Foreman, Section Foremen, Clerical Personnel.

SUMMARY: Plans, controls, and supervises, through key personnel, all inspection functions pertaining to manufactured parts and tools of the Quality Control Department.

DUTIES

1. To recommend plans for space, facilities, manpower, and organizational requirements for the inspection of all products manufactured in the Air Armament Division.

2. To prepare for approval budget forecasts for facilities, manpower, and operating expenses and to control these expenditures within budget limits.

3. To confer with Production Planning personnel in the establishment of inspection schedules and to insure adherence to these schedules.

4. To confer with those on the same level of authority to plan and coordinate inspection functions; with subcontractors and vendors on matters involving mechanical inspection techniques; and with customers' representatives to resolve inspection problems.

5. To direct the study of new inspection techniques for the development of improved methods and equipment and the establishment and maintenance of inspection standards and procedures.

6. To supervise, through key personnel, inspection of parts, materials, processes, tools, fixtures, and gauges manufactured by or procured for the Division; procurement of special inspection gauges and equipment; surveillance and approval of inspection fixture and gauge designs by Manufacturing Engineering personnel; scheduling of gauge and measuring-equipment calibration for inspection and manufacturing operations; storage and movement of rejected materials; inspection of parts and assemblies in Process Packaging and inspection surveillance of product shipments; and recording and maintenance of inspection data on all the foregoing in conformance with product and part drawings, engineering and MIL specifications, standard practice instructions, cost estimates, and production schedules.

7. Prepares, through key personnel, training information for the up-grading of employees and creates examinations for testing their competence.

8. Conducts the management development program and other such programs; observes subordinate supervisors so that their over-all effectiveness may be strengthened in preparation for more responsible positions in the management organization.

9. Maintains harmonious employee relations and insures employee compliance with Company policy, rules, safety regulations, systems, and procedures.

10. Advises subordinates in the handling of first-step grievances and participates in second-step grievance cases.

11. Gives intermediate approval to recommendations for hiring, salary increases, promotions, demotions, and dismissals according to work-loads and within authorized limits.

SENIOR TEST ENGINEER

An Electronics Company

GENERAL DESCRIPTION OF WORK PERFORMED: Supervises one or more Test Engineers in the performance of production-line test activity. Is responsible to the Production Test Manager for a project or several related projects.

PRINCIPAL DUTIES AND RESPONSIBILITIES

1. Maintains Engineering–Manufacturing liaison during the pre-release period and throughout a given project.

2. Sets up new test lines in preparation for production runs; determines quantity of stations and capability level of technicians required.

3. Collaborates in design and construction of special test equipment. Determines limits on "Company" specifications, as well as such additional tests as are needed to insure satisfactory operation of the end-item equipment.

4. Controls test labor costs and is responsible for scheduling test personnel and equipment in such a manner that production is not delayed.

5. Assists Employment Office through technical interviews of prospective employees to evaluate capabilities.

6. Provides for job performance review, on a continuing basis, of all personnel under his supervision.

FACTORS

1. *Job Knowledge*: Must have a thorough knowledge of electronics and manufacturing techniques, to include quality and reliability programs, as well as a complete and detailed knowledge of test-equipment standards. Must keep abreast of new techniques related to his profession through review of technical literature and trade magazines as well as participation in special study courses. A B.S. degree in engineering or mathematics, or equivalent military or commercial electronics experience, is required.

2. *Mental Application*: Under general guidance of Production Test Manager, solves complex technical problems related to electronic design failure, tolerance build-up, and specification compliance on production items and test equipment. Collaborates in the development of new unique test equipment and procedures, and recommends design changes on product and associated test equipment as needed. Originates and modifies, utilizing his own experience and background, new and untried "Company-controlled" test procedures prior to formal draft, so as to meet end-term military specifications.

3. *Responsibility for Costs*: Should be capable of making accurate bid proposals for test labor costs, and is directly responsible for test labor efficiency in meeting schedules within the project budget. Recommends special tests for components to minimize assembly and rework costs due to high failure rates in tests.

4. *Responsibility for Contacts*: Maintains liaison between Engineering and Manufacturing regarding project problems of design or manufacture. Makes skillful first-hand presentation of test data to develop and maintain customer confidence in the test capabilities of the Company. Prepares and presents analytical reports on complex test problems for use by both Quality Control and Engineering.

5. *Responsibility for Directing Others*: Is accountable for planning and organizing line flow and test stations in addition to training and directing one or more Test Engineers and 5 to 20 Senior or Special Apparatus Technicians on the project level. Interprets corporate and departmental policy in dealing with test personnel problems. Initiates, subject to higher approval, all types of personnel actions.

INSPECTION FOREMAN

A Large Steel Company

PRIMARY FUNCTION: To supervise the inspection and classification of all Foundry products.

DUTIES AND RESPONSIBILITIES

1. To supervise a crew of six or more Inspectors to inspect, gauge, measure, and otherwise classify steel castings according to standard A.S.T.M. quality classifications and special customers' specifications. To maintain inspection services on whatever days and shifts the Foundry Finishing Subdivision is in operation in each of the following areas:

    a. Chip Shop: Large castings molded on the slinger floor.

    b. Minute Department: Small castings moulded on the bench floor.

    c. Drawbar and Sideframe Floor: Large-volume production from Herman and Cincinnati moulding machine.

    d. Diesel Shop: Locomotive frames and other large castings machined to finished dimensions.

2. To determine inspection procedures in addition to normal visual and dimensional checks for castings being shipped to distant customers to minimize the cost of returning castings for repairs. (Additional procedures may include laying out the casting for machining according to drawings provided.) To determine when castings should be given radiographic examination to protect the Company's interests.

3. To examine sample castings produced by Foundry and approve production runs if quality is satisfactory. To examine defective castings returned by a customer, authorize credit to customer, and determine whether castings should be repaired or replaced.

4. To instruct Inspectors in order to establish acceptable quality standards for new and unusual orders and to spot-check their performance. To make final decisions as to the acceptability of castings of borderline quality which have been set aside by Inspectors. To determine if it is possible to repair seriously defective castings or if they should be scrapped. To interpret results of X-ray examinations to classify castings.

5. To ascertain that jobs on all shifts are manned and to prepare shift working schedules. To arrange with Chief Inspector to increase or decrease the workforce, temporarily or permanently, as required.

6. To handle personnel problems of the workforce. To recommend promotions, demotions, rate changes, leaves of absence. To approve days off or shift changes. To answer inquiries or complaints and take action on cases requiring disciplinary measures after consulting the Chief Inspector if the matter is a difficult or unusual one.

7. To report inspection findings promptly to Foundry Superintendent and/or Moulding Subdivision Supervisors to enable remedial steps to be taken on balance of order or on a future order.

8. To review inspection procedures with visiting Customers' Representatives and facilitate the work of resident Customers' Inspectors.

9. To assist the Casting Service Representative to provide technical advice to customers and to investigate quality complaints in the field, as required.

10. To requisition tools and supplies as required.

11. To instruct employees in safe working methods and insure that activities are carried on safely.

12. To keep informed on expected standards of yield and quality performance. To compare day-to-day performance with standards and strive to minimize waste or excessive downgrading of product in the performance of the inspection function.

RELATIONSHIPS

1. Reports to the Chief Inspector, Inspection Department.

2. Collaborates closely with the General Foreman and Foremen of the Finishing Subdivision to inspect castings prior to shipment and authorize repairs or scrapping of defective castings.

3. Collaborates closely with the General Foreman and Foremen of Moulding, Core Room, and Pattern Subdivisions and with the Quality Man to report inspection results and suggest corrective measures for casting defects.

4. Cooperates with the Foundry Metallurgist and his staff, the Casting Service Representative, and the Casting Sales personnel to insure that castings meet customers' quality requirements, to minimize scrap losses, and to repair costs.

FOREMAN–PRODUCTION TESTING

A. O. Smith Corporation

REPORTS TO: General Foreman.

PRIMARY FUNCTION: To supervise final production test of petroleum-handling products (except service station pumps and lube equipment).

DUTIES AND RESPONSIBILITIES

1. To schedule daily production of Production Testing Section in accordance with routing cards received from Production Control. To alter production schedule in order to meet shipping schedules and in accordance with the availability of machines, material, and/or manpower.

2. To supervise the operational processes of the Sections, including the performance of pressure and/or accuracy tests on petroleum-handling products (exclusive of hand pumps) and the performance of operating and pressure tests on meters and accessories such as valves, eliminators, and the like.

3. To observe operating condition of manufacturing equipment. To make minor adjustments and repairs. To report major repairs on pumps, motors, test stands, to Maintenance Man and follow up to insure that repairs are made.

4. To recommend improvements in manufacturing methods, such as improved setup of valves on test rack.

5. To maintain daily record of meters tested and rejected for Quality Control.

6. To compare employees' time cards against job cards to insure that employees have made proper entries.

7. To maintain a stock of materials and equipment required in testing operation and the necessary fittings and solvents. To requisition any shortages and expedite their delivery when necessary.

8. To assist Industrial Engineering in the development of test procedures when requested.

9. To supervise the Production Testers in their functions and in their decisions as to the quality of the product. To personally make final decision on quality of those units of questionable quality within specified limits. To cooperate with Quality Control Department in the development of improved quality of products and tests.

10. To administer Company personnel policies as they affect employees under his supervision with reference to vacations, disciplinary action, training in safety and meter-testing techniques, housekeeping, and so on. To retain recommendatory authority with reference to firing within his Section.

UNIT FOREMAN, ASSEMBLY INSPECTION

An Electronics Company

GENERAL DESCRIPTION OF WORK PERFORMED: Supervises the inspection of electronic assemblies to assure agreement with specifications within the scope of the Military Products Division Quality Control Manual.

REPORTS TO: General Foreman–Assembly Inspection.

PRINCIPAL DUTIES AND RESPONSIBILITIES

1. Trains inspectors to perform inspection according to required quality standards.
2. Prepares inspection instructions, using applicable specifications and quality standards.
3. Maintains inspection records and data.
4. Initiates corrective action where quality improvements are required.
5. Evaluates inspection results to assure optimum quality level.
6. Assists production in assembly of quality equipment.
7. Maintains drawings and records to assure that modifications and all equipment acceptances are to drawing requirements.
8. Surveys all manufacturing areas to assure proper storage and handling of parts and equipment, segregation of defective material, and performance of assembly operations within the scope of Company customer quality requirements.
9. Investigates failures and defects and initiates corrective action to prevent recurrence.
10. Submits equipment to customer for acceptance, after verifying that all specifications and quality requirements have been complied with.

11. Coordinates with customer to correct any defects generated within the assembly area.

12. Coordinates with Quality Control staff to correct defects beyond jurisdiction of Assembly Inspection.

13. Performs preliminary review and process of defective material. Takes corrective action as indicated to reduce scrap costs.

14. Supervises a group of Inspectors to assure conformance to Company Policy Manual and the Union agreement.

15. Contacts assembly supervision, engineering personnel, and customer representatives as required to maintain quality level outlined in the Quality Control Manual.

16. Operates Inspection function within cost requirements, and assists in reducing cost of assembly and inspection.

FACTORS

1. *Job Knowledge*

   a. Requires a thorough knowledge of quality requirements for assembly of military electronics equipment, military specifications and standards, workmanship standards, mechanical measuring devices, and methods of operation applicable to the military electronics industry. Basic familiarity with electronics fundamentals is required in order to understand the effect that improper assembly would have on the operation of the completed product.

   b. Requires a high-school diploma and completion of a trade-school electronics course, in addition to a minimum of four years' experience in the inspection or assembly of small military electronics equipment, of which at least three years have been in inspection supervision.

2. *Mental Application*: Under the general guidance of supervision, and basing his actions on personal experience and regulations prescribed by the Quality Control Manual, the Unit Foreman implements inspection requirements and maintains quality standards on one or more projects. Initiates requests for corrections or drawing changes on items not conforming to specifications due to improper assembly, poor workmanship, engineering-print errors, or defective parts.

3. *Responsibility for Cost*: Is responsible for maintaining consistently high inspection standards for all completed pieces of equipment, in order to reduce cost through elimination of defective parts and/or assemblies, while remaining within the established budget. Errors in application of proper inspection techniques and judgment will lead to considerable cost in equipment repair and impair the Company's reputation with the customer.

4. *Responsibility for Contacts*: Exercises tact and persuasiveness with supervisory and technical personnel of most manufacturing departments in pointing out equipment defects and suggesting improved assembly methods. Has constant contact with customers while performing corrective action and presenting equipment for acceptance.

5. *Responsibility for Directing Others*: Exercises direct first-line supervision over a group of 6 to 50 Inspectors. Is accountable for assigning duties; monitoring output; measuring efficiency, training, and guidance. Initiates, with approval of superiors, all types of personnel actions.

Manufacturing Engineering and Research

Positions in both the manufacturing engineering and the manufacturing research areas have to do with the development of new and/or improved manufacturing processes, equipment, and related activities.

MANAGER, MANUFACTURING ENGINEERING

Amphenol–Borg Electronics Corporation

GENERAL RESPONSIBILITIES: Under the direction of the Operations Manager, plans, organizes, and directs the activities of employees engaged in Manufacturing Engineering work, including the maintenance of physical plant, tool room cost estimating, and plant layouts; the establishment of manufacturing processes and equipment; the establishment of standard data and the making of time studies; the development of machinery and facilities; and the making of special studies for process or product improvement, methods improvement, cost reduction, and the like. Does related work as required.

TYPICAL DUTIES

1. Supervises the preparation of estimates of the cost of manufacturing proposed new products; participates in and assists with the preparation of cost estimates for the more complex or unusual new products; and suggests design changes, as necessary, to facilitate manufacture, improve quality, or reduce costs.

2. Directs the development of manufacturing processes and equipment

for new products; directs the continuing review, revision, and improvement of processes and equipment for existing products; and participates in finding solutions to the more complex and unusual problems relating to manufacturing processes.

3. Directs the establishment of standard data for use in determining production rates; directs the establishment of the production rates on the basis of both standard data and time study; and participates in resolving disputes involving production rates.

4. Directs the review and analysis of daily production efficiency reports to identify cases where the standard, the performance, the tools, or other elements of production appear to be unsatisfactory.

5. Supervises the rendering of advice and assistance to Manufacturing Departments in connection with the solution of manufacturing difficulties; participates in finding solutions to the more complex manufacturing problems that arise; confers with Product Engineers where design problems are involved.

6. Assigns special studies and projects relating to plant layouts, equipment, product and process improvements, cost reduction, and the like to Production Engineers; outlines scope, objectives, and approach to be taken for such projects; reviews progress from time to time; and reviews results. May present findings to management for consideration.

7. Where major considerations are involved, recommends to management policies and procedures relating to cost estimating, maintenance, manufacturing processes and equipment, facilities, standards, and the like.

8. Plans and directs maintenance of building, facilities, machinery, equipment, and grounds.

9. Supervises tool room operations.

10. Interviews, selects, and hires personnel for key manufacturing engineering positions; participates in reviewing the performance of key personnel and in recommending salary adjustments where merited; counsels employees on performance deficiencies; recommends transfers, promotions, and separations as required.

11. Reviews proposed budgets prepared by subordinate Department Heads; suggests revisions as necessary; participates in discussions between Department Heads and the Budget Director at which final budgets are developed for submission to management.

12. Directs preparation and maintenance of process instruction sheets for all products.

13. Acts as management representative in labor grievances involving production rates, process sequence, or equipment determination.

MINIMUM QUALIFICATIONS REQUIRED

1. Graduation from college with a degree in industrial or mechanical engineering and eight years of experience in industrial engineering work, at least two years of which shall have been in a responsible supervisory capacity and which shall have included experience in methods and standards engineering, time study, plant layout, and process engineering work.

2. Thorough knowledge of industrial engineering principles and practices; thorough knowledge of the methods, processes, tools, and equipment involved in manufacturing division products; ability to plan, organize, and direct the development of effective operations and processes for a relatively complex manufacturing operation.

MANAGER–PROCESS DEVELOPMENT

A Proprietary Products Company

BASIC FUNCTION: Works under the general supervision of the Director of Product and Process Development. Directs a staff of Chemical Engineers in the development of appropriate processes for the manufacture of new products and for the improvement or modification of existing processes. Conducts studies regarding the engineering design of new or replacement equipment for use in laboratory processing operations.

MAJOR DUTIES AND RESPONSIBILITIES

1. Supervises process research and development for new and improved products, and for new processing principles, in order to arrive at more efficient processing methods. Schedules pilot runs on new processes and evaluates the results of such research work, recommending the addition, expansion, or discontinuance of projects.

2. Coordinates process research work with product development, processing, equipment engineering, and packaging activities.

3. Evaluates new equipment and recommends improved utilization of existing equipment, facilities, and techniques.

4. Supervises the preparation of samples for the conducting of wide panel surveys by the Product Counselor group.

5. Is responsible for "troubleshooting" of laboratory processing problems in areas of packaging and processing.

6. Conducts ingredient studies on formulations made in Pilot Laboratory quantities when the effect of certain ingredients cannot be judged properly by bench or analytical tests.

7. Reviews studies made of pertinent product parameters in relation to manufacturing control and consumer functionality.

8. As directed, supervises the training of technical personnel engaged in national and international operations.

9. Cooperates with Technical Services Manager in supervising the preparation of product and process standards and operating procedures.

10. Keeps the proper members of the Research and Development staff advised of significant developments in the general fields of product and process development and other areas of mutual interest and responsibility.

11. Serves upon Research and Development committees, at the direction of superior, to secure collective judgment on research policies and to maintain proper coordination of product and process development activities with other operations of the Company.

12. Coordinates the efficient control of the process-research programs within approved budget limitations.

MANAGER, MANUFACTURING BRANCH

International Harvester Company

GENERAL STATEMENT OF DUTIES AND MANAGERIAL RESPONSIBILITIES: As managerial head of the Manufacturing Research Department, is held directly responsible for its over-all management, the tone and character of its organization, the efficiency and adequacy of operations and facilities, and the maintenance of harmonious internal and external relations. Performs related duties as required.

Initiates and endorses the hiring, promotion, discharge, layoff, transfer, and pay rates of employees under his direction.

Is responsible for the administration of Company policies and objectives, formulates rules necessary for the efficient functioning of all Manufacturing Research activities, and collaborates with staff members in the disposition of employees' personal problems.

TYPICAL DUTIES

1. Be responsible for the execution of approved Manufacturing Research policies and programs, determining the courses of action to be followed and directing and coordinating staff personnel in the effectuation of prescribed objectives and procedures.

2. Be responsible for the efficient and economical execution of all Manufacturing Research activities, coordinating and integrating all Department activities to assure unification of operations.

3. Be responsible for the establishment and control of Department operating budgets, costs, and expenses, planning the organization within the general pattern and adjusting its size and character in conformity with changing requirements.

4. Coordinate the activities of staff and supervisory personnel on matters pertaining to procedures, costs, personnel, safety, and working conditions, devising and authorizing the adoption of methods designed to simplify and standardize practices.

5. Review equipment propositions; analyze for relationship to Company policies, procedures and regulations, research programs, business trends, operational costs, and related items; determine those which appear to be practicable and which will provide more efficient operations.

6. Confer with higher management concerning the approval of equipment propositions, giving the reasons for such requests and pointing out the advantages of the suggestions in regard to cost, efficiency, and improved operations.

7. Confer with staff and Department Heads to review new, present, or proposed research programs, projects, policies, methods, or Department operational functions; evaluate such items; and approve those that appear to be feasible and workable.

8. Analyze the progress of Manufacturing Research activities and functions: organize and plan operations to effect unity of action; clarify Company policy, thinking, and regulations; outline proper procedures, and prescribe effective remedial measures.

9. Review recommendations regarding changes in Department operational functions, approving meritorious recommendations or suggestions and directing their installation.

10. Review building programs, expansions, and related items, acting in a consulting capacity and making recommendations to higher management concerning major projects which involve large capital expenditures.

11. Consult local Accounting management about procedures and methods, operation costs, budget programs, wage and related matters;

receive information, suggestions, and opinions pertinent to Accounting Department activities in relation to Research functions; offer advice and assistance in diagnosis of problems and develop methods and ways to obtain solutions to over-all problems.

12. Organize, formulate plans for, and appoint committees or individuals to develop various special programs and systems, authorizing the establishment of those which are practicable and suitable to Research operations.

SUPERVISOR OF PRODUCTION ENGINEERING

An Electronics Company

GENERAL FUNCTIONS: Supervise Production Engineering staff in South Plant, plan and schedule work for the staff, make recommendations pertaining to the personnel and functions of the Department, and train staff members. Be responsible for the production of Company products to meet cost, quality, and delivery requirements; provide Departments with proper drawings, parts, and assemblies; and ascertain that Manufacturing is kept up to date on changes, modifications, and waivers.

SPECIFIC DUTIES

1. Supervise Production Engineering staff consisting of approximately four employees.

2. Plan, schedule, and assign work for staff.

3. Be responsible for administration, conduct, quality, and quantity of work in Department.

4. Recommend pay increases, promotions, transfers, and dismissals for members of staff.

5. Institute and/or recommend changes and procedures in operations performed by the staff.

6. Train members of staff in duties and functions of job.

7. Advise and assist the Chief Engineer in formulating proposals for policies on (and recommend procedures to) manufacturing, maintenance, and quality; administer such policies and procedures, when approved, in the South Plant.

8. Investigate high costs of excessive shrinkage and assist Foremen in taking corrective steps.

9. Be responsible for maintaining specifications in accordance with approved designs.

10. Cooperate closely with Quality Control in maintaining quality standards.

11. Encourage suggestions for improvements in manufacturing equipment and processes from Foremen, Foreladies, and Group Leaders; help train them to encourage and give full credit to employees who make suggestions for improvements.

12. Reduce manufacturing cost.

13. Provide all Departments under his jurisdiction with the proper drawings, parts, and assemblies and ascertain that Manufacturing is kept up to date on changes, modifications, and waivers.

14. Keep adequate records with respect to engineering tests and assist the Chief Engineer in the preparation of the annual budget for his Section.

15. Advise and assist the Chief Production Engineer in the preparation of the annual budget for his Section.

16. Recommend approval of expenses of personnel in his Department.

17. May be required to perform allied duties, fill in on other jobs, perform higher-classification functions such as promotional training, and perform duties as directed by a superior classification function. Also may be required to perform any work done in like or lesser job classifications.

DIRECTOR OF PRODUCT AND PROCESS DEVELOPMENT

A Proprietary Products Company

BASIC FUNCTION: Directs the technical research and development activities of the Company and provides coordinative guidance to the following Departmental Operating Divisions: Product Development, Semi-Basic Research, Process Development, National Product Quality, and Technical Services.

MAJOR DUTIES AND RESPONSIBILITIES

1. Develops and recommends such technical and research policies and programs as are necessary to support profitable growth and to implement the general policies and goals of the Company.

2. Coordinates research activities among Departmental Operating Divisions.

3. Provides stimulus and encouragement to Department personnel to increase the adequacy and quality of their research and service programs.

4. Arranges for dissemination of information on Division research activities among the other Departmental Divisions through reports, meetings, and the like.

5. Informs Departmental Divisions of scientific and technological developments of potential interest to the Company.

6. Represents the Company, as delegated by a superior, on technical research matters in professional societies, industry associations, and other such organizations.

7. Advises and assists Departmental Divisions to see that all research programs are executed efficiently and in accordance with schedule.

8. Sees that Department personnel keep informed on scientific and technical matters.

9. Formulates capital expenditure program for Department.

10. Executes all other general administrative responsibilities of the Department.

GENERAL SUPERVISOR, MATERIALS RESEARCH

International Harvester Company

GENERAL STATEMENT OF DUTIES AND MANAGERIAL RESPONSIBILITIES: As managerial head of Materials Research activities, is held directly responsible for investigative research studies on the use and application of materials, with a view to converting from existing materials to other types and kinds of equal or superior quality and performance without adversely affecting economy of production; performs related duties as required.

Directs, disciplines, instructs, and assigns work to the employees under his supervision and initiates the hiring, promotion, discharge, layoff, transfer, and rates of pay of such employees with the aid of Service Departments.

Is responsible for carrying out Company policies; formulates rules necessary for the efficient performance of the activities under his supervision; and receives and acts on employees' personal problems that may be presented to him.

TYPICAL DUTIES

1. Initiate and direct the study and development of alternate materials, for use in Company products, which will maintain or improve quality, performance, and economy of manufacture.

2. Make surveys, studies, and investigations of individual parts, submitting recommendations relative to substitutions of materials and methods of manufacture.

3. Coordinate the activities of the various Research Sections in the development of comparative costs relative to the conversion of materials and methods of manufacture.

4. Cooperate with and advise the Purchasing Department regarding substitutes for materials in short supply.

5. Cooperate with the Patent Department concerning patent possibilities, copyrights, royalties, and related matters involving materials and methods which may be developed for substitutions or conversions.

6. Act as liaison representative between Materials Research and the various Engineering Departments on problems pertaining to conversions and substitutions of materials.

7. In cooperation with Engineering Department, arrange for the conducting of necessary field tests, evaluating the results and formulating new or revised materials.

8. Follow the progress of developments in processing cost studies of conversions and substitutions of materials.

9. Furnish reports to management, with recommendations and supporting data, pertaining to substitutions of materials for the express purpose of maintaining production schedules.

10. Keep abreast of the development of new materials by reviewing articles in technical publications and maintaining contacts with other Company groups, industries, and technical societies.

GENERAL SUPERVISOR,
MANUFACTURING STANDARDS RESEARCH

International Harvester Company

GENERAL STATEMENT OF DUTIES AND MANAGERIAL RESPONSIBILITIES: As the managerial head of Manufacturing Standards Research activities, is held directly responsible for establishing manufacturing standards on methods, procedures, tools, tooling, and related items for the purpose of improving manufacture of the product. Performs related duties as required.

Directs, disciplines, instructs, and assigns work to employees under his supervision and initiates the hiring, promoting, discharge, layoff, transfer, and rates of pay of such employees with the aid of service departments.

Is responsible for carrying out Company policies; formulates rules necessary for the efficient performance of the activities under his supervision; receives and acts on employees' personal problems that may be presented to him.

TYPICAL DUTIES

1. Plan and supervise the work of employees engaged in developing, compiling, analyzing, and distributing manufacturing standards material and information, including the development and maintenance of manufacturing standards specifications.

2. Coordinate the activities of the Manufacturing Standards Section with other Sections for the purpose of obtaining information and data which may be developed into standards, consulting and advising on matters pertinent to standards and standardization.

3. Contact Works and Engineering personnel regarding manufacturing problems and other matters which may require established standards for efficient production operations.

4. Consult with and advise Works personnel in the establishment and proper usage of standards material.

5. Participate, as Company representative, in the activities of technical and other organizations, especially on national standards committees, collecting and screening material which can be adopted or revised for use by the Company.

6. Consult with and advise Purchasing Department personnel on subjects relating to standardization of perishable tools and other purchased items.

7. Visit other industries and organizations for the purpose of exchanging ideas and information on manufacturing processes, procedures, methods, tools, tooling, and related matters which might be incorporated into Company standards.

MANUFACTURING OPERATIONS ANALYST, SENIOR

Olin Mathieson Chemical Corporation

REPORTS TO: Plant Manager or Superintendent of Manufacturing.

MAJOR FUNCTIONS: Under general direction as to scope of operations and objectives to be accomplished, supervises or performs complex mechanical engineering investigations concerned with specific phases of the design and/or development of miscellaneous complete units or components related to new and/or improved plant equipment and processes. Recommends methods for improving and maintaining product quality and production standards in areas where major difficulties are encountered.

RESPONSIBILITIES INCLUDED

1. Implementing the objectives of assigned projects through the application of fundamental and specialized engineering principles and complex standard and specialized methods and techniques. Developing new methods and techniques as well as modifying existing methods applicable to assigned projects.

2. Investigating and/or approving deviation waivers for quantities of manufactured components that do not meet production standards. Determining operations basically responsible for failure of components to meet production standards and determining whether the process, tools, fixtures, gauges, machines, or production employees are at fault. Formulating and/or directing corrective repair programs for salvaging quantity lots of components that do not meet production standards.

3. Initiating purchase orders necessary to replace old, worn, or damaged tools, fixtures, and gauges. Initiating change orders, work orders, or

repair orders so as to outline design changes, repairs, process changes, and the like for tools, fixtures, and gauges.

4. Recommending the use of cutting tools of advanced design and/or of special material to replace tools which wear out quickly. Observing the success of recommended tooling and maintaining records of it for periods of time sufficient to verify its superiority.

5. Arranging for the timely purchase, repair, or replacement of highly perishable jig and fixture components so as to prevent production stoppages or delays.

6. Requesting changes in manufacturing tolerances and/or processes when these changes will simplify production operations, reduce costs, or improve product quality.

7. Determining need for and developing new and/or improved equipment and tooling by reviewing and analyzing existing or proposed process changes, product revisions, or production operations.

8. Conferring with representatives of tool and equipment vendors in regard to items that could be profitably incorporated into existing manufacturing processes or concerning the delivery of repair or special tools that are critical in maintaining production flow.

9. Establishing and maintaining internal contacts with all levels of engineering and manufacturing supervision in order to obtain, exchange, interpret, or supply information of mutual interest.

10. Establishing schedules and cost estimates for the completion of assigned projects and providing information concerning the effect of programs of change or repair upon production schedules.

11. Recommending selection, hiring, change in status, or termination of assigned employees.

SUPERVISION EXERCISED: Directly, 3-5. Indirectly, 1-3.

EDUCATION REQUIRED: College degree in mechanical engineering, or equivalent.

PREVIOUS EXPERIENCE PREFERRED: Minimum of five years' engineering experience in manufacturing activities.

RELATED EXPERIENCE ACCEPTABLE: Experience as process engineer or design engineer.

Production Planning and Control

While line management is, of course, basically responsible for getting out the work, most companies today have specialized staff or services for production planning, inventory control, and the like.

MANAGER OF PRODUCTION PLANNING AND CONTROL

A Tubing and Forged Products Company

PURPOSE OF THE POSITION: The Manager of Production Planning and Control shall be responsible for planning, scheduling, initiating, and following up plant production, warehousing, and shipping activities in accordance with customer service requirements, production and inventory forecasts, and Manufacturing Department policy and procedure. He shall also be responsible for participating in the over-all planning of activities as a member of the Vice President of Manufacturing's staff.

ORGANIZATIONAL RELATIONSHIPS

Reports to: Vice President of Manufacturing.
Supervises directly: Chief Scheduler.
                     Production Analyst.
                     Material Analyst.
                     Production Control Clerk.
                     Scheduling Clerk.
                     Material Control Clerk.
                     Expediter.
                     Secretary.

MAJOR DUTIES AND RESPONSIBILITIES

A. Production Planning and Control for the _____ *Plants.*
     1. Establish and maintain material, supply-in-process, and finished-product inventory levels in accordance with Manufacturing Division inventory control procedures.

2. Order material and supplies in the quantities necessary to satisfy production forecasts and inventory standards.

3. Plan utilization of production facilities necessary to meet current product demand and to provide for the preservation of proper inventory levels.

4. Coordinate the dispatching of production orders and material and supply requisitions to the Production Department.

5. Dispatch shipping orders to the Shipping Section in accordance with customer requirements, Company service standards, and Manufacturing Division policy and procedure.

6. Maintain follow-up and expedite procedures in regard to all orders issued.

7. Determine the need for stock replenishment through use of the daily perpetual inventory report.

8. Advise the Vice President of Manufacturing and the Sales Department of obsolete and slow-moving product items.

9. Provide the Sales Department with shipping promises on individual orders as necessary.

10. Maintain and distribute control records and reports as specified in the Manufacturing Division standard procedures manual.

11. Review performance of all Plant Production Planning and Control employees and recommend changes in status, including salary changes, to the Vice President of Manufacturing.

B. *Organizational Planning*

1. Participate in the over-all planning of Plant organization as requested by the Vice President of Manufacturing.

2. Review Plant Production Planning and Control Department organization, policy procedure, and standards on a continuing basis, and recommend changes to the Vice President of Manufacturing.

C. *Coordination of Plant Production Planning and Control Activities*

1. Internal: Coordinate the activities of all Production Planning and Control personnel through application of procedures for planning, indoctrination, training, execution, communication, and control.

2. External: Keep Manufacturing Division management, Plant Department Heads, and functionaries of Divisions other than Manufacturing informed of related activities to facilitate over-all coordination.

D. Control of Plant Production Planning and Control Activities

   1. Compare Production Planning and Control operating results and performance of Department personnel with established standards, budgets, and procedures.

   2. Institute action necessary to assure compliance with Manufacturing Division policy, procedure, and standards.

MANAGER, PRODUCTION CONTROL

Allegheny Ludlum Steel Corporation

BASIC FUNCTION: To plan and schedule production in detail to assure on-schedule completion of orders so as to permit maximum customer goodwill. Is responsible to the Manager of Operations for directing the Works' Production Control activities within the Corporation's policy.

MAJOR DUTIES AND RESPONSIBILITIES

  1. *Organization and Personnel*

    a. To maintain and direct an organization which is adequate for the performance of the Works' Production Control functions.

    b. To insure that the duties and responsibilities of subordinates are clearly defined and fixed, and to approve position descriptions of immediate subordinates.

    c. To recommend to the Manager of Operations major changes in the form and size of the Works' Production Control Department required to meet changing conditions.

    d. To see that personnel in the Production Control organization are kept fully and currently informed of all pertinent Corporate policies and that such policies are followed in the Department.

    e. To recommend to the Manager of Operations the employment, promotion, dismissal, or change in compensation of immediate subordinates.

    f. To direct the Corporation's personnel policies within the Works' Production Control Department.

    g. To approve the employment, promotion, dismissal, or change in compensation of personnel reporting directly to his immediate subordinates.

    h. To review and appraise periodically the qualifications and performance of each subordinate as prescribed by Corporation policy.

    i. To administer his assigned organization within established policies and programs for personnel performance rating, manpower forecasting, training, and salary administration.

2. *Production Planning*

    a. To develop and transmit to the Customer Service Department realistic production capacity data for each product made by the Works.

    b. To cooperate with the Customer Service Department in its responsibility for meeting promised delivery dates.

    c. To direct the establishment and maintenance of adequate master-planning records of operation-load status.

    d. To direct planned production and schedules or load Department facilities on a general schedule basis to meet delivery dates.

    e. To direct the requisitioning of semi-finished material from the various Works of the Corporation as required for meeting established production schedules.

    f. To direct the maintenance of appropriate records of semi-finished inventories available for application to customer orders.

    g. To direct the application of semi-finished inventories to orders where it is in the Corporation's best interest to do so.

    h. To direct the maintenance of ingot and semi-finished inventory balance at levels established by the Works' management.

    i. To recommend to the Manager of Operations and the Coordinator, Production Control, semi-finished inventory levels requisite for effective delivery service.

3. *Production Scheduling*

    a. To direct in detail the scheduling of Department facilities to complete operations as established by Department loading.

    b. To direct the sequential loading of individual equipment for the completion of operations as established by Department loading.

    c. To direct, in conjunction with the Department Foreman, the dispatching of tasks or assignments to individual equipment as established by the equipment-load schedule.

    d. To direct the expediting of orders through production in accordance with the established schedules and to report regularly on the status of current schedules to the Production Status Section of the Division.

4. *Production Status*

   a. To direct the maintenance of appropriate records covering future and current production loads and the status of current production orders.

   b. To direct the development and preparation of order status and delay order reports.

   c. To direct the development and preparation of weekly shipping performance reports.

   d. To direct the typing, duplicating, and distribution of manufacturing orders as established by standard procedures.

   e. To cooperate with the Customer Service Department in its responsibility for servicing customer orders.

5. *Budgets*

   a. To prepare a Department budget covering all anticipated expenses and submit it to the Manager of Operations for approval.

   b. To see that operations of his Department are conducted within approved budget limits and to review periodically actual performance in relation to such limits.

6. *General*

   a. To cooperate with the Coordinator, Production Control, on Corporate policy and production control functions.

   b. To cooperate with the Works' Customer Service Department and with Sales Division personnel in all activities related to their areas of responsibility.

   c. To see that his organization is currently informed on Corporate affairs.

   d. To recommend to the Manager of Operations and to the Coordinator, Production Control, revisions in Department policies and procedures when advisable to maintain effective production control.

   e. To approve, as established by Corporate procedures, the expense accounts of immediate subordinates.

   f. To approve, as established by Corporate procedures, requisitions within the Production Control Department for equipment, supplies, services, or any other expenditures.

   g. To review, as requested, proposals for facilities to produce new products or for changes in existing facilities which materially affect capacities for existing products; to recommend appropriate action to the Manager of Operations and the Coordinator, Production Control.

h. To perform any additional duties which may be requested by the Manager of Operations.

SUPERINTENDENT–COMPONENT MANUFACTURING PRODUCTION CONTROL

Olin Mathieson Chemical Corporation

REPORTS TO: General Superintendent–Production Control.

MAJOR FUNCTIONS: Under the general direction of the General Superintendent–Production Control as to objectives to be accomplished, supervises, directs, and coordinates the activities of Production Control Area Supervisors engaged in administering and monitoring component planning and scheduling for all manufactured parts in the plant. Develops and establishes reporting procedures and controls to insure a smooth flow of work through the various manufacturing operations so as to meet projected production requirements. Performs related duties as required.

RESPONSIBILITIES INCLUDED

1. Developing, establishing, and maintaining the component manufacturing reporting systems and procedures necessary to insure conformance to established production schedules. Directing and coordinating through subordinates the activities of Area planners and schedulers, expediters, dispatchers, and tool and gauge crib attendants so as to facilitate the flow of work through various manufacturing operations.

2. Evaluating delays in the production process in order to determine their effect on various parts of the production schedule. Revising plans and schedules for in-process components as warranted and advising model planners in Assembly Group channels to determine the net effect of these delays on the over-all production schedule.

3. Directing the detailed investigation and interpretation of machinery or manning requirements for the manufacture of new products as compared with existing products. Insuring the proper modification

of existing plans and schedules to phase in these changes properly without an interruption in the normal flow of work.

4. Developing detailed shop plans and schedules in order to meet component schedules. Following up, expediting, and reporting on projected versus actual production rates and assisting in devising methods of making up lost time due to unforeseen delays. Expediting the flow of critical parts, tools, materials, and supplies through the required sequences. Analyzing status reports, move reports, and load schedules in order to determine any potential trouble areas.

5. Cooperating and conferring with Production Supervision in order to expedite and meet production schedules in the most consistent and economical manner. Conferring with supervisory personnel of other Service and Operating Departments in order to obtain, interpret, supply, or exchange information of mutual interest.

6. Directing the maintenance of a current file of work standards of all operations in any area in order to schedule appropriate machine loadings. Maintaining reporting controls on manufacturing orders to insure that the Area has received the order with sufficient lead time to meet the schedules. Determining that the workload is properly distributed within each shop and in relation to other shops.

7. Preparing and submitting for approval the annual budget requirements for his area of responsibility. Monitoring the expenditure of appropriated funds by implementing standard budgetary controls and limitations.

8. Recommending the selection, hiring, change in status, and/or termination of assigned employees. Assisting in the administration and interpretation of Corporate and Division policies and procedures as they may affect his employees.

SUPERVISION EXERCISED: Directly, 4-7. Indirectly, 30-45.

EDUCATION REQUIRED: College degree in engineering or industrial administration, or equivalent, with additional courses in manufacturing methods and procedures.

PREVIOUS EXPERIENCE PREFERRED: Minimum of 5 to 7 years' experience as scheduler and planner, including supervisory responsibilities.

RELATED EXPERIENCE ACCEPTABLE: Experience as expediter, industrial engineer, or manufacturing supervisor.

PRODUCTION PLANNING SUPERVISOR

The Morgan Engineering Company

BASIC FUNCTION: To be responsible to the Vice President–Manufacturing for master schedules and shop schedules which coordinate Engineering, Estimating, Manufacturing, and Sales; for developing lead time and establishing delivery dates on new orders; for Manufacturing Division's contacts with customers' representatives; for recommending changes in workforce, hours, and/or machine utilization to meet changing conditions within the Manufacturing Division; for dispatching and production expediting; and for reports and records.

BASIC OBJECTIVE: To administer the functions of the Production Planning Department in such a manner that optimum schedules and services are provided which aid the Manufacturing Division to meet Corporate objectives.

MAJOR DUTIES AND RESPONSIBILITIES

1. Organization and Personnel

a. To maintain and direct an organization which is adequate for the performance of the Production Planning functions.

b. To insure that the duties and responsibilities of subordinates are clearly defined and fixed, and to approve position descriptions of immediate subordinates.

c. To recommend to the Vice President–Manufacturing major changes in the form and size of the Production Planning Department to meet changing conditions.

d. To see that personnel in the Production Planning Department are kept fully and currently informed of all pertinent Company policies, and that such policies are observed.

e. To recommend to the Vice President–Manufacturing the employment, promotion, dismissal, change in status, or compensation of personnel under his immediate supervision.

f. To direct the Company's personnel policies within the Production Planning Department.

g. To approve the employment, promotion, dismissal, change in status, or compensation of personnel reporting to his immediate subordinates.

h. To periodically review and appraise the performance and qualifications of subordinates as prescribed by Industrial Relations policies.

    i. To hold periodic meetings with subordinates to discuss and review operating policies, plans, performance, and problems.

2. *Master Scheduling*

    a. To prepare, maintain, and distribute master schedules to include all firm orders.

    b. To consult Division Vice Presidents, as required, in order to coordinate and incorporate divisional activities into master schedules.

    c. To review factory work orders and coordinate their lead-time requirements into a master schedule.

    d. To coordinate Material Control scheduling relationships with Shop lead-time requirements.

    e. To establish tentative and firm delivery dates.

    f. To submit to the Vice President–Manufacturing periodic work-load reports and manpower and machine requirement forecasts.

3. *Shop Scheduling*

    a. To prepare, maintain, and distribute periodic shop and machine-load schedules for all Production Departments.

    b. To see that factory work order processing masters and shop route sheets are prepared for each order, using data established by Processing group.

    c. To prepare detail lead-time requirements for Purchase Material in conjunction with Material Control group.

    d. To establish machine and equipment loading.

    e. To see that progress reports, job-status records, and other miscellaneous records are maintained and prepared as a control of established schedules, including hours worked on factory work orders and the like.

    f. To reschedule work when original schedules are not met.

4. *Dispatching*

    a. To see that factory work orders are issued by shop supervision in accordance with master and shop schedules.

    b. To see that move orders are issued as required.

    c. To see that actual time expended is properly recorded on job-time cards and factory work order cards.

5. *Production Expediting*

    a. To contact and confer with various Divisions and Departments to receive or supply information concerning schedules and/or shipping dates.

   b. To meet customers' representatives, supply requested information, and maintain such established contacts as required.

6. *Budgets*

   a. To assist the Supervisor, Cost Accounting, Budgets, and Timekeeping in the preparation of the annual Production Planning Department budget and to submit it to the Vice President–Manufacturing. To supply the Supervisor, Cost Accounting, Budgets, and Timekeeping with the direct labor hour requirement estimate for his use in establishing Manufacturing Department budgets.

   b. To operate the Production Planning Department within the approved budget.

   c. To assist the Plant Engineering Department in the preparation of the annual budget for capital expenditures within the Production Planning Department and to submit it to the Vice President–Manufacturing.

   d. To periodically meet with the Vice President–Manufacturing and review actual operating performance in relation to budgets.

7. *Production Control*

   a. To supervise the services of the Production Planning Department, including:

     (1) Central Control status and progress of shop orders.

     (2) Determination of shop workload requirements.

     (3) Distribution of workload to shop.

     (4) Dispatching of shop orders.

     (5) Expediting of production shop orders.

   b. To coordinate all established schedules and work station loadings with the General Manufacturing Superintendent, in order that the various Shop Superintendents and Foremen can maintain schedules and shipping dates.

8. *General*

   a. To recommend to the Vice President–Manufacturing revisions in Department policies and procedures when advisable to achieve more effective production control.

   b. To approve requisitions within the Production Planning Department for equipment, supplies, services, and any expenditures as authorized in the purchasing requisition procedure; to recommend to the Vice President–Manufacturing amounts in excess of authorized limits.

   c. To confer with the Industrial Relations Division with respect to orientation and training of personnel in the Production Planning Department.

d. To perform any additional duties as requested by the Vice President–Manufacturing.

SUPERVISOR OF PRODUCTION CONTROL

Controls Company of America

PRIMARY FUNCTION AND RESPONSIBILITY: The Supervisor of Production Control is responsible for supervising the activities of the Plant Production Control function in planning and executing factory assembly and parts schedules and maintaining customer service. He has managerial and functional responsibility for assuring that the production schedules are met, together with good inventory turnover and satisfactory customer service.

RELATIONSHIPS

Line: Reports to Plant Manager. Advises him of all matters that will affect the activities of the plant. Supervises Product Production Planners; Chief Dispatcher; Receiving, Stocking, and Shipping Leader; Order Clerks; Expediters; Stockroom personnel, and miscellaneous clerical help.

Staff: Cooperates with Sales, Material Control, Purchasing, Plant Superintendent, Quality Control, Manufacturing Engineering, and others as required.

Outside: Participates, when practical, in professional societies and associations to insure knowledge of new and improved production control techniques.

DUTIES AND RESPONSIBILITIES

1. To prepare assembly and parts schedules for the plant operation, order fabricated material to support these schedules, and follow up to see that schedules are met. Also, to expedite material control for purchased parts and raw material.

2. To assist in the establishment of inventory turnover budget and allowable inventories by product line in order to minimize work-in-process materials and control the inventory.

3. To evaluate customer schedules and the sales forecast in terms of capacity, facilities, and material availability and make his recommendations to the Plant Manager.

4. To administer an effective and efficient over-all Production Control program as dictated by the requirements of the business, assuring that plant output schedules and budgets are met and efficient scheduling and dispatching methods are employed so that products are produced in the shortest possible time and with the least possible expense.

5. To assure that inactive and obsolete parts and raw materials are inventoried, analyzed, and reported to the proper parties, who will advise scrap, rework, or resale to the best advantage of the Corporation.

6. To develop, with the Manager–Production Control, new and improved routines, methods, and procedures aimed at the reduction of overhead expense.

7. To direct the activities of the Receiving, Stocking, and Shipping personnel to insure accurate identification and count of materials, and to achieve optimum space utilization.

8. To negotiate with Sales personnel on all delivery schedules.

9. To maintain a high level of schedule promises kept and establish a reputation of trust and dependability with regard to meeting shipping dates and keeping Sales properly informed of the status of orders.

10. To organize and maintain a balanced and trained organization with the flexibility and potential to meet both short- and long-range requirements.

11. To administer the Company policy concerning personnel administration as it relates to Personnel of the _____ Manufacturing–Production Control function. This includes such activities as hiring and termination, recommendations for changes in rates and working conditions, the handling of grievances, and the training of personnel in procedures.

GENERAL: The Supervisor of Production Control controls the flow of all production material within the plant; therefore, the position requires over-all knowledge as well as detailed knowledge of inventory control, production control, material handling and stockkeeping, and manufacturing processes. Considerable judgment is required to prevent financial loss to the Corporation and customer dissatisfaction because of inability to meet shipments plus the accumulation of excessive inventories. Ability to make both long- and short-range plans involving production and inventory control functions and procedures, systems, and personnel is essential. The quality and timeliness of recommendations to the Plant Manager are a direct measure of the performance of the Supervisor of Production Control.

SUPERVISOR–INVENTORY CONTROL

A Machinery Maker

FUNCTION: To supervise, directly and through section heads, the activities of the department engaged in insuring that stocks of goods are adequate but not excessive for operating requirements, in accordance with established practice and policy procedures; to provide a basis for recording inventories and movement of goods in the most economical manner consistent with Corporation's procurement and accounting requirements; to determine the most economical quantities and varieties to be carried; to promote more rapid turnover and minimize the investment in inventories to reduce taxes, insurance, storage and handling expense, and minimum losses from obsolescence and physical deterioration, assuring an available supply of materials when needed to facilitate production operations, minimize cost of idle time, and render better service to customers.

ORGANIZATIONAL RELATIONSHIPS

1. Reports to: Manager of Manufacturing. Supervises: Warehousing, internal transportation, and stock ledgers.

2. The Inventory Control Supervisor reports directly to the Manager of Manufacturing. His duties require close collaboration with all Manufacturing, Engineering, and Sales Departments to achieve production schedules.

SPECIFIC RESPONSIBILITIES: The Inventory Control Supervisor shall be accountable for the following broad responsibilities that he shall fulfill through delegation of responsibility and authority and by initiation and execution of action in keeping with the authority vested in his office and the applicable Corporation policies and procedures.

1. To control the delivery of material requirements as to time and quantity, and the purchasing, receiving, storage, and handling of material; to store finished parts, ship finished products, and provide all records necessary to keep track of these materials; to establish

inventories of the raw materials and parts items to be carried in stock; to set up order points for the various items based on purchasing and manufacturing lead times in accordance with specified practice; to requisition items when available balance falls below order point.

2. To prepare reports on inventory activities on request.

3. To schedule and conduct meetings to review current status of production schedules and work jointly with the Departments involved to overcome any problems.

4. To provide internal transportation between Warehousing and Production Departments as needed to maintain production schedules.

5. To be constantly on the alert for opportunities to improve methods, materials, and procedures so as to effect economy in the operation of the Department and Division. To prepare and submit recommendations, outlining the features and anticipated savings, to management for approval.

6. To train, instruct, and assign work to employees. To administer the Corporation personnel policies within the Department, enforce safety and health regulations, and take prompt action on employee complaints to encourage good morale. To maintain current status with respect to employee morale and keep management informed about it. To review job performance of subordinates and advise them of their good points and shortcomings; to counsel them on growth potential.

7. To plan and schedule work and make effective use of employees' time. To keep Department operating expense within budget allowance.

AUTHORITY: The Inventory Control Supervisor is vested with the following authority to be exercised in keeping with all established Corporation and Division policies and procedures in carrying out the responsibilities of the office.

1. To hire authorized personnel and recommend salary-rate or employee-status changes in the Department.

2. To penalize or discharge any employee in the Department who is guilty of an infraction of Corporation rules which calls for such penalty.

3. To settle complaints or grievances in the Department within the limits of Corporation personnel policy and labor contract terms.

MANAGER, FINISHED PRODUCT INVENTORY CONTROL

The Carborundum Company

GENERAL RESPONSIBILITY: Is responsible for control of the level of finished product inventories and for control of the quantity and allocation of these inventories to the plant warehouse and district warehouses, all in accordance with Company policy; for the coordination and monitoring of finished product inventory record keeping and the order-processing phase of finished inventory control with Data Processing, the Division Accounting Branch, Manufacturing Branch, the Sales Branches, and the Marketing Division; for manually intervening in the Data Processing finished inventory control system to cover exceptions to the general pattern of automatic inventory control; for implementing all established changes of policy in the Division Manufacturing Branch, Sales Branches, Accounting Branch, and plant and district warehouses that affect Division finished product inventory control; for acting as liaison between functional staff and Division management and their subordinates and as liaison between the Sales Branches and the Manufacturing Branch in all matters pertaining to finished product inventory control; for making studies and initiating recommendations for improvement and extension of the Data Processing finished inventory control system and expansion of use of finished inventory data to improve customer service, factory scheduling, and the balance between inventory and setup costs; and for making studies and recommendations regarding changes in the cost data used in the inventory control system.

ORGANIZATIONAL RELATIONSHIPS

A. *Line.* Responsible to: Manager, Production Control Department. Supervises: Unit salaried employees.

B. *Staff.* Advises and receives advice from Finance Division Manager and his subordinates, Marketing Division Manager and his subordinates, Coated Abrasives Division Manager and his subordinates, District Sales Managers, and District Office Managers.

SPECIFIC DUTIES

KIND OF ACTIVITY	SCOPE	TYPE OF ACTION
A. *Line or Operational*		
1. Finished product inventory levels.	Coated Abrasives Division.	Directs the control of finished product inventories, including maintenance of inventory

III. SPECIFIC DUTIES (cont'd)

KIND OF ACTIVITY	SCOPE	TYPE OF ACTION
A. *Line or Operational* (cont'd)		
		ceilings, and coordination with Data Processing and line supervision on economic manufacturing quantities and stock levels and with Sales management on service levels.
2. Allocation of finished product inventories.	Coated Abrasives Division.	Directs the allocation of finished product inventories to either plant or district warehouses in line with transportation and storage costs, service levels, and division policies.
3. Automatic inventory control.	Inter-Division.	Manually intervenes in the daily processing of automatic inventory control to question, investigate, and take action on all exceptions to the normal pattern. Contacts District Sales Managers, Office Managers, and Manufacturing supervision for specific data, and decides courses of action.
4. Implementing established policy changes.	Coated Abrasives Division.	Implements established policy changes regarding finished product inventory control.
B. *Staff or Functional*		
1. Order handling and finished product inventory procedures.	Coated Abrasives Division.	Conducts studies leading to improvement in automatic order handling and inventory control procedures and recommends to Manager, Production Control, programs, policies, and procedures pertaining to these improvements.
2. Liaison with Data Processing.	Coated Abrasives Division.	Consults with Manager, Data Processing Branch, and his subordinates on all matters pertaining to inter- and intra-

III. SPECIFIC DUTIES (cont'd)

KIND OF ACTIVITY	SCOPE	TYPE OF ACTION
B. *Staff or Functional* (cont'd)		
		Division finished product inventory control. Updates cost data used in the Data Processing automated inventory control system.
3. Liaison with Sales and other Division Branches.	Coated Abrasives Division.	Maintains liaison with Sales, Manufacturing, Accounting, and Technical Branches regarding finished product inventory control as related to inventory records, order processing, obsolescence, and so on.
4. Expansion of data.	Coated Abrasives Division.	Consults with Branch heads and their subordinates; at the direction of Manager, Production Control, conducts studies leading to use of finished inventory data in plant scheduling, work in process, and raw material inventories.

SUPERVISOR–DETAIL SCHEDULING AND MANUFACTURING COORDINATOR

A. O. Smith Corporation

REPORTS TO: Supervisor–Production Control.

PRIMARY FUNCTION: Supervises the coordination of the machine loading in the Manufacturing Department necessitated by parts shortages and production priorities. Effects detailed scheduling and rescheduling of parts fabrication and assembly operations and movement and storage of raw materials, parts, subassemblies and finished goods, tooling, and blueprints within the Manufacturing Departments.

DUTIES AND RESPONSIBILITIES

1. Supervises the coordination of the machine loading in the Manufacturing Department. This includes the following services:

   a. The maintenance of surveillance over machine-load cost centers and the rerouting of production through less busy cost centers.

   b. The establishment of machining priorities necessary to complete assembly schedules.

   c. The splitting of full job packets for partial production as required by available raw materials, machine loading, and the like.

   d. Assistance to the Foreman and the Stores Department in the issuance of materials required by the manufacturing cost centers.

   e. Informing of Production Control relative to those items which will not meet promised shipping dates for the purpose of establishing new delivery dates.

   f. The preparation of periodic reports by cost centers relative to the number and schedule status of jobs in the shop. Also, reports by cost center relative to PRN and red-tag orders.

2. Administers Company personnel policies as they affect employees under his supervision with reference to training, safety, vacations, merit increases, housekeeping, and the like. Retains authority to recommend firing.

4. The Colorado Fuel and Iron Corporation

By way of completing this selection of managerial position descriptions in manufacturing, we present—in an unabridged version —the "Organization Guide" of the Roebling Plants of The Colorado Fuel and Iron Corporation.

HOW TO USE THE GUIDE

The position descriptions included in the Guide, which have been worked out with the participation of the individuals involved, set forth certain new responsibilities which have been recognized as needed for the development of the Corporation, as well as formalizing the objectives, scope, responsibilities, and relationships of various positions.

The effectiveness and teamwork of the organization will increase as it becomes versed in operating under the conditions agreed upon. Reference to the Guide should be helpful in answering questions concerning the handling of particular matters and should serve to define organizational problems whose solution should be included in revisions to the Guide.

Each executive and supervisor whose position is described should extend application of the Guide by developing similar descriptions covering his subordinates. This process will bring the following benefits:

1. Agreement will be reached between executives and supervisors and subordinates as to the division of activities and the establishment of objectives, responsibilities, and relationships for each position.

2. Each subordinate will gain a better understanding of his own responsibilities and the orientation of his activities to those of the organization as a whole.

3. The Guide will provide a framework for the selection, training, and promotion of subordinates. Duties of a position can be more easily translated into a specification of qualifications, training, and experience required. The Guide establishes an objective basis on which performance can be reviewed regularly. It spells out the requirements of higher positions for the training of those who are under consideration for promotion.

RESPONSIBILITIES OF EVERY EXECUTIVE

The term "executive" or "supervisor" is just another name for management—the executive or supervisor assists in formulating, and executes, policies which guide the enterprise. Good executives are mentally and emotionally alert and active; they demonstrate initiative, imagination, and creative thinking and thus inspire enthusiasm for getting a job done well.

Every executive has certain responsibilities which he must perform because he is an executive—and which he must perform according to established policies if he is to be a successful executive.

Stated simply, every executive must do these things in connection with carrying out the job assigned to him:

1. Every executive must make plans for carrying out the job he has been given to do. In order to avoid making a whole lot of little plans, the executive establishes a "policy," which is a plan of action to guide subordinates so they won't have to keep checking with him on details.

2. Every executive must assign duties to the subordinates who will help him carry out his assigned job. He must decide how many subordinate positions are needed, what each is to cover, and what authority each is to have. This is the development of the plan of organization, or the plan for administering his job.

3. Every executive must select personnel to fill the subordinate positions which have been set up. Obviously, the people selected must have the personal qualifications to do the particular job. Then these subordinates must be directed, trained, coached, and inspired to do their best work. Subordinates must be made to feel that there

are opportunities for advancement and that their personal interests are being properly considered.

4. Every executive must provide, within the limits of his authority, the necessary physical facilities for carrying out the job assigned to him. These facilities may be plants, operating equipment, storage space, and office facilities.

5. Every executive must see that the necessary procedures are set up so subordinates may carry on their jobs with maximum effectiveness and at low cost. These procedures consist of the best ways for doing each individual job under his direction.

Stated more fully and more technically, these responsibilities require every executive to do these things:

A. In Establishing Policies

1. See that policies are established for all activities under his jurisdiction.

2. Administer approved policies.

3. Receive recommended revisions in established policies from associates and subordinates.

4. Review recommendations with appropriate executives.

5. Recommend changes to superiors.

B. In Establishing Organization

1. Make certain that all necessary functions are provided for and are properly coordinated.

2. Receive recommended revisions in the established plan of organization from associates and subordinates.

3. Review recommendations with appropriate executives.

4. Recommend changes to superiors.

C. In Directing Personnel

1. Plan and delegate to subordinates regular and special assignments, and maintain aggressive follow-through to assure proper performance by subordinates.

2. Train subordinates in the use of facilities and in procedures, personnel relations, and administration policies.

3. Interpret policies and the plan of organization to subordinates.

4. Approve the selection of candidates proposed by the Administrator of Employment.

5. Develop understudies for the successful continuity of the activity, and coach them in doing the best possible job.

6. Maintain discipline, adjust grievances, and counsel with subordinates to increase morale.

7. Measure effectiveness of effort and approve salary adjustments of subordinates.

8. Give attention to the personal interests of subordinates so as to assure them of proper opportunities for advancement and recognition.

9. Approve transfers and discharges.

D. *With Respect to Facilities*

1. Provide adequate facilities for economical operations.

2. Determine the proper location of facilities for optimum operating results and possible expansion.

3. Provide proper safeguards to persons and properties in the operation of facilities.

4. Provide for protection and maintenance of facilities.

5. Receive from associates and subordinates recommendations as to changes in type of facilities, their locations, safety devices, protection, and maintenance.

6. Review recommendations with appropriate executives.

7. Recommend changes to superior.

E. *With Respect to Methods, Procedures, and Techniques*

1. Provide adequate methods, procedures, and techniques for economical operations and for rendering required services.

2. Prepare written guides covering established methods, procedures, and techniques for instruction of personnel.

3. Assure compliance with these methods, procedures, and techniques.

4. Receive recommended changes from associates and subordinates.

5. Review recommendations with appropriate executives.

6. Recommend changes to superior.

DEFINITION OF TERMS

1. LINE AND FUNCTIONAL RESPONSIBILITY

The organization plan for the Corporation combines line and functional responsibility for various activities. If each executive is to have a clear understanding of the scope of his authority and the ways in which the authority is to be exercised in relation to others, he must recognize the difference between these two types of responsibility.

Line responsibility (and good organization always provides equal "authority" with "responsibility") is concerned with determining the need, time, and place for action and with issuing direct orders to line subordinates. Direction of day-to-day operations involves line responsibility for getting things done.

Functional authority (sometimes called "technical" authority) is simply the accountability for seeing that operations carried on in other departments adhere to procedures and methods which have been established by the department having the functional or technical authority for the specific activity.

Once methods and procedures have been established for operation of a particular activity in another department, that department assumes responsibility for their adoption, as the department with functional authority has no line authority over the persons who are to operate or use the procedures. Since adoption must be secured through regular line organization channels, success of the functional authority depends to a great degree on power of persuasion and on acceptance of Company policy by everyone.

From a technical organization standpoint, however, the executive to whom both the line and functional supervisors report in effect gives blanket direction that the procedures of the functional department shall be followed. Thus the functional executive or supervisor, or the technical specialist, actually has line backing for his technical work.

When the methods and procedures have been adopted, functional authority also follows through with accountability for seeing that established methods and procedures are adhered to in actual operation.

In essence the above might be summarized in this way. The line authority says, "Do," and the functional authority says, "When you do, do it this way and in accordance with this plan."

2. COLLABORATION AND COOPERATION

Collaboration indicates an equal assumption of responsibility for the action on which two or more individuals work together.

Cooperation implies the lending of assistance (without any assumption of responsibility) by one or more individuals to the party in whom responsibility is vested.

Line Positions

The following pages present a selection of the key positions in The Colorado Fuel and Iron Corporation's line.

WORKS MANAGER

BASIC FUNCTION

The Works Manager is responsible for directing and coordinating the Corporation's local manufacturing activities.

SCOPE

The Works Manager is responsible for directing and coordinating the Corporation's local manufacturing activities; he directly supervises:

Superintendent–Wire Rope Mill.
Superintendent–Cold Rolling Mill.
Superintendent–Steel Production.
Superintendent–Wire Mills.
Superintendent–Planning and Industrial Engineering.
Chief Plant Engineer.
Superintendent–Quality Control.
Superintendent–Industrial Relations.

OBJECTIVES AND RESPONSIBILITIES

Although additional duties may be assigned to him, his specific responsibilities include these major activities. To:

1. Participate with other major executives in the establishment of long-term objectives of the Corporation, and be responsible for formulation of production programs to accomplish these objectives.

2. Develop and maintain sound labor and personnel relations in accordance with approved policies established by Industrial Relations and the Publicity Department.

3. Review pertinent management control and other reports in relation to approved plans and take corrective action when necessary.

4. Direct maintenance operations for facilities and equipment as economically as possible, consistent with proper maintenance.

5. Coordinate and direct, through Superintendents, cost reduction studies on products which are not competitive due to high manufacturing cost.

6. Review Divisional Sales Plans, through Superintendent–Planning and Industrial Engineering and Superintendents, with respect to labor and equipment requirements and demands on joint facilities and approve manufacturing programs developed from Sales Plans.

7. Review and approve divisional manufacturing overhead expense budgets and operating expense budgets.

8. Review requests for capital expenditures and make recommendations to Director of Operations and, through Superintendent–Planning and Industrial Engineering and Manufacturing Superintendents, cooperate with Controller in preparation of capital expenditure budgets.

9. Review actual production as compared with planned production, and supervise efforts by Manufacturing Managers to correct deviations.

10. Supervise all traffic and transportation activities through the Superintendent-Transportation.

RELATIONSHIP WITH OTHER UNITS OF ORGANIZATION

1. Cooperates with other executives to insure that manufacturing programs are synchronized to greatest extent possible with sales, financial, and purchasing programs.

2. Collaborates with Vice President–Engineering in purchase of new equipment to insure that equipment is technically suitable.

3. Collaborates with Director of Purchases, through Superintendent–Planning and Industrial Engineering and Manufacturing Superintendents, in the formulation of purchasing programs.

SUPERINTENDENT–WIRE MILLS

BASIC FUNCTION

The Superintendent–Wire Mills is in charge of operations and productive facilities of his mill in accordance with Corporation policies. He is responsible for the manufacture, in accordance with Standard Manufacturing Practices, of all products to approved specifications and quality standards; for the economy of manufacturing operations of the mill, and for making recommendations to management for improving same when to take such action exceeds the limits of his authority.

SCOPE

The Superintendent–Wire Mills reports to the Works Manager, and the following supervisory personnel report to him:

Assistant to Superintendent–Wire Mills.
Superintendent–Production.
Superintendent–Planning and Cost Control.
Product Engineer.
Divisional Engineer.

OBJECTIVES AND RESPONSIBILITIES

Although additional responsibilities may be assigned to him by the Works Manager, his specific duties include the following:

A. Cost, Schedule, and Quality Requirements

1. Direct and coordinate operation of equipment and personnel to obtain lowest cost practicable, consistent with equipment limitations and quality standards.

2. Direct the manufacture of products according to approved Production Programs and Schedules and manufacturing practices (as established in conjunction with Metallurgical Engineering).

3. Assume responsibility for manufacture of products at standard cost or better, except as affected by volume or raw material price variances.

4. Direct cost reduction efforts and the adjustment of variable overhead expense to match volume levels.

5. Prepare operating expense budgets with assistance of Controller.

6. Review management control and other operating and inspection reports in relation to approved plans, and take corrective action when necessary.

7. Under the functional direction of the Controller and with his assistance, design and install cost control procedures using expanded Standard Manufacturing Practices, improved cost reporting, and analysis.

8. Prepare and submit to Superintendent–Planning and Industrial

Engineering anticipated plant capacity data, considering such factors as equipment, labor, and materials available.

9. Review applicable sales plans with Works Manager, and Superintendent–Planning and Industrial Engineering, with respect to labor and equipment requirements.

10. Direct Superintendent–Planning and Cost Control in development of Production Programs to meet Sales Plans, and approve such programs. Review for approval the schedules developed for execution of such programs.

11. Direct own supervisory personnel to make effective use of inspection services, and develop requirements for inspection service in conjunction with Quality Control Engineer.

12. Through Quality Control Engineer, control production to meet approved standards of quality.

B. *Product Specification and Design*

1. Through the Quality Control Engineer, formulate decisions relating to acceptance, modification, or rejection of customer product specifications for insulated wire products.

2. Through the Quality Control Engineer, develop processes for manufacture of steel wire and conduct research to improve processes.

C. *Wage and Salary Administration*

1. Direct activities of Mill Industrial Engineer in accordance with approved policies and practices.

2. Review for approval job descriptions, classifications, and evaluations to be used in Mill.

3. Assume responsibility for application of approved job classes to all employees in Mill.

4. Merit rate technical, clerical, and supervisory personnel on the Mill payroll.

5. Assume responsibility for accurate production and time recording and proper application of incentive rates.

D. *Equipment and Facilities*

1. Assist in development of approved plans for modification or addition of equipment and facilities. Initiate requests for capital expenditures and other works orders chargeable to the mill.

E. *Personnel Relations*

1. Assume responsibility for maintaining adequate and proper employee relations within mill in the execution of Corporation policies and programs.

2. Assume responsibility for on-the-job employee training, including prospective foremen.

3. Assume responsibility for shop discipline, including accident prevention.

4. Participate, as required, in the grievance procedure.

5. Assist in developing and executing the manufacturing phase of various training programs.

RELATIONSHIP WITH OTHER UNITS OF THE COMPANY

1. Cooperate with Quality Control Engineering in establishing Standard Manufacturing Practices for all wire products, such Standard Manufacturing Practices to be jointly approved before installation.

2. Collaborate with Quality Control Engineering in making decisions relating to the acceptance, modification, or rejection of questionable customer wire requirements.

3. Collaborate with Quality Control Engineering when needed on disposition or conversion of off-standard wire products.

4. Request Quality Control Engineering studies directed toward reduced material and processing costs, and improved quality or solution of metallurgical problems relating to life or performance of material and equipment.

5. Co-sign, with Quality Control Engineering, customer complaint investigation reports on wire.

6. Review and develop plans with Plant Engineer and Central Plant Engineering personnel for major Plant Engineering and Maintenance projects.

7. Discuss problems of Maintenance service and cost with Plant Engineer. Cooperate in setting up planned Maintenance program for mill and in scheduling down-time on machines for overhaul.

8. Work closely with Superintendents of Industrial Relations–Trenton and Roebling to be fully informed of the interpretation and administrative requirements of the Corporation's labor relations policies and Union contracts. Make recommendations to Superintendents of Industrial Relations–Trenton and Roebling concerning labor contract terms.

9. Through the Quality Control Engineer, provide technical service to Sales on a budgeted basis.

ASSISTANT TO SUPERINTENDENT–WIRE MILLS

BASIC FUNCTION

The basic function of the Assistant to Superintendent–Wire Mills is to assist the Superintendent on a variety of special assignments. He is not charged with the administration of any major line or staff activity.

SCOPE

He reports to the Superintendent. Unless otherwise specified, he has charge of no regularly assigned personnel.

OBJECTIVES AND RESPONSIBILITIES

His responsibilities vary with assignment from the Superintendent, but his specific duties may include the following:

1. Handle personnel problems, representing the Superintendent to effect required solutions.
2. Represent the Superintendent in Union meetings.
3. Conduct special cost reduction studies in material usage, manufacturing methods, and overhead expense areas.
4. Set up controls on Maintenance expense, and conformity with schedules.
5. Expedite shipments of special orders.
6. Investigate causes of customer complaints.
7. Direct training projects for mill personnel.
8. Carry out portions of Plant Safety Program.
9. Direct the compilation of data for special production, cost, or personnel reports.
10. Investigate conditions which create excessive scrap or rework of material.

RELATIONSHIP WITH OTHER UNITS OF ORGANIZATION

The Superintendent may delegate a wide variety of responsibilities involving contacts with any other Departments of the Corporation.

SUPERINTENDENT–PRODUCTION

Basic Function

The Superintendent–Production has delegated to him by the Superintendent–Wire Mills the responsibility for the manufacture of all products as required by approved schedules and in accordance with approved operating policies and practices, including specification, cost, and quality standards.

Scope

He reports to the Superintendent–Wire Mills, and to him report assigned Supervisors–Night Operations, General Foremen, and Foremen.

Objectives and Responsibilities

Although additional responsibilities may be assigned to him by the Superintendent–Wire Mills, his specific duties include the following:

A. Cost, Schedule, and Quality Requirements

1. Under the general direction of the Superintendent–Wire Mills, supervise the operation of facilities and production personnel to meet standard costs and approved schedules.

2. Initiate and/or carry out assignments relating to reduction of manufacturing costs, reviewing labor and material costs, and instituting corrective action when necessary.

3. Assume responsibility for correcting variable overhead expense under his control when volume fluctuates.

4. Take an active part in assisting Superintendent–Wire Mills to establish basis for mill expense budgets.

5. Approve overtime operation.

6. Schedule personnel, facilities, and materials as required in order to meet approved production schedules.

7. Work with Superintendent–Planning and Cost Control to modify schedules as a result of unforeseen conditions.

8. Keep abreast of quality trends, including rejects and reworks, loss of production, etc., as shown in inspection reports. Institute measures to improve the quality of output and reduce rejects and rework.

9. Work with Quality Control personnel in correcting and maintaining level of quality in production.

B. *Wage Administration*

1. Supervise accurate reporting of time and production data.

C. *Methods and Standard Manufacturing Practices*

1. Assume responsibility for maintaining standard conditions and procedures under which time standards were set and are subsequently administered.

2. Supervise the manufacture of products according to Standard Manufacturing Practices.

3. Recommend changes in manufacturing processes or methods in the interest of lower costs, improved quality, or higher production rates.

4. Provide technical and manufacturing advice to Product, Quality Control, or Sales Engineers where questions of manufacturing technique are involved.

D. *Maintenance of Equipment*

1. Approve requests for Maintenance service not requiring work orders.

2. Make and/or approve recommendations for units to be included in planned Maintenance programs.

E. *Personnel Relations*

1. Under direction of Superintendent–Wire Mills, assume responsibility for executing the Company's labor relations policies and programs through subordinate supervisory personnel.

2. On assignment from the Superintendent–Wire Mills, represent him in meetings with Union members or other mill personnel.

3. Direct the carrying-out of on-the-job training for production personnel.

RELATIONSHIP WITH OTHER UNITS OF ORGANIZATION

The Superintendent–Wire Mills may delegate a wide variety of responsibility for contacts with other Departments, particularly on production problems.

GENERAL FOREMAN

BASIC FUNCTION

The General Foreman is the operating supervisor on the day shift in charge of an assigned area or group of departments within a plant. He is responsible for the operation of equipment according to approved schedules at the lowest cost consistent with quality.

SCOPE

He reports to the Superintendent–Production. To him report assigned Assistant General Foremen, Foremen, clerks, and hourly-paid personnel.

OBJECTIVES AND RESPONSIBILITIES

Although additional responsibilities may be assigned to him by the Superintendent–Production, his specific duties are as follows:

A. *Cost, Schedule, and Quality Requirements*

1. Under the direction of the Superintendent–Production, supervise the operation of assigned facilities and personnel to meet cost, quality, and schedule requirements. Coordinate and administer the activities of assigned Departments to attain these requirements.

2. Assume responsibility for attainment by subordinate foremen of standard costs of manufacture of labor and machine hours and material usage.

3. Attain complete familiarity with expense budgets.

4. Recommend adjustment of variable overhead expense to coincide with volume level budget.

5. Review cost and performance reports, recommend corrective measures, or take approved action indicated as necessary.

6. Operate within limits of expense budgets for repairs, supplies, and small tools.

7. Interpret schedule requirements for personnel, facilities, and material. Direct subordinate personnel in taking steps to meet such requirements.

8. Maintain close check on quality trends, cost of rejects and rework, loss of production, etc., as shown in inspection reports.

9. Recommend or undertake approved measures to correct off-standard conditions and work with Quality Control Engineering personnel to maintain level of quality in production.

B. *Wage Administration*

1. Assume responsibility for proper administration by subordinate personnel of incentive standards and job class assignments.

2. Assist assigned Foremen in settling problems arising from rate and wage administration.

3. Furnish information as required for description and classification of new and changed jobs.

C. *Methods and Standard Manufacturing Practices*

1. Assume responsibility for observance of all Standard Manufacturing Practices by subordinate Foremen.

2. Assist assigned Foremen in meeting operating, technical, and quality problems created by requirements of Standard Manufacturing Practices.

3. Recommend changes in Standard Manufacturing Practices and methods of operation to reduce costs and/or improve quality.

D. *Maintenance of Equipment*

1. Request Maintenance service on assigned machines, equipment, and facilities.

2. Cooperate with Maintenance personnel assigned to area. Following consultation with Superintendent–Production, work out suitable down-time schedules on machines and equipment for overhaul.

3. Make recommendations on replacement of machines and equipment.

E. *Personnel Relations*

1. Oversee and coordinate the administration of the Corporation's labor relations policies by assigned Foreman. This includes training, safety, grievance procedures, shop discipline, and morale. Assist subordinate supervisory personnel to carry out their responsibility for these elements. Apply authorized interpretations of labor contracts where needed.

SUPERVISOR–NIGHT OPERATIONS

BASIC FUNCTION

The Supervisor–Night Operations is responsible for the operation of his assigned plant or areas during second- or third-shift operation as directed by the Superintendent–Production. On the day shift, he serves as an assistant to the Superintendent–Production on special assignments.

SCOPE

He reports to the Superintendent–Production. On second- and third-shift operation he serves as supervisor or coordinator of all operating facilities and assigned Foremen, clerks, and hourly-paid personnel within the Division, as designated by the Superintendent–Production. On the day shift, subordinate supervisory personnel report to him only on special assignment from the Superintendent–Production.

OBJECTIVES AND RESPONSIBILITIES

Although additional responsibilities may be assigned to him by the Superintendent–Production, his specific duties include the following:

A. *Cost, Schedule, and Quality Requirements*

1. Under the direction of the Superintendent–Production, supervise the operation of assigned facilities and personnel to meet cost, quality, and schedule requirements.

2. Assume responsibility for attainment by subordinate Foremen of standard costs of manufacture of labor and machine hours and material usage.

3. Attain complete familiarity with expense budgets.

4. Recommend adjustment of variable overhead expense to coincide with volume level budget.

5. Review cost and performance reports, and recommend corrective measures.

6. Operate within limits of expense budgets for repairs, supplies, small tools, etc.

7. Coordinate work of related departments to meet scheduled requirements.

8. Maintain close check on quality trends, cost of rejects and rework, loss of production, and so forth, as shown in inspection reports.

9. Recommend measures to correct off-standard conditions.

10. Work with Quality Control Engineering personnel to maintain level of quality in production.

B. *Wage Administration*

1. Assume responsibility for proper administration by subordinate personnel of incentive standards and job class assignments.

2. Assist assigned Foremen in settling problems arising from rate and wage administration.

3. Furnish information as required for description and classification of new and changed jobs.

4. Make first approval of down-time on machines and equipment.

C. *Methods and Standard Manufacturing Practices*

1. Assume responsibility for observance of all Standard Manufacturing Practices by subordinate Foremen.

2. Assist assigned Foremen in meeting operating, technical, and quality problems created by requirements of Standard Manufacturing Practices.

3. Recommend changes in Standard Manufacturing Practices and methods of operation to reduce costs and/or improve quality of products.

D. *Maintenance of Equipment*

1. Request Maintenance service necessary to maintain maximum level of production and efficiency of equipment.

2. Request down-time on machines and equipment for overhaul.

3. Make recommendations on replacement of machines and equipment.

4. Cooperate with Maintenance personnel assigned to area.

E. *Personnel Relations*

1. Oversee and coordinate the administration of the Corporation's labor relations policies by assigned Foremen. This includes training, safety, grievance procedures, shop discipline, and morale. Assist subordinate supervisory personnel to carry out their responsibility for these elements. Apply authorized interpretations of labor contracts where needed.

F. *Miscellaneous Duties*

1. Carry out special assignments for Superintendent–Production while working on day shift. These special assignments include the following:

   a. Investigations to reduce product scrap and rework.

   b. Expediting of required product material.

   c. Causes of poor labor and machine performance.

   d. Overhead cost reduction studies.

   e. Other miscellaneous types of assignments.

FOREMAN–PRODUCTION

The Foreman–Production is the operating supervisor directly in charge of hourly-paid personnel in an assigned area or department. He is directly responsible for the carrying out of all approved schedules at standard material and labor costs.

SCOPE

He reports to a General Foreman, Supervisor–Night Operations, or Superintendent–Production; to him report assigned clerks and hourly personnel.

OBJECTIVES AND RESPONSIBILITIES

Although additional responsibilities may be assigned to him by his superior, his specific duties include the following:

A. Cost, Schedule, and Quality Requirements

1. Directly supervise personnel and the operation of machines and equipment to meet cost, quality, and schedule requirements.
2. Assume direct responsibility for control of labor hours, material usage, and machine output, checking actual current output and usage figures against standard requirements.
3. Operate within limits of expense budgets for repairs, supplies, and small tools.
4. Furnish information for and assistance in preparation of expense budgets as required.
5. Execute prepared production schedules where supplied on individual machines and by individual products. Prepare own schedules where none are provided.
6. Order production materials and operating supplies required by schedule.
7. Plan and schedule personnel assignments. Adjust operating plans to meet changes in conditions.
8. Request services from other Departments incidental to accomplishment of approved schedules.
9. Assume direct responsibility for quality of product produced in his area and condition of package when it leaves the area. Review inspection reports, tests, and product samples to note quality

trends, and take corrective action to keep quality within required limits.

10. Where required, direct the taking of control samples according to the needs of Quality Control Engineer.

B. *Wage Administration*

1. Assume direct responsibility for application of approved job classes to assigned employees. Furnish information as required for description and classification of new and changed jobs.

2. Review, explain, and administer incentive plans used in the area. Recommend the setting of standards on unrated work.

3. Report all changes in methods and materials according to established procedures.

4. Approve all day work and other allowances for incentive workers.

5. Assume direct responsibility for providing accurate production, scrap, and time reports, and in the case of incentive jobs furnish information necessary for the application of proper incentive rates from the rate schedules.

C. *Methods and Standard Manufacturing Practices*

1. Recommend changes in methods of operation to reduce costs or increase production.

2. Enforce all Standard Manufacturing Practices and methods in assigned area.

3. Cooperate with Industrial Engineering personnel in development and installation of improved methods.

4. Encourage and follow up employee suggestions.

D. *Maintenance of Equipment*

1. Assume direct responsibility for equipment and machinery and its proper service and maintenance by Maintenance Department personnel. Check inspection, lubrication, and adjustment of machines.

2. Initiate requests for Maintenance service. Anticipate Maintenance requirements and make recommendations for meeting them. Report abnormal mechanical conditions.

3. Assume responsibility for cleanliness and orderly appearance of assigned area.

E. *Personnel Relations*

1. Handle all grievances at first-step level of grievance procedure.

2. Carry out on-the-job training of new employees.

3. Enforce rules covering plant discipline, including safety. Maintain a record of each assigned employee's conduct, noting any exceptional instances.

4. Assume responsibility for employee compliance with safety precautions and practices. Make record of all accidents for analysis to assure the future safety of employees and for possible reference in compensation cases.

5. Transmit authorized information to employees promptly and clearly as instructed by supervisor.

FOREMAN–RECEIVING, WAREHOUSING, AND DISTRIBUTION

BASIC FUNCTION

The Foreman–Receiving, Warehousing, and Distribution is the operating supervisor responsible for receiving, warehousing, and controlling the issue and distribution of raw materials and supplies.

SCOPE

He reports to the Superintendent–Planning and Cost Control; to him report assigned clerks and hourly personnel.

OBJECTIVES AND RESPONSIBILITIES

Although additional duties may be assigned to him by the Superintendent–Planning and Cost Control, his specific duties include the following:

A. Cost, Schedule, and Quality Requirements

1. Supervise personnel engaged in receiving, moving, and storing raw materials in storage areas.

2. Assume responsibility for establishing materials handling and delivery procedures.

3. Assume direct responsibility for efficient distribution of raw materials to production machines as required by production schedules, and the condition of the package when it leaves the area.

4. Assume direct responsibility for the proper storage of raw materials and supplies to eliminate damage and waste in storage areas.

5. Furnish accurate reports to Superintendent–Planning and Cost Control on the issue of raw materials and supplies.

6. Furnish accurate physical counts of inventory on hand to Superintendent–Planning and Cost Control as required to provide the basis for checking book inventory records.

7. Develop new methods and procedures to reduce the cost of unloading and storing materials.

8. Furnish information to Superintendent–Planning and Cost Control on inventory status to insure against the possibility of material shortages.

9. Advise Superintendent–Planning and Cost Control of defective raw materials and supplies as received or as found in stock to permit return to vendor for credit or to scrap.

10. Report dead or obsolete stock to Superintendent–Planning and Cost Control. Report storage areas cleared of such items.

11. Furnish information for and assistance in preparation of expense budgets as required. Operate within limits of expense budgets for repairs, supplies, and small tools.

12. Plan and schedule personnel assignments and adjust operating plans to meet changes in conditions.

B. *Wage Administration*

1. Assume direct responsibility for application of approved job classes to assigned employees. Furnish information as required for description and classification of new and changed jobs.

2. Review, explain, and administer incentive plans used in the area. Recommend the setting of standards on unrated work.

3. Report all changes in methods and materials according to established procedures.

4. Approve all day work and other allowances for incentive workers.

5. Assume direct responsibility for providing accurate production, scrap, and time reports, and in the case of incentive jobs furnish information necessary for the application of proper incentive rates from the rate schedules.

C. *Methods and Standard Manufacturing Practices*

1. Recommend changes in methods of operation to reduce costs or increase production.

2. Enforce all Standard Manufacturing Practices and methods in assigned area.

   3. Cooperate with Industrial Engineering personnel in development and installation of improved methods.

   4. Encourage and follow up employee suggestions.

D. Maintenance of Equipment

   1. Assume direct responsibility for equipment and machinery and its proper service and maintenance by Maintenance Department personnel. Check inspection, lubrication, and adjustment of machines.

   2. Initiate requests for Maintenance service. Anticipate Maintenance requirements and make recommendations for meeting them. Report abnormal mechanical conditions.

   3. Assume responsibility for cleanliness and orderly appearance of assigned area.

E. Personnel Relations

   1. Handle all grievances at first-step level of grievance procedure.

   2. Carry out on-the-job training of new employees.

   3. Enforce rules covering plant discipline, including safety. Maintain a record of each assigned employee's conduct, noting any exceptional instances.

   4. Assume responsibility for employee compliance with safety precautions and practices. Make record of all accidents for analysis to assure the future safety of employees and for possible reference in compensation cases.

   5. Transmit authorized information to employees promptly and clearly as instructed by supervisor.

FOREMAN–WAREHOUSING AND SHIPPING

BASIC FUNCTION

A Foreman–Warehousing and Shipping is the operating supervisor directly in charge of receiving from production and warehousing, and shipping finished goods produced in the Division.

SCOPE

He reports to the Superintendent–Production; to him report assigned clerks and hourly personnel.

OBJECTIVES AND RESPONSIBILITIES

Although additional duties may be assigned to him by the Superintendent–Production, his specific duties include the following:

A. *Cost, Schedule, and Quality Requirements*

1. Directly supervise personnel engaged in receiving, warehousing, and shipping finished goods.

2. Accumulate weights for specific destinations to be used as a basis for ordering railroad freight cars and commercial freight trucks.

3. Accumulate footages and weights to complete a truckload or carload order, when delivery to the warehouse of this order is spread over a number of days.

4. Assume responsibility for proper loading and blocking of commercial freight trucks and railroad freight cars, and for the condition of package when it leaves the area.

5. Assume responsibility for preparing all shipping papers originating within the mill.

6. Recommend new methods and procedures for unloading, storage, and shipping to reduce costs.

7. Supervise spot checks of physical inventory to verify book inventory figures maintained by Sales Department.

8. Assume responsibility for selecting correct products, weights, and footages of finished goods applied against a specific shipping authorization received from Sales Department.

9. Furnish information for and assistance in preparation of expense budgets as required. Operate within limits of expense budget for repairs, supplies, and small tools.

10. Plan and schedule personnel requirements and adjust operating plans to meet changes in conditions.

B. *Wage Administration*

1. Assume direct responsibility for application of approved job classes to assigned employees. Furnish information as required for description and classification of new and changed jobs.

2. Review, explain, and administer incentive plans used in the area. Recommend the setting of standards on unrated work.

3. Report all changes in methods and materials according to established procedures.

4. Approve all day work and other allowances for incentive workers.

5. Assume direct responsibility for providing accurate production, scrap, and time reports, and in the case of incentive jobs furnish information necessary for the application of proper incentive rates from the rate schedules.

C. *Methods and Standard Manufacturing Practices*

1. Recommend changes in methods of operation to reduce costs or increase production.

2. Enforce all Standard Manufacturing Practices and methods in assigned area.

3. Cooperate with Division Standards Engineering personnel in development and installation of improved methods.

4. Encourage and follow up employee suggestions.

D. *Maintenance of Equipment*

1. Assume direct responsibility for equipment and machinery and its proper service and maintenance by Maintenance Department personnel. Check inspection, lubrication, and adjustment of machines.

2. Initiate requests for Maintenance service. Anticipate Maintenance requirements and make recommendations for meeting them. Report abnormal mechanical conditions.

3. Assume responsibility for cleanliness and orderly appearance of assigned area.

E. *Personnel Relations*

1. Handle all grievances at first-step level of grievance procedure.

2. Carry out on-the-job training of new employees.

3. Enforce rules covering plant discipline, including safety. Maintain a record of each assigned employee's conduct, noting any exceptional instances.

4. Assume responsibility for employee compliance with safety precautions and practices. Make record of all accidents for analysis to assure the future safety of employees and for possible reference in compensation cases.

5. Transmit authorized information to employees promptly and clearly as instructed by supervisor.

Staff Positions

The following pages present a selection of the key positions in The Colorado Fuel and Iron Corporation's staff.

Plant Engineering Department

CHIEF PLANT ENGINEER

BASIC FUNCTION

The Chief Plant Engineer directs the operation of Plant Engineering and Maintenance activities according to approved policies. He is responsible for executing plant and equipment addition or modification programs. He is also responsible for administering a continuous economy program in Plant Engineering and Maintenance activities.

SCOPE

He reports to the Works Manager. The following report to him:

Assistant Chief Plant Engineer.
Chief Project Engineer.
Administrative Assistant.
Combustion Engineer.
Utilities Engineer.

OBJECTIVES AND RESPONSIBILITIES

Although additional responsibilities may be assigned to him by the Works Manager, his specific duties include the following:

1. Organize and direct the activities of Plant Engineering and Maintenance services in the Plants.
2. Develop and summarize recommended Corporation programs for addition or modification of equipment, machines, and facilities and submit for approval.
3. Direct the execution of such programs as approved.
4. Develop engineering studies by members of engineering staff to

develop means of modifying and improving existing Corporation practices in such fields as electric power distribution and use, steam generation, lubrication, and other areas.

5. Develop plans covering preventive maintenance and generally oversee the development and execution of such programs in Manufacturing Divisions.

6. Review and analyze Maintenance control and expense reports; direct studies on Maintenance problems and attain lowest possible costs consistent with service requirements.

7. Analyze progress reports on major work orders and design projects and initiate corrective measures when cost or completion goals are not being met.

8. Prepare operating expense budgets for Department with assistance of Controller.

9. Through the Chief Project Engineer, direct the design and development of new types of machines and equipment to keep the Corporation's processes on a competitive basis.

10. Initiate and/or approve requests for work orders; analyzing each for completeness, adequacy of cost estimate, economic (or other) justification, practicability, conformance with approved programs, and completion date.

11. Review and approve plans for execution of major work orders.

12. Approve procedures covering drafting practices.

Relationship with Other Units of Organization

1. In conjunction with Assistant Chief Plant Engineer, Chief Project Engineer, Plant Engineers and Superintendents, review and work out agreement on major Plant Engineering and Maintenance projects.

2. Review with Engineering Department heads the product specifications of the respective Manufacturing Divisions to determine need for and design requirements of new facilities, equipment, and machines.

3. Work closely with the Superintendent of Industrial Relations–Roebling and the Superintendent of Industrial Relations–Trenton to be fully informed of the interpretations and administrative requirements of the Corporation's labor relations policies and Union contracts. Make recommendations to above Superintendents concerning labor contract terms.

Plant Engineering Department

ADMINISTRATIVE ASSISTANT–CHIEF PLANT ENGINEER

BASIC FUNCTION

The Administrative Assistant–Chief Plant Engineer provides engineering services in the evaluation of requests for appropriation for equipment and facilities, and in the analysis of the factors justifying them, such as cost reduction, increased production, safety, quality, etc. He is responsible for coordinating the administrative functions of the Department; for supervising clerical functions in the Central Engineering Office; and for correlating Plant Engineering activities with other Plants.

SCOPE

He is responsible to the Chief Plant Engineer. To him report assigned Junior Engineers and Central Plant Engineering office clerical personnel.

OBJECTIVES AND RESPONSIBILITIES

Although additional responsibilities may be assigned to him by the Chief Plant Engineer, his specific duties include the following:

1. Administer Plant Engineering Department procedures, prepare reports, and maintain records according to approved Plant and Corporation requirements.

2. Accumulate and summarize data leading to and supporting appropriation requests for both capital and expense items in excess of $500. This includes the following:

   a. Determine whether formal appropriation request is necessary to cover job.

   b. Review estimated costs and provide breakdown to permit segregation of capital and expense components.

   c. Make first review of necessity for work and estimated savings and set up savings in auditable form.

   d. Review priority and certificate of necessity possibilities.

3. Set up work order and work progress sheets. Accumulate costs of work and prepare in report form.

4. Accumulate, codify, and summarize data leading to preparation of Annual Equipment Replacement and Development Program.

5. Prepare reports as required including:

    a. Quarterly report on actual and anticipated rate of expenditure on major appropriations.

    b. Analyses on machine repair costs.

6. Exercise functional control over maintenance procedures in Manufacturing Departments and Maintenance Shops.

7. Develop and recommend Plant Engineering procedures.

8. Train Plant Engineering personnel in Corporation procedures related to Department activity.

9. Carry out a variety of assignments of administrative nature for Chief Plant Engineer.

RELATIONSHIP WITH OTHER UNITS OF ORGANIZATION

1. Work closely with Finance and Accounting Departments on accounting and financial aspects of works orders, shop orders, and appropriation requests.

2. Provide Purchasing Department with information on orders, quotation requests, and priority and certificate of necessity applications which are pending or in force.

Plant Engineering Department

CHIEF PROJECT ENGINEER

BASIC FUNCTION

The Chief Project Engineer is responsible for assigned engineering design and preparing plans for major plant engineering projects covering the modification, construction, and expansion of the Corporation's facilities, equipment, and machines. He also provides technical and drafting assistance to various Plant Engineering staffs.

SCOPE

He reports to the Chief Plant Engineer. To him report assigned Project Engineers and the Chief Draftsman. On related major projects, the Chief Plant Engineer may assign the Utilities or Combustion Engineer to work as Project Engineer under the direction of the Chief Project Engineer.

OBJECTIVES AND RESPONSIBILITIES

Although additional responsibilities may be assigned to him by the Chief Plant Engineer, his specific duties include the following:

1. Through the Project Engineers and Chief Draftsman, direct the development of designs, drawings, and bills of material on major projects as assigned by the Chief Plant Engineer.

2. Direct the preparation of cost and time estimates on contemplated major projects.

3. Verify the practicability of new designs from the standpoint of design principles, performance, cost, and completion dates. Develop alternate designs to test each project on these factors.

4. Assume general supervision of the execution of those approved Plant Engineering projects to which he is assigned by the Chief Plant Engineer.

5. Maintain a close check on important Plant Engineering projects, checking designs and estimates, and lend assistance as needed.

6. Supervise the training of Junior Engineers and Draftsmen assigned to Central Plant Engineering.

7. Develop and present for approval procedures covering administrative requirements in design and drafting work, such as progress reports on design work, checking of drawings, numbering of drawings, and other drafting room procedures. Administer such procedures as approved.

Plant Engineering Department

ASSISTANT CHIEF PLANT ENGINEER

BASIC FUNCTION

The Assistant Chief Plant Engineer directs the activity of Maintenance personnel and Plant Engineering personnel regularly assigned to Manufacturing Departments, and assists the Chief Plant Engineer in the general over-all operation of the Plant Engineering Department.

SCOPE

He reports to the Chief Plant Engineer, and the following personnel report to him:

Plant Engineer–C. R. P. D.
Plant Engineer–W. R. D.
Plant Engineer–H. M. D. and W. M. D.
Superintendent, maintenance and construction shops–Trenton.
Superintendent, maintenance and construction shops–Roebling.
Superintendent, plant protection.
Superintendent, box and reel making.

OBJECTIVES AND RESPONSIBILITIES

Although additional responsibilities may be assigned to him by the Chief
Plant Engineer, his specific duties include the following:

1. Direct engineering studies in each Manufacturing Department to
   ascertain need to rehabilitate, replace, modify, or expand facilities,
   machines, or equipment.

2. Direct the completion of designs and layouts of approved capital
   programs that are assigned to Plant Engineering staffs.

3. Direct the preparation of estimates on projects assigned to Plant
   Engineering staffs and approve same.

4. Direct the preparation of monthly progress reports on all engineering projects handled by the Plant Engineering and Shop Superintendents' staffs.

5. Direct Maintenance activities through Plant Engineers and Central
   Shops Superintendents, coordinating Central Shop and Maintenance
   functions.

6. Direct preparation and execution of preventive maintenance programs in Manufacturing Departments.

7. Through assigned Superintendent, direct operation of Central Maintenance Shops to provide required services to Plant Engineering
   Department and Manufacturing Departments at lowest possible
   costs.

8. Keep close watch on maintenance expense; review individual job
   costs, works order costs, maintenance backlog reports, and monthly
   expense statements prepared by Controller. Institute, review, and
   approve cost reduction studies and initiate indicated action.

9. Direct program to simplify and standardize maintenance methods,
   parts, and materials.

10. Assume responsibility for the execution of the Corporation's labor
    relations programs and policies, including safety in the Plant Engi-
    neering Department.

RELATIONSHIP WITH OTHER UNITS OF ORGANIZATION

1. Establish and maintain close working relationships with Manu-

facturing Superintendents. Secure their approval on Plant Engineering programs that concern their Departments; cooperate with them to work out problems of maintenance service and job scheduling. Cooperate in setting plant maintenance expense budgets.

2. Work closely with the Superintendent of Industrial Relations–Trenton and the Superintendent of Industrial Relations–Roebling to be fully informed of the interpretation and administrative requirements of the Corporation's labor relations policies and Union contracts. Make recommendations to above Superintendents of Industrial Relations concerning labor contract terms.

Plant Engineering Department

DIVISIONAL PLANT ENGINEER

Basic Function

The Plant Engineer is assigned to one or more Manufacturing Departments to direct and coordinate Plant Engineering and Maintenance work.

Scope

He reports to the Assistant Chief Plant Engineer. Within the assigned area, the following report to him:

Staff Engineer.
Assigned Junior Engineers, Draftsmen, and clerical personnel.
General Maintenance Foremen.
Maintenance Foremen.

Objectives and Responsibilities

Although additional responsibilities may be assigned to him by the Assistant Chief Plant Engineer, his specific duties include the following:

A. *New Plant Engineering Work*

1. Understand processes, machines, equipment, and facilities of assigned Department (s).

2. Direct or make engineering studies of machines and equipment to

determine need for replacement and possibilities for increasing output and/or reducing maintenance and other costs.

3. In conjunction with and as approved by the Superintendent, direct the development of, or develop designs for, equipment, machines, and construction projects within the Department (s) and write up required specifications, as assigned by Assistant Chief Plant Engineer.

4. Analyze economics of alternative engineering plans, preparing necessary cost estimates.

5. Expedite engineering projects in the Department (s) to complete on or before planned dates. This requires the coordination of production needs, engineering considerations, shop work and assembly, erection, and initial production.

6. Direct the work of the Staff Engineer and assigned Junior Engineers and Draftsmen.

7. Direct the preparation of drawings for maintenance work and for plant engineering projects handled in the Department (s) by his staff. Maintain progress reports on all projects within his Department (s).

8. Work closely with and receive assistance from the Chief Project Engineer and other Central Office Plant Engineering personnel on major or specialized projects.

9. Supply the Chief Project Engineer and other Central Office Plant Engineering personnel with technical assistance on major or specialized projects as required.

B. *Maintenance*

1. Assume responsibility for the cost and effectiveness of maintenance service in assigned Department (s).

2. Review and analyze maintenance expense statements for Department (s) furnished by the Controller as well as individual job costs and institute corrective measures.

3. Assist the General Maintenance Foreman in isolating and correcting causes of high maintenance cost.

4. Assume primary responsibility for setting up Department preventive maintenance programs and procedures.

5. Direct the carrying out of programs to simplify and standardize maintenance practices.

6. Assume responsibility for safety program covering men and equipment under his jurisdiction.

7. Be familiar with and execute the Corporation's labor relations policies.

RELATIONSHIP WITH OTHER UNITS OF ORGANIZATION

1. Provide Superintendent with required plant engineering and maintenance service.
2. Cooperate with Superintendent in reviewing, analyzing, and reducing Department maintenance costs.
3. Reach agreement with Product and Industrial Engineers in developing plans for facilities, equipment, and machine design.

SUPERINTENDENT–PLANNING AND COST CONTROL

BASIC FUNCTION

The Superintendent–Planning and Cost Control is in charge of production scheduling and inventory control in his assigned Department. He is also responsible for the establishment, analysis, and interpretation of control reports relating to Department manufacturing costs.

SCOPE

The Superintendent–Planning and Cost Control reports to the Superintendent. He plans, schedules, and supervises the work of an assigned Cost Control and Scheduling group.

OBJECTIVES AND RESPONSIBILITIES

Although additional duties may be assigned to him by the Manufacturing Manager, his specific responsibilities include the following:

1. Develop Manufacturing Programs to meet Sales Plans for long-term planning of operations, insofar as is practicable within the productive limitations of the plant and facilities and the availability of raw materials.
2. Recommend revisions in Sales Plans which will permit more effective use of production facilities to meet short-term sales requirements.
3. Recommend changes in manufacturing capacities to meet long-range Sales Plans more effectively.

4. Schedule production to fulfill approved Manufacturing Programs and special requirements of sales orders.

5. Develop raw material requirements for long- and short-term production plans and provide purchase requisitions to meet such plans.

6. Maintain inventory records for raw materials, in-process, and finished goods.

7. Provide the necessary follow-up of production to insure fulfillment of schedules.

8. Assume responsibility for the development and installation of Standard Manufacturing Practices in conjunction with the Industrial Engineer, Quality Control, and Product Engineer, as required. Audit compliance with Standard Manufacturing Practices, noting deviations and reasons for possible changes in manufacturing sequence, material usage, etc., to reduce costs and/or improve quality of product. Confer with the Quality Control or Product Engineer and the Industrial Engineer on revisions in process and operating standards as they relate to production schedules and standard costs.

9. Prepare production reports as directed, and assist the Superintendent in developing operating budgets.

10. Supervise the taking of physical inventories in accordance with procedures established by the Controller.

11. Assume responsibility for receiving and storing of all raw materials and finished goods.

12. Advise Shipping Department to ship finished products in accordance with Sales Department needs.

13. Assume responsibility for assembling and distributing reports as needed. May distribute production, payroll, and timekeeping records.

14. Review the adequacy and accuracy of time and production reports.

15. Under the functional direction of the Controller, collaborate with his staff in developing the forms, procedures, sources of data, and reports used in cost control programs, particularly concerning labor and materials.

16. Analyze and interpret production and cost control reports for Superintendent's review and action. This review covers current reports and prior reports in order to appraise trends of peformance.

17. Assume a principal role in training line supervisory personnel in the understanding and use of cost control and performance reports.

18. Audit the reporting and control of labor performed on unrated work.

SUPERVISOR–PRODUCTION PLANNING AND SCHEDULING

Basic Function

The Supervisor–Production Planning and Scheduling is responsible for planning raw material requirements and scheduling production to meet plans and forecasts of the Sales Department, as approved by the Superintendent–Production Planning and Cost Control.

Scope

He reports to the Superintendent–Production Planning and Cost Control; to him report assigned Scheduling Clerks and Expediters and the Chief Clerk of the Department.

Objectives and Responsibilities

Although additional responsibilities may be assigned to him by the Superintendent–Production Planning and Cost Control, his specific duties include the following:

1. Direct the work of personnel assigned to production planning and scheduling.
2. Determine raw material and production capacity needs to meet requirements of Sales Plans.
3. Supervise the preparation of required production schedules for the Plant (s).
4. Supervise the scheduling of production for individual Departments to maintain balanced output according to requirements.
5. Supervise the maintenance of Department records, including the following:
   a. Unfilled order backlog.
   b. Finished goods inventory.
   c. Manufacturing orders in process.
   d. Status of actual production against delivery promises.
   e. Production.
6. Direct the preparation and distribution of the following:
   a. Raw material requirements.
   b. Weekly and week end operating schedules of equipment and manpower.
   c. Production reports.
   d. Material requisitions.
   e. Material usage reports.
7. Direct the issue of manufacturing orders to Production Departments.
8. Develop delivery promises on orders and inquiries.
9. Furnish information for and assistance in preparation of expense

      budgets for Department and operate within limits of approved budget.

10. Recommend changes in clerical procedures to reduce costs or increase clerical production in Department.

11. Report variation from Standard Manufacturing Practices and methods in production.

12. Assume responsibility for maintenance and service of office equipment and machinery.

Plant Engineering Department

SUPERINTENDENT–MAINTENANCE AND CONSTRUCTION

BASIC FUNCTION

The Superintendent–Maintenance and Construction Shops (Trenton or Roebling) has delegated to him by the Assistant Chief Plant Engineer the responsibility for operating these Shops at a minimum cost to provide services required by approved schedules, and in accordance with approved operating policies and practices including specification, cost, and quality standards.

SCOPE

He reports to the Assistant Chief Plant Engineer, and to him report assigned General Foremen, Foremen, Junior Engineers, and clerical personnel.

OBJECTIVES AND RESPONSIBILITIES

Although additional responsibilities may be assigned to him by the Assistant Chief Plant Engineer, his specific duties include the following:

A. Cost, Schedule, and Quality Requirements

1. Supervise assigned Shops, assuming responsibilities for cost, quality, amount of work performed, and compliance with schedules.

2. Assist assigned Foreman in working out operating plans and schedules, establishing proper workloads, and balancing crew requirements.

3. Initiate and/or carry out assignments relating to reduction of manufacturing costs and reviewing labor and material costs; institute corrective action when necessary.

4. Assume responsibility for correcting variable overhead expense under his control when volume fluctuates.

5. Make frequent audits of job costs—actual costs against estimated costs—in each shop.

6. Analyze statements of maintenance expense and establish cost reduction goals for each shop.

7. Plan facilities and equipment requirements; initiate requests for such expenditures with supporting analyses.

8. Study Plant Engineering plans for work requiring services from his area and arrange to provide such services.

9. Take a principal role in developing program to simplify and standardize maintenance methods, parts, and materials.

10. Provide assistance to Maintenance supervision in Manufacturing Departments as requested. Provide assistance to the Chief Project Engineer and other Central Office Plant Engineering personnel as requested.

11. Take a principal part in developing craft-apprentice training programs in his general area.

B. *Wage Administration*

1. Supervise accurate reporting of time and production data.

C. *Methods and Standard Practices*

1. Assume responsibility for maintaining standard conditions and procedures under which time standards were set and are subsequently administered.

2. Supervise the manufacture of products according to Standard Manufacturing Practices.

3. Recommend changes in manufacturing processes or methods in the interest of lower costs, improved quality, or higher production.

4. Provide technical and manufacturing advice to Product, Quality Control, or Sales Engineers where questions of manufacturing technique are involved.

D. *Personnel Relations*

1. Assume responsibility for safety program covering men and equipment under his jurisdiction.

2. Under direction of Assistant Chief Plant Engineer, assume responsibility for executing the Corporation's labor relations policies and programs through subordinate supervisory personnel.

Plant Engineering Department

UTILITIES ENGINEER

BASIC FUNCTION

The Utilities Engineer is responsible for the generation of steam and electric power in the Trenton and Roebling Plants. He is responsible for the pumping, storage, and distribution of utilities up to the point of entry into the buildings. He provides service relating to utilities to the Plant Engineering Department.

SCOPE

He reports to the Chief Plant Engineer. Where major utilities projects are involved, he may be assigned to work under the direction of the Chief Project Engineer. The following personnel report to him:

Staff Engineer–Utilities.
Foreman–Trenton boiler houses.
Power Plant Engineer–Roebling power plant.
Assigned Junior Engineers and Draftsmen.

OBJECTIVES AND RESPONSIBILITIES

Although additional responsibilities may be assigned to him by the Chief Plant Engineer, his specific duties include the following:

1. Work on projects in his technical field in the various Production Departments as assigned by the Chief Plant Engineer.

2. Make engineering studies and write reports covering findings, conclusions, and recommendations to modify and improve existing corporate practice in utilities.

3. Assist Plant Engineers in working out problems in the fields of steam distribution, heating, plumbing, air, oil, gas, and water supply.

4. Write specifications for machines, equipment, and facilities related to utilities requirements.

5. Develop basic plans and designs on utility facilities and carry forward to such a point that Project Engineers can complete them (under his direction in the Project Engineering Section).

6. Prepare cost estimates on engineering proposals and analyze economics of alternative engineering plans in his assigned areas.

7. Assume responsibility for inspection of all fire-protective equipment up to the point of entry into the buildings. Request maintenance service to keep in proper operating condition.

8. Assist Plant Engineers in working out problems pertaining to fire-protective equipment in their departments.

9. Review, analyze, and make disposition of Insurance Company inspection reports and surveys.

10. Make reports of fires and other compensable damage to plant property.

11. Maintain map records to show all plant utility service lines.

12. Assume general responsibility for safety program covering men and equipment under his jurisdiction.

13. Be familiar with and execute Corporation's labor relations policies.

Plant Engineering Department

SUPERINTENDENT–PLANT PROTECTION

BASIC FUNCTION

The Superintendent–Plant Protection is generally responsible for the security of the Corporation's properties against illegal actions, fire, and damage to machines and equipment during shutdown periods. He is also responsible for the security of personnel within the Plant's premises except as they are covered by the Plant's safety regulations.

SCOPE

He reports to the Assistant Chief Plant Engineer. To him report Roundsmen in the Trenton area, the Inspector–Fire Equipment at Trenton, and the Chief Roundsman at Roebling.

Objectives and Responsibilities

Although additional responsibilities may be assigned to him by the Assistant Chief Plant Engineer, his specific duties include the following:

A. *Police Functions*

　1. Assume general responsibility for securing Plant property against unlawful entry, theft, and sabotage.

　2. Enforce regulations against gambling on Plant property.

　3. Suppress disorder on Plant property.

　4. Make investigations including reports, when required, of any acts covered by the above items.

B. *Fire Prevention*

　1. Serves as head of Fire Department–Trenton area.

　2. Detect and prevent fires. Report poor housekeeping and fire hazards to responsible personnel.

　3. Inspect fire equipment through the Inspector–Fire Equipment at Trenton, and test working condition. Report the condition of fire equipment and suggest changes or additions where needed.

　4. Answer all Trenton Plant fire alarms, instruct fire fighters, and issue fire-line passes at Trenton.

　5. Investigate causes of all fires at Trenton and make necessary reports.

C. *Employee Protection*

　1. Establish traffic control stations for employees' safety and assume general responsibility for the direction of traffic.

　2. Point out unsafe yard conditions and request their correction.

　3. Direct the distribution of safety glasses to plant visitors when passes are issued by the Police Department.

　4. May direct the transporting of injured or ill employees for treatment to first-aid stations.

D. *Identification*

　1. Direct the issuance of Police Department passes to plant visitors.

　2. Administer programs covering employee identification badges, finger prints, and photographs.

　3. Administer identification program according to Federal and state requirements.

E. *Plant Inspection During Shutdown*

　1. Direct the examination of property, equipment, and machines by plant protection personnel during periods of shutdown to detect

such things as overheated motors, pipe line leaks, overheated furnaces, machines that should be shut down, etc.

F. *Civil Defense*

1. Assist in organizing the Plant's Civil Defense group and serve as member of committee to develop program.

G. *Miscellaneous Service*

1. Direct the issuing and receiving of time cards during certain hours at plant entrances.
2. Direct the operation of telephone switchboard during off hours.
3. Assist the Safety Department when required.
4. Supervise the operation of the Plant parking lots where required.
5. Supervise receipt of call-ins from employees who cannot report for work.
6. Supervise notification of employees to report for work.
7. Direct the lighting up of certain electric and gas-fired equipment directly before first shift of week.

INDEXES

Index by Job Description

D

T

Index by Company Name